The American Crisis Series

Books on the Civil War Era

Steven E. Woodworth, Associate Professor of History,
Texas Christian University
SERIES EDITOR

The Civil War was the crisis of the Republic's first century —the test, in Abraham Lincoln's words, of whether any free government could long endure. It touched with fire the hearts of a generation, and its story has fired the imaginations of every generation since. This series offers to students of the Civil War, either those continuing or those just beginning their exciting journey into the past, concise overviews of important persons, events, and themes in that remarkable period of America's history.

Volumes Published

James L. Abrahamson. *The Men of Secession and Civil War, 1859–1861* (2000). Cloth ISBN 0-8420-2818-8 Paper ISBN 0-8420-2819-6

Robert G. Tanner. *Retreat to Victory? Confederate Strategy Reconsidered* (2001). Cloth ISBN 0-8420-2881-1 Paper ISBN 0-8420-2882-X

Stephen Davis. *Atlanta Will Fall: Sherman, Joe Johnston, and the Yankee Heavy Battalions* (2001). Cloth ISBN 0-8420-2787-4 Paper ISBN 0-8420-2788-2

Paul Ashdown and Edward Caudill. *The Mosby Myth: A Confederate Hero in Life and Legend* (2002). Cloth ISBN 0-8420-2928-1 Paper ISBN 0-8420-2929-X

Spencer C. Tucker. *A Short History of the Civil War at Sea* (2002). Cloth ISBN 0-8420-2867-6 Paper ISBN 0-8420-2868-4

Richard Bruce Winders. *Crisis in the Southwest: The United States, Mexico, and the Struggle over Texas* (2002). Cloth ISBN 0-8420-2800-5 Paper ISBN 0-8420-2801-3

Ethan S. Rafuse. *A Single Grand Victory: The First Campaign and Battle of Manassas* (2002). Cloth ISBN 0-8420-2875-7 Paper ISBN 0-8420-2876-5

John G. Selby. *Virginians at War: The Civil War Experiences of Seven Young Confederates* (2002). Cloth ISBN 0-8420-5054-X Paper ISBN 0-8420-5055-8

Edward K. Spann. *Gotham at War: New York City, 1860–1865* (2002). Cloth ISBN 0-8420-5056-6 Paper ISBN 0-8420-5057-4

Anne J. Bailey. *War and Ruin: William T. Sherman and the Savannah Campaign* (2002). Cloth ISBN 0-8420-2850-1 Paper ISBN 0-8420-2851-X

Gary Dillard Joiner. *One Damn Blunder from Beginning to End: The Red River Campaign of 1864* (2003). Cloth ISBN 0-8420-2936-2 Paper ISBN 0-8420-2937-0

Steven E. Woodworth. *Beneath a Northern Sky: A Short History of the Gettysburg Campaign* (2003). Cloth ISBN 0-8420-2932-X Paper ISBN 0-8420-2933-8

John C. Waugh. *On the Brink of Civil War: The Compromise of 1850 and How It Changed the Course of American History* (2003). Cloth ISBN 0-8420-2944-3 Paper ISBN 0-8420-2945-1

Eric H. Walther. *The Shattering of the Union: America in the 1850s* (2004). Cloth ISBN 0-8420-2798-X Paper ISBN 0-8420-2799-8

On the Brink of Civil War

Henry Clay addresses the Senate in 1850
(Painting by Peter Frederick Rothermel)
U.S. Senate Historical Office

On the Brink
of Civil War
The Compromise of 1850
and How It Changed
the Course of
American History

The American Crisis Series
BOOKS ON THE CIVIL WAR ERA
NO. 13

John C. Waugh

A Scholarly Resources Inc. Imprint
Wilmington, Delaware

Scholarly Resources Inc.
104 Greenhill Avenue
Wilmington, DE 19805-1897
www.scholarly.com

Library of Congress Cataloging-in-Publication Data

Waugh, John C.
  On the brink of Civil War : the Compromise of 1850 and how it
changed the course of American history / John C. Waugh.
     p. cm. — (The American crisis series ; no. 13)
  Includes bibliographical references and index.
  ISBN 0-8420-2944-3 (cloth : alk. paper) — ISBN 0-8420-2945-1
(pbk. : alk. paper)
  1. Compromise of 1850. 2. United States—Politics and
government—1849–1861. 3. United States—History—Civil War,
1861–1865—Causes. I. Title. II. Series.
E423 .W26 2003
973.7'113—dc21

2002156718

∞ The paper used in this publication meets the minimum require-
ments of the American National Standard for permanence of paper
for printed library materials, Z39.48, 1984.

To my good friend

Jeff Bingaman of New Mexico—

carrying on the tradition of

senatorial statesmanship

About the Author

John C. Waugh is a journalist who stopped reporting the twentieth century in 1989 and began reporting the nineteenth. In the years since, he has written six books about the Civil War era: *The Class of 1846*, *Reelecting Lincoln*, *Surviving the Confederacy*, *Sam Bell Maxey and the Confederate Indians*, *Last Stand at Mobile*, and this one. He spent most of his newspaper years as a staff correspondent and bureau chief of *The Christian Science Monitor*. Waugh has also served on the senior staffs of two national politicians, Nelson Rockefeller of New York and Jeff Bingaman of New Mexico.

CONTENTS

ACKNOWLEDGMENTS

Peering back into the past and putting what you see between the covers of a book is too much of a job for just one pair of eyes or hands. The glare of potential error, the chance of a mishandling of truth are too great. I therefore have other hands and other eyes to thank in this journey back to the year of 1850, the time of one of the most dramatic passages in American history, when some of the very greatest men in our country struggled with one of its greatest crises.

Thanks first must go to a trio of distinguished historian-friends who helped me along the way. Steven E. Woodworth, of Texas Christian University, recruited me to write a book for this American Crisis Series and enthusiastically endorsed my choice of a subject. Two other outstanding masters of our past read the manuscript and offered invaluable suggestions: Richard Allan Baker, the eminent U.S. Senate Historian, whose eye for this drama is unequaled; and Edwin Cole Bearss, the chief historian emeritus of the National Park Service, whose all-encompassing grasp of our past and its meaning is staggering.

I am deeply indebted to the very able and congenial editors at Scholarly Resources with whom I have been privileged to work on this project, in particular Matthew R. Hershey and Linda Pote Musumeci. Their professional care and skill have made this a much better book than it might have been.

And what would any of us who write of the past do without libraries and librarians? For months I virtually lived at the Mary Couts Burnett Library at Texas Christian University poring over the *Congressional Globe* for the Thirty-first Congress in which this great drama played out. I drew material constantly, as well, from the two other fine libraries in the Dallas-Fort Worth Metroplex, where I live—Southern Methodist University and the University of Texas in Arlington. I am also indebted to the library resources of Rice University in Houston and the University of Texas in Austin. And when I could not find what I needed at any of those libraries there was Priscilla Cardwell, the interlibrary loan librarian at the Arlington, Texas, Public Library System, who never failed to find what I wanted somewhere else in the country and put it into my hands.

Last, but certainly never least, I must always thank my wife, Kathleen Dianne Lively, who put up once again with my daily disappearances into the nineteenth century. She has come to understand that there is great drama being acted out there by great characters, and that to write of them is my joy.

CHAPTER ONE

STORM CLOUDS RISING

IT WAS THE END of one decade and the beginning of another, and Washington City was bracing in early December 1849 for the coming of the newly elected Thirty-first Congress.

At midcentury the waiting federal capital looked, to one who knew it, "like an overgrown, tattered village which some late hurricane had scattered along the river's edge."[1] This random village-capital in the District of Columbia on the banks of the Potomac seemed to straddle two worlds—one dynamic and forward moving, the other a throwback to the brawling frontier. It was a time in the Union of heady material prosperity, and Washington was not only the political power center of the country, but also a growing magnet for science and art. As one young Washingtonian said, the city was "too well acquainted with Talent and Genius."[2] David Outlaw, a North Carolina Whig congressman who would rather have been home, called it "this city of magnificent distances, and of hollow hearted and ambitious men, and selfish scheming women."[3]

In the decade just ending, the population in the country had jumped 36 percent, from a little over 17 million to over 23 million. The coming census would show Washington with 40,001 of those inhabitants: 29,730 whites, and 10,271 colored—8,158 free blacks and 2,113 slaves—and civic expenditures in 1848–49 of $122,140.

The new young nation after but three-quarters of a century since independence was becoming a major player in world commerce, riding on the taut sails and sleek hulls of its clipper ships, the swiftest large sailing vessels ever put on the water. The age of steam, newly emerging, foretold ever more speed and ever more prominence and prosperity. On land, the country at midcentury was stitched with 9,000 miles of iron lines, laid down to accommodate that new transportation marvel, the railroad train. It was a figure that would double within five years, triple within ten. The telegraph—another miracle of technology—was newborn, but it already linked the capital to most of the major cities in the country.[4] Fortunes were being made everywhere. Americans were rushing to the newly discovered gold fields of California. Steamboats and sailing vessels, testifying to the prosperity, were putting in and out of Washington's docks, plying up and down the river to Alexandria, Mount Vernon, and Hampton Roads to the sea.[5]

But Washington had its blemishes as well. Its broad, unpaved streets were mud-bogs in winter, dust-bins in summer. Poverty, squalor, prejudice, backwardness, and violence resided side by side with the elegance of rising wealth and political power.[6] The only footpath or carriage road into Virginia and the South was still over the Long Bridge, built in President Andrew Jackson's time. The sole railroad approach to the city was through Baltimore on the Baltimore & Ohio line.[7] Gas streetlamps were few, and the houses were unnumbered. Finding a residence required a hack driver with a memory.[8]

Washington was also a sump. The canal that cut through the village was an open cesspool. Drainage was faulty or nonexistent—and disease inducing. Householders dumped their garbage and slop into the alleys and roadways, to the satisfaction of regiments of free-roaming hogs who scavenged and dug wallows in the roads and defiled the city's buildings and fences. Miasmic odors from slaughterhouses polluted the air. Rats and cockroaches infested dwellings, the president's house not excepted. In the summer, legions of flies rose from dung in the stables and offal in the streets. Mosquitoes by the millions swarmed into the heat and humidity from stagnant ponds pitting the city.[9]

The nation's capital was clearly a work in progress. A symbol of its unfinished state was the stub of the uncompleted monument to George Washington, begun in 1848 after years of discussion.[10] It was but "a huge stone stump" at midcentury, surrounded by stacks of memorial stones waiting to make walls—gifts from a mix of individuals, societies, companies, states, and foreign powers. The stone donated by Pope Pius IX disappeared one night and was never found.[11]

The city was dominated by two centers of political power—the White House and the Capitol. There were 6,345 private residences and boardinghouses, accommodating 6,730 families, but few powerful men in the government owned homes in Washington. They boarded. They and their power were transient. But when in town, there was ample opportunity to communicate with a higher power. They could worship, if they chose, in thirty-eight churches, thirteen of them Methodist.[12]

The Capitol sat atop Jenkins Hill, Washington's highest, appearing alone, serene, and aloof. Its copper-sheathed wooden dome dominated the city. The idea of a dome, unknown in America, had pleased George Washington, for he had believed it would lend the capitol "beauty and grandeur."[13] The building's "milk-white walls . . . swathed in moonlight," surrounded by encircling fountains and shrubbery, "looked more like a creation of fairy-land than a substantial reality."[14]

The copper-domed Capitol in Washington, DC, as it looked in 1850
U.S. Senate Historical Office

But a reality it was, and its outward serenity belied the untranquil political reality gripping the nation. In this early December, in the waning days of 1849, at the end of a decade of great events, there was the darkening shadow of impending crisis. Members of the new Thirty-first Congress were arriving under a heavy, brooding sense of ever-present and imminent national catastrophe.

The country was learning—again—that a huge land deal and Negro slavery were a nation-splitting combination. When the United States went to war with Mexico in the middle of the decade just ending, its main aim—driven by Manifest Destiny—was to acquire the vast territories of New Mexico, Utah, and California, then belonging to Mexico. The war, won decisively when the U.S. army marched into Mexico City in mid-September 1847, succeeded spectacularly. A treaty was hammered out and signed, and overnight the United States grew in girth from 1,753,588 square miles to 2,944,337 square miles—a nearly 68 percent ballooning that with the settlement of the Oregon question expanded the country all the way to the Pacific.[15]

It was a stunning national triumph and a staggering acquisition. And it was now threatening the very life of the nation. It had renewed a bitter sectional standoff that was again imperiling the delicate political equilibrium between the slaveholding and nonslaveholding states that had long kept North and South linked in tenuous union. Senator Andrew P. Butler of South Carolina believed these new acquisitions from Mexico "have brought with them many dangers, and they present temptations well calculated to make a change in the original character of our institutions."[16]

President Zachary Taylor, the Mexican War hero in the White House, was not being perfectly candid when he said in early December that "the United States of America at this moment present to the world the most stable and permanent Government on earth."[17] In truth, as the elected members of the Thirty-first Congress converged on Washington, the country seemed in critical danger of shattering over the issue of whether slavery would or would not be permitted in these new territories. One observer spoke of "the great comet of dissolution that has been blazing upon us for so long, coming nearer and nearer."[18]

That summer, Henry L. Benning, a Georgia lawyer and keen student of public affairs, put the trouble in sharp focus when he wrote that "it is apparent, horribly apparent, that the slavery question rides insolently over every other everywhere . . . the whole North is becoming ultra anti-slavery and the whole South ultra proslavery." He wrote a congressman, "I no more doubt that the North will abolish slavery the very first moment it feels itself able to do it without too much cost, than I doubt my existence."[19]

Hearts and minds were hardening daily. Every Northern legislature but one had urged Congress to act to bar slavery from all the territories. Several had urged the abolition of slavery and the slave trade in the District of Columbia. Southern legislators, believing this position constituted warfare on their rights, had gone on record with like unity against all of it. Warring resolutions from statehouses North and South mirrored positions that were becoming dangerously fixed and polarized.[20] If barred with their slaves from new territory that they believed belonged to the South equally, many

Southern leaders seemed ready to secede from what they saw as a fanatic, abolition-driven North bent on destroying the Southern way of life—"fanatical assailants of our peculiar institutions," threatening "our dearest interest."[21]

The alternatives as Congress was about to convene were either some kind of compromise that the South could live with or secession and disunion. Massachusetts Congressman Robert C. Winthrop believed "the country has never been in more serious exigency than at present." The South, he said, "is angry, mad."[22] George Templeton Strong, a Wall Street lawyer and astute observer of the times, wrote in his diary, "the South is very rampant and a good deal in earnest. . . . Things are not in a comfortable state, and it is not easy to see our way out of the complication." He called it "the great Southern problem."[23] The blunt-writing Horace Greeley of the *New York Tribune* thought this Southern problem, this slavery question, a "threadbare topic."[24] But "never did a thunder-cloud exhibit an angrier aspect," a worried congressman, Henry W. Hilliard of Alabama, said; "it touched every part of the horizon, and threatened the destruction of the Union."[25]

Senator Henry S. Foote of Mississippi, another Southerner who generally put things in more florid prose than Hilliard and thought he knew who ought to be blamed, remarked that a decade ago "the cloud of abolition was no bigger than a man's hand." Now "that cloud has overspread the whole firmament," and "red lightning is already gleaming in our faces and the thunder is rolling above our heads."[26] Henry Clay, the great senator from Kentucky, spoke of the "twenty odd furnaces," federal and state, "in full blast in generating heat, and passion, and intemperance, and diffusing them throughout the whole extent of this broad land."[27] Longtime Senator Thomas Hart Benton of Missouri, who would soon be a major actor in the drama about to open in the Senate chamber, spoke of "the cry of danger" in the country, of "an incompatibility of interest between the two sections," but insisted that "separation is no remedy."[28]

The prevailing opinion in the North, crossing all the parties— Democrat, Whig, and Free-Soil—was that slavery should not be allowed into these new territories under any circumstances. While Northerners generally—extreme abolitionists excepted—would leave slavery alone in the states where it already existed, they wanted these new territories to remain slave free. Horace Mann, the ardent Free Soil congressman from Massachusetts, who also saw "dark clouds . . . full of lightning" overhanging the future, nonetheless was saying, "better disunion, better a civil or a servile war—better anything that God in his providence shall send, than an extension of the boundaries of slavery."[29]

Southerners were answering such incendiary thunderbolts with flame of their own. They believed that the common territory of the nation—territory they had sent more men than the North to fight and die for in Mexico—should be open equally to slavery, until new states carved out of the territory specifically outlawed it. They argued, as Congressman Thomas L. Clingman of North Carolina did, that the South would insist on its right "to participate fairly in the benefits of the national territory." "Do us justice," Clingman warned the North, "and we continue to stand with you; attempt to trample on us, and we separate."[30]

One worried observer, citing "the constantly generating gases at Washington," said of the congressional session ahead, "We shall undoubtedly have the Union dissolved forty times before its close, if political storm and tempest, the thunder and lightning of the Senate, the volcanic eruptions of the House, the flashing clouds of the State legislatures, and the artificial earthquakes and phosphorescent fire of letter-writers, can accomplish it."[31]

Everybody was likely to be testy. That had been evident in the last Congress when Robert W. Johnson of Arkansas got into an angry dispute with Orlando B. Ficklin of Illinois. Johnson sprang forward to clutch Ficklin, and Samuel W. Inge of Alabama, uninvolved until then, rushed in and struck Ficklin two or three blows with a cane. Later, when order was restored, one of Inge's neighbors asked, "Why, Inge, what did you fall upon Ficklin for?" "Why, I thought that the fight between the North and the South had commenced, and I might as well pitch in."[32]

Undergirding this passionate feeling of Southerners was the greater worry that the long-standing sectional balance, the sole bulwark between them and Northern political dominance, was about to collapse with all this new territory threatening to remain free. It appeared that not a single acre would be translated into a slave state. There was the prospect that seventeen new states would be carved from this territorial land bonanza—and not a single one of them a slave state. It would throw the traditional balance, already eroded, into a yawning imbalance. Already the South had been overlapped by the North in population. It had never had equal footing in the House of Representatives. Only in the Senate, equally split between North and South—fifteen states apiece with two senators each—did the equilibrium remain protected and intact. With seventeen new free states hewn from the territories, this balance would be irredeemably shattered, the South put at the utter mercy of the North, and slavery placed in fatal jeopardy.

"The injury to the South is already great," the *Jackson Mississippian* editorialized in September 1849. "Absolute ruin to the South is inevitable, unless this question is settled at once, and on such a basis that the agitation of it shall cease on the floor of Congress, or unless the South discontinues a Union with her enemies. . . . They not only insist on excluding us from a common territory, but they knowingly pursue a course which, if continued, must lead to insurrection and ruin. They avow a policy which is incompatible with the constitution, and with our institutions and safety. The Union has ceased to be a Union."[33]

In early 1849, Southern members of the Thirtieth Congress had caucused frequently to consider what they saw as aggression against their section by the North and how to stop it, or, if that could not be done, how to chart secession and dissolution. Behind these meetings was the angry iron hand and whip-like mind of South Carolina Senator John C. Calhoun, a Democrat. It produced a manifesto, written by him and called the "Southern Address." Ardent Northern legislators saw it to be "in the highest degree inflammatory."[34] Its aim had been to rally the slaveholding states around a new political banner. It had urged Southerners to abandon their traditional party moorings to form a new sectional party that would act as a bloc to defend Southern rights. The address had recapped the sectional struggle over slavery and accused the North of violating slavery's constitutional guarantee and looking to its total destruction. Calhoun had cried for united Southern action as the only way to meet this persistent Northern aggression.[35]

The "Southern Address" was by no means embraced by every Southerner. Democrats and Whigs enjoyed about equal strength in the South and had throughout the decade. Forty of the eighty-eight Southerners whom Calhoun asked to sign it refused—nearly all of them Southern Whigs. Most Whigs in the South were large cotton, tobacco, rice, and sugar planters with strong ties to slavery and states' rights. But they were also Union-loving. Only two of them had signed Calhoun's address. But out of it had come a call for a convention of Southern states to meet in Nashville in June 1850 to consider unified resistance.[36]

Many Northerners did not credit this Southern rage. They saw it as false bravado unworthy of serious notice. Ohio Congressman Joshua Giddings, a rabid antislavery Free-Soiler, called the cry of dissolution gasconade, "the dernier resort of Southern men for fifty years, whenever they desired to frighten doughfaces [pro-Southern Northerners] into a compliance with their measures."[37]

But the dissolution seed was definitely in the soil. A correspondent of the *New York Tribune* wrote, "In the Senate there are eight Southern senators and in the House thirty members from the same section who are organized as disunionists and are opposed to any compromise whatever looking to the perpetuity of the Union."[38] One angry Northerner wrote, "the South is mole-eyed and mad . . . blind to the fact that the womb of time is quick with the coming birth of universal freedom."[39]

The new Congress would be split four ways over any compromise to stem this gathering tide of rebellion. First, there were the procompromise Democrats. They favored a solution that had become known as "popular sovereignty," which argued that Congress should stay out of the controversy and let the territories decide for themselves as they became states whether or not to be slave or free. Second, there were the procompromise Whigs, who did not favor popular sovereignty but wanted some kind of compromise. They believed the Constitution gave the Congress power over slavery in the territories, and rightly so—but it should be very carefully exercised.

Third, there were the anticompromise Free-Soilers, a loose melding of radical northern Whigs, Democrats, and Free-Soil Party members who agreed that Congress had power over slavery in the territories but that a higher moral power demanded slavery be excluded. There was to be no surrender to the southern "Slaveocracy." And finally, there were the anticompromise Democrats. These were the Southern radicals, the "fire eaters," who believed that Congress had no business in the territory business but was a mere caretaker. They held to a strict states' rights philosophy, that slavery in the territories was a state preserve and that slaveholders had a constitutional right to take their slaves into those territories at will and that the federal government was duty bound to protect that right.[40]

⁓ For a handful of men of the new Congress, this storm cloud overspreading the political firmament was déjà vu. They had seen one like it threatening the Union, horizon to horizon, thirty years before. The three U.S. senators who had dominated national politics for nearly half a century—Clay, Calhoun, and Daniel Webster of Massachusetts, together again in the Senate one last time in the twilight of great careers—had seen it all before in 1820. The split had not been so virulent then, but it had been bad enough. Then as now the same deadly combination—a huge acquisition of land (the Louisiana Purchase) and Negro slavery—had threatened to shatter the Union.

The problem reached back in time even before 1820. Legislation in 1790 had established the rule that slaveholding was allowable anywhere in federal territories where not positively barred by federal law. And for thirty years that rule had held undisturbed. But the nation in the intervening time had acquired the Louisiana territory, that vast 828,000 square miles of western land beyond the Mississippi—a purchase that doubled the size of the young republic. There had been urgent stirrings in the North against slavery since then, and the bonds of Union had begun to fray. As late as April 1818 a proposal to bar slavery in all states thereafter admitted was snuffed out in the House. It was but the prelude to bigger trouble.[41]

The U.S. Constitution had made Congress the maker and enforcer of all necessary rules and regulations governing the territories, which generally passed through an internship in democracy while waiting for their populations to grow to sufficient size for statehood. Congress laid the tinder for a political firestorm when it upgraded Missouri, a part of the Louisiana Purchase, to a territory of the highest rank in 1816. Missouri had been growing rapidly in population since the War of 1812. By 1816 it had reached 40,000 and had been in training for statehood for thirteen years.

Memorials of admission began reaching Congress from Missouri in late 1817. A select committee in the House reported a bill authorizing the territory to form a constitution and state government on April 3, 1818. In December, Henry Clay, then Speaker of the House, presented the Missouri bill, and in February 1819 it was taken up by the Committee of the Whole.

By then the Missouri territory's population had swelled to 56,000 freemen and 10,000 slaves, and it was generally believed it would enter the Union as a slave state. It formally applied as such in 1819, in the second session of the Fifteenth Congress. It was the first in the Trans-Mississippi territory, after Louisiana, to seek admission, and it opened the fight over whether the vast American heartland was to be slave or free. Both sections wanted their brand imprinted on the new West, its resources made their own.

Not pleased with Missouri's bid were antislavery congressmen from the North. One of these was James Tallmadge Jr., a freshman Democrat representing the Poughkeepsie district from New York. Tallmadge was forty-one, a veteran of the War of 1812 and a rising politician in the Empire State. He had married his second cousin, Laura Tallmadge, in 1810. Their only daughter, Mary Rebecca, born in 1816 and said to be stunningly beautiful, would be presented at various courts in Europe as a young woman. There she would become a favorite of Queen Victoria, not so stunningly beautiful, who, soon after ascending the English throne, said one morning over breakfast that she would exchange her crown for Miss Tallmadge's dazzling beauty.[42]

What Tallmadge did on February 12, 1819, when the Missouri enabling bill reached the floor in the Fifteenth Congress, was less than dazzling to Southerners. Calling slavery "this monstrous scourge of the human race . . . this bane of man, this abomination of heaven,"[43] he moved to amend the bill to prohibit the further introduction of slaves into Missouri and to free all children of slaves born in the state, after admission, at age twenty-five. A measure for gradual abolition, it would radically cripple slavery in Missouri.

The amendment was anathema to the South, and it ignited a political firestorm. Southern members of Congress almost unanimously denounced it. The hotheads among them threatened dissolution of the Union if the restriction held. Thomas W. Cobb of Georgia accused Tallmadge of "kindling a fire which all the waters of the ocean could not extinguish. It could be extinguished only in blood!"[44]

Despite the Southern outcry, the amendment passed the House in two parts: the prohibition of slavery in Missouri, 87–76; freedom after age twenty-five, 82–78. The voting was distinctly sectional. The Senate, refusing to agree to it, struck the amendment from the bill by a 22–16 vote. The House refused to back down. The Fifteenth Congress expired in deadlock over statehood, the House refusing to admit Missouri without the restriction, the Senate refusing to admit Missouri with it.

In the hiatus between the Fifteenth and Sixteenth Congresses tempers continued to fray. Northern legislatures passed resolutions against admitting Missouri unless slavery was barred. Southerners threatened dissolution if it was outlawed. Clearly there had to be a compromise if this Union-periling deadlock was to be resolved.

Wags had taken to calling it the "Misery Debate."[45] And the misery and the debate resurfaced immediately in the new Sixteenth Congress, this time first in the Senate, where Northerners now saw slavery " 'rolling onward with a rapid tide toward the boundless regions of the West,' threatening to doom them to sterility and sorrow."[46] Speech clashed with speech, Northerner with Southerner, as the debate rocked on in the Senate. Threats of secession became the common talk of Southern senators. The dreaded words "civil war" and "disunion" were "uttered almost without emotion."[47]

The major break toward compromise came when Illinois Senator Jesse B. Thomas introduced the idea of a dividing line for the territories—every state south of 36° 30' in the Louisiana Purchase to be slave, every state north free, excepting Missouri, which lay north of the line. Otherwise slavery would be barred, in the present and future, north of the divide in the territory but permitted south of it.

But there was another problem. Political equilibrium between the North and South was a basic Southern tenet. Southerners demanded a balance between free and slave states, believing it the only way to protect their rights and preserve their political clout. In the past, therefore, by tacit agreement states slave and free had been admitted to the Union in pairs. Vermont had entered in tandem with Kentucky, Tennessee with Ohio, Louisiana with Indiana, Mississippi with Illinois. Abolition wits were saying that "things had come to such a pass that a white baby could no longer be born into the Union unless a black one was born at the same time."[48] When Missouri's Territorial Assembly petitioned Congress for statehood there were twenty-two states, eleven free and eleven slave. If Missouri entered unaccompanied by a free state it would skewer the balance.

There was, however, a free state available. Maine had recently broken from Massachusetts and applied for admission. In the House, Speaker Clay, a man intent on finding the middle ground, bound the two states into a single package. Maine would enter the Union free, Missouri slave. That bill was sent to the Senate, where it was narrowly adopted. After several failed attempts to connect them, Thomas's 36° 30' line was attached to it, and the two compromise measures were adopted. When this bill was sent back to the House, Tallmadge's slavery prohibition was jettisoned—narrowly, by three votes, 90–87. The compromise bill then passed.

It had not happened quietly. It had come only after a "prolonged and bitter contest; after a debate, then without parallel in the history of the Congress," with threatened disunion hanging over all throughout.[49] Maine was admitted the next day, March 3, 1820. On March 6, Missouri was authorized to form a constitution and state government without a slavery restriction.

Delegates to the aspiring state's First Constitutional Convention met from June 12 to July 19 in the Mansion House Hotel in St. Louis, a large three-story brick building at Third and Vine Streets. In the hotel's big dining room, the principal ballroom of the city, where theatrical companies often performed, the delegates generated drama of their own, which would start the debate raging anew with more doomsday threats of disunion, requiring yet another compromise. Resenting the delay and bridling at the Northern attempt to tell them they could not have slavery, they showed an early mulishness for which Missourians would later become renowned. They defiantly wrote into their new constitution a clause that would require the General Assembly, when the territory became a state, to pass laws "to prevent free negroes or mulattoes from coming to or settling in this State, under any pretext whatever."[50]

The Missourians laid their newly minted constitution, with that incendiary clause riding in conspicuous attendance, on November 20. Opponents of Missouri's admission, particularly in the House, which was generally opposed to its statehood in the first place, seized on the clause as a pretext to kill it. Clay, no longer Speaker but with as keen an eye for compromise as ever, waded into the middle of the problem again. After listening to hours and days of endless and fruitless wrangling over the issue on the House floor, he created compromise language for this new upchurning. He wrote that Missouri should not pass any laws preventing anybody of any description from settling there who were citizens of other states, since to do so was starkly unconstitutional. If Missouri would accept this "fundamental condition," it would be admitted by proclamation of President James Monroe without further action by Congress.[51]

The House rejected Clay's compromise 83–80, and by the middle of February 1821 Congress was deadlocked again over this "distracting question," "this trying question," "this ominous and ill-boding question."[52] The House was in session every day into the night without adjournment and without rest or food. "It is long since I have dined except by candle-light," one member complained.[53]

A writer noted that "only a magician could be expected to pull a compromise rabbit from a parliamentary hat like this."[54] Clay, the would-be magician, moved in again with yet another compromise strategy. He proposed that a House Committee of Twenty-three be named to confer with a Senate committee to hammer out an accord of some kind that would let Missouri in. Named to head the House committee, he put before the joint committee what was basically a dusted-off version of his earlier rejected compromise plan. This time it passed, 87–81, in the House and was approved two days later by the Senate. Missouri somewhat grudgingly agreed to delete the offensive clause and was admitted into the Union on August 10. Clay was widely hailed for his "artful measure" and was acclaimed as the "Great Pacificator."[55]

Thirty-seven Southern representatives voted against the compromise, and Virginia's John Randolph called it a "dirty bargain."[56] Thirty years later it would still be thought so by many Southerners, and Senator James Mason, another Virginian, would say the 36° 30' line had been "acquiesced in, nothing more."[57] But the compromise was widely thought of at the time as a pro-Southern solution. It had won the South an immediate slave state and ensured for it yet another—Arkansas, standing by and ready. It gave slavedom another state, and the vast territory in the North where slavery was henceforth barred was unsettled and likely to remain so for decades to come. So antislavery Northerners saw the compromise as a surrender.[58]

Indeed, the South had won most of what it wanted, since the fight had been over Missouri statehood. The 36° 30' line had been tacked on for the North—to make the medicine go down. Still, many Southerners looked on it in dismay, accepting it only as the lesser of evils—to avert disunion. The *Richmond Enquirer*, seeing it as but a prelude to further future Northern aggression, wrote: "We scarcely ever recollected to have tasted a bitterer cup."[59]

The struggle for compromise over Missouri marked the first clear split of the two sections of the Union and the beginning of the South's urgent, unremitting obsession with political equilibrium. For the first time the slave states were now clearly separated from the free—by a distinct geographical line. Slaveholders stopped looking to slavery's ultimate extinction, the tacit viewpoint before, but instead to its indefinite perpetuation and extension. Sectional power became a paramount must in the South to that end. It became pressingly urgent for the region to add more slave states. The South had come to believe by 1849 that its political identity and destiny were riding on the struggle for more such states. Political equilibrium had come to mean equilibrium for slavery. Equal rights in the territories had come to mean equal rights for slavery. That was now the issue, and it had become sharply defined and nation-dividing.[60]

Although the compromise was looked upon as a bargain struck between the two sections rather than a permanent solution of the slavery issue, the bitter cup had been a lasting one. Pairing free states and slave in the Louisiana Purchase territories north and south along the 36° 30' line was the pattern that had kept the political balance and the Union intact for nearly three decades until this next great land acquisition from the Mexican War.

But the Missouri Compromise had turned out to be only a "dress rehearsal" for what seemed ahead for this Thirty-first Congress convening in late 1849 in the train of the huge land acquisition from the Mexican War. The same issues present in 1820 had all resurfaced. They had simply festered in thirty years into a more festering wound. The Missouri problem had flushed out the full-blown Northern attack on slavery expansion in the territories and now it was there again, more lethal than ever. Also present in 1849, ratcheted up to a much higher tension, was the threatening peril of possible—even likely—dissolution of the Union if a compromise was not again struck.[61] And compromise would be more difficult this time. In 1820, Northern feeling against slavery had not hardened as it had by 1849. It had been before the South felt truly mortally threatened.[62] But abolitionist societies had proliferated in the North since then, the outcry against slavery had jumped to a far higher decibel, and the bonds of union had frayed further.

In 1820 one venerable American political sage who knew much about nation making and nation splitting had looked on the turmoil, saw what it portended, and despaired for the future of the country. Thomas Jefferson, in the evening of his life, had written to a friend: "It [the Missouri question] is the most portentous one which ever yet threatened our Union. In the gloomiest moment of the revolutionary war I never had any apprehensions equal to what I feel from this source." To Jefferson, the question was "like a firebell in the night" that had awakened him and filled him with terror. "I considered it at once as the knell of the Union. It is hushed, indeed, for the moment. But this is a reprieve only, not a single sentence. A geographical line, coinciding with a marked principle, moral and political, once conceived and held up to the angry passions of men, will never be obliterated; and every new irritation will mark it deeper and deeper." He said, "we have the wolf by the ears, and we can neither hold him, nor safely let him go."[63]

Had this great political prophet lived to see what was about to happen in Washington in 1850, he would have believed that the fire and the wolf had indeed consumed the Union.

NOTES

1. Byron Sunderland, "Washington as I First Knew It," *Records of the Columbia Historical Society* 5 (1902): 195.

2. Constance McLaughlin Green, *Washington: Village and Capital, 1800–1878* (Princeton, NJ, 1962), 224.

3. David Outlaw to Emily Outlaw, January 5, 1850, David Outlaw Papers, Southern Historical Collection, University of North Carolina, Chapel Hill.

4. This information is distilled from a discussion of these matters in Elbert B. Smith, *The Presidencies of Zachary Taylor and Millard Fillmore* (Lawrence, KS, 1988), 4–5.

5. Sunderland, "Washington as I First Knew It," 201.

6. Green, *Washington: Village and Capital*, 228.

7. Sunderland, "Washington as I First Knew It," 201.

8. Frederick W. Seward, *Seward at Washington as Senator and Secretary of State: A Memoir of His Life, with Selections from His Letters* (New York, 1891), 104.

9. For this picture of Washington's other side I am heavily indebted to Green, *Washington: Village and Capital*, 211–12.

10. Francis O. French, *Growing Up on Capitol Hill: A Young Washingtonian's Journal, 1850–1852* (Washington, DC, 1997), 48.

11. Sunderland, "Washington as I First Knew It," 199.

12. Ibid., 196, 203–4.

13. William C. Allen, *History of the United States Capitol: A Chronicle of Design, Construction, and Politics* (Washington, DC, 2001), 18, 169, 178.

14. Alexander Mackay, *The Western World; or Travels in the United States in 1846–47*, 3 vols. (1849; reprint ed., New York, 1968), 1:171.

15. These figures are from Smith, *The Presidencies of Zachary Taylor and Millard Fillmore*, 2.

16. *Congressional Globe*, 31st Cong., 1st sess., Appendix, 1253.

17. James D. Richardson, ed., *A Compilation of the Messages and Papers of the Presidents, 1789–1897*, 10 vols. (Washington, DC, 1897), 5:9.

18. James S. Pike, *First Blows of the Civil War: The Ten Years of Preliminary Conflict in the United States from 1850 to 1860* (New York, 1879), 19.

19. Ulrich B. Phillips, ed., "The Correspondence of Robert Toombs, Alexander H. Stephens, and Howell Cobb," in *Annual Report of the American Historical Association for the Year 1911*, vol. 2 (Washington, DC, 1913), 97 n, 169, 171.

20. Allan Nevins, *Ordeal of the Union*, Vol. 1, *Fruits of Manifest Destiny, 1847–1852* (New York, 1947), 255.

21. Robert P. Brooks, ed., "Howell Cobb Papers," *Georgia Historical Quarterly* 5 (June 1921): 41.

22. Herbert Darling Foster, "Webster's Seventh of March Speech and the Secession Movement, 1850," *American Historical Review* 27 (January 1922): 257.

23. George Templeton Strong, *The Diary of George Templeton Strong: The Turbulent Fifties, 1850–1859*, ed. Allan Nevins and Milton Halsey Thomas (New York, 1952), 5, 19.

24. Horace Greeley, *The Autobiography of Horace Greeley, or Recollections of a Busy Life* (New York, 1872), 227.

25. Henry W. Hilliard, *Politics and Pen Pictures at Home and Abroad* (New York, 1892), 216.

26. *Congressional Globe*, 31st Cong., 1st sess., 403.

27. Ibid., Appendix, 116.

28. Thomas Hart Benton, *Thirty Years' View; or a History of the Working of the American Government for Thirty Years, from 1820 to 1850*, 2 vols. (1856; reprint ed., New York, 1968), 2:132.

29. Mary Tyler Mann, *Life of Horace Mann* (Boston, 1888), 288; *Congressional Globe*, 31st Cong., 1st sess., Appendix, 224.

30. Thomas L. Clingman, *Selections from Speeches and Writings of Honorable Thomas L. Clingman of North Carolina* (Raleigh, NC, 1877), 260, 254.

31. Pike, *First Blows of the Civil War*, 6.

32. Greeley, *Autobiography*, 232–33.

33. Quoted in U.S. National Archives and Records Administration, Center for Legislative Archives, "Westward Expansion and the Compromise of 1850," in *Congress and the Shaping of American History*, Vol. 1, *1789–1869* (Washington, unpublished), 42.

34. Mann, *Life of Horace Mann*, 273.

35. The address and its signees are in John C. Calhoun, *The Papers of John C. Calhoun*, vol. 26, *1848–1849*, ed. Robert L. Meriwether and Clyde N. Wilson (Columbia, SC, 1959–), 225–43.

36. Nathan Sargent, *Public Men and Events from the Commencement of Mr. Monroe's Administration, in 1817, to the Close of Mr. Fillmore's Administration, in 1853*, 2 vols. (Philadelphia, 1874), 2:343–45; Carl N. Degler, "There Was Another South," *American Heritage* 11 (August 1960): 54; Arthur Charles Cole, *The Whig Party in the South* (Washington, 1913), 104.

37. Joshua R. Giddings, *Speeches in Congress* (Boston, 1853), 409–10.

38. *New York Tribune*, February 2, 1850, quoted in James Ford Rhodes, *History of the United States from the Compromise of 1850 to the McKinley-Bryan Campaign of 1896*, 8 vols. (1892–1919; reprint ed., Port Washington, NY, 1967), 1:136n.

39. Pike, *First Blows of the Civil War*, 12.

40. This concise summary of the four main positions on compromise owes much to the National Archives' excellent unpublished "Westward Expansion and the Compromise of 1850," 30–31.

41. Don E. Fehrenbacher, *The South and Three Sectional Crises* (Baton Rouge, LA, 1980), 12–13.

42. Arthur White Talmadge, *The Talmadge, Tallmadge and Talmage Genealogy* (New York, 1909), 181, 217.

43. *Annals of Congress*, 15th Cong., 2d sess., 1205, 1206.

44. Ibid., 1437.

45. Thomas Hart Clay, *Henry Clay* (Philadelphia, 1910), 111.

46. Horace Greeley, *The American Conflict: A History of the Great Rebellion*, 2 vols. (Hartford, CT, 1864–1866), 1:76.

47. Glover Moore, *The Missouri Controversy, 1819–1821* (1953; reprint ed., Gloucester, MA, 1967), 92.

48. Oliver Dyer, *Great Senators of the United States Forty Years Ago* (New York, 1889), 35.

49. James Albert Woodburn, "The Historical Significance of the Missouri Compromise," in *Annual Report of the American Historical Association for the Year 1893* (Washington, 1894), 264–65.

50. Floyd Calvin Shoemaker, *Missouri's Struggle for Statehood, 1804–1821* (1916; reprint ed., New York, 1969), 166, 166n, 291; Woodburn, "The Historical Significance of the Missouri Compromise," 265.

51. Moore, *The Missouri Controversy*, 147.

52. *Annals of Congress*, 16th Cong., 2d sess., 1101, 1124, 1128.

53. Everett Somerville Brown, ed., *The Missouri Compromises and Presidential Politics, 1820–1825* (St. Louis, MO, 1926), 36.

54. Moore, *The Missouri Controversy*, 154.

55. Ibid., 154–56, 159, 168–69. The "artful measure" quote is from Brown, *The Missouri Compromises and Presidential Politics*, 31.

56. Rhodes, *History of the United States*, 1:37.

57. *Congressional Globe*, 31st Cong., 1st sess, Appendix, 224

58. Rhodes, *History of the United States*, 1:37; Moore, *The Missouri Controversy*, 114.

59. *Richmond Enquirer*, February 10, 1820, in Fehrenbacher, *The South and Three Sectional Crises*, 19–20.

60. This assessment is distilled from Woodburn's excellent "The Historical Significance of the Missouri Compromise," 294–96.

61. This description of the renewal of the controversy owes much to Moore, *The Missouri Controversy*, 342, 348, 350.

62. James MacGregor Burns, *The Vineyard of Liberty* (New York, 1981), 243.

63. Thomas Jefferson, *The Works of Thomas Jefferson*, 12 vols., ed. Paul Leicester Ford (New York, 1905), 12:157–59.

CHAPTER TWO

DAVID WILMOT'S BOMBSHELL

DAVID WILMOT, a freshman Democratic congressman from Pennsylvania, was not generally known as a troublemaker. But when he rose in a hectic House chamber on August 8, 1846, and clamored for recognition he had an amendment full of mischief on his mind.

Wilmot was a rural country lawyer from Pennsylvania's Twelfth District, noted for his unkempt dress, unruly hair, cussing ability, and ever-present wad of chewing tobacco. But beneath that uneven veneer was an ambitious thirty-two-year-old politician, and a regular and faithful party man.[1] He had backed all the key Democratic measures—the annexation of Texas in 1845, the compromise for Oregon territory, even President James Polk's tariff reduction program—when many other Democrats had not.[2]

The young congressman was of average height with an over-ample girth—one observer described him as stout and "Dutch-built"—but with a face "as fair and smooth as a woman's" and a rich, melodious voice capable of impressive eloquence. His hair hung loosely about his eyes, but he was a charming conversationalist armed with a delightful laugh. He was as laid back in demeanor as he was in appearance, tending to leave things "both in his private affairs and profession, rather loosely arranged," much like his hair. He was considered to be a man of "much native talent, but acts on the spur of the moment," and it generally took great occasions to arouse his ardor. But when aroused, he was powerful and formidable.[3]

On that sultry Saturday in early August, he was aroused. The war had been raging in faraway Mexico for four months, and President Polk wanted $2 million to use to persuade the Mexicans to let go of their northern territories. His request for the money was before the House when Wilmot stood to be recognized. Saying that he was opposed "now and forever, to the extension of this 'peculiar institution' that belongs to the South," Wilmot slapped a one-sentence amendment onto Polk's request that would bar slavery from all the new land acquired in the war.[4] It was not so much that

Wilmot was morally outraged. He cared little about the welfare of slaves one way or the other. What he wanted were the new territories kept as free soil for white labor. It was clear he saw his incendiary amendment as a white man's proviso.[5]

David Wilmot
Library of Congress

Wilmot was being Tallmadge all over again nearly thirty years later, with a measure Southerners considered far more virulent. To them "this odious proviso"[6] would be a wholesale ransoming of their rights to the entire rest of the country. It immediately became "a Gorgon's head—a chimera dire—a watchword of party, and the synonyme [sic] of civil war and the dissolution of the Union."[7] Michigan Senator Lewis Cass, who was to be the Democratic nominee for president in 1848, predicted that if passed "it would be death to the [Mexican] war—death to all hopes of getting an acre of Territory, death to the administration, and death to the Democratic party."[8] John C. Calhoun called it an "apple of discord."[9] It was widely feared that if it passed—and there was a chance it could—the South would secede.

Styled the Wilmot Proviso, it made the obscure, back-country, back-bench politician an instant household name and re-raised the curtain, more dramatically than ever, on the sectional drama. "As if by magic," the *Boston Whig* wrote on August 15, "it brought to a head the great question which is about to divide the American people."[10]

In truth it was a proviso that had not originated in Wilmot's mind alone. It was not even a new idea. He introduced it early Saturday evening when the House was rocking to the chaos that attended the dying moments of the first session of the Twenty-ninth Congress, as it was grinding out last-minute bills before scheduled adjournment at noon on the following Monday. It was an oppressive night at the end of a very hot day. Newspaper fans and ice water were in heavy demand on the floor and in the galleries.[11] Throughout the day Wilmot had been in conference with like-minded Northern colleagues opposed to slavery's extension in the territories.

At noon, over dinner in a hotel nearby, he had raised the subject of an amendment to Polk's money bill with other congressmen at his table. Wilmot told them that it was clear that the $2 million Polk wanted was but a first installment to purchase the vast territory from Mexico. If so, Wilmot said he intended to move an amendment that slavery should be excluded from all of it. Later, in front of the hotel, he met with several other members. They agreed to "advise with our northern friends generally," and when Congress reassembled that evening, if the soundings were positive, an amendment should be pressed.

When their soundings met strong approval from other Northern Democrats, several members gathered to agree on "the form and terms" of the proposed amendment. Several of them, Wilmot among them, drafted language. After various drafts the wording was agreed upon. The language was basically that of the Northwest

Ordinance of 1787: "There shall be neither slavery nor involuntary servitude in the said territory, otherwise than in the punishment of crimes whereof the party shall have been duly convicted." It was the free-soil formula for the territories authored by Thomas Jefferson.[12] Wilmot would later say that his amendment "asserted no new principle. I was but the copyist of Jefferson."[13]

It was agreed that Wilmot was the one to introduce the amendment, since he was the most likely of them all, being such a faithful party man, to be recognized in the confusion on the floor, when time was running out and recognition was hard to come by.[14] When his bombshell hit the floor in the rush to adjourn, the House passed it on that very day. But in the ebbing moments of the session an unsympathetic and more sectionally balanced Senate let it die behind a filibuster by Massachusetts Senator John Davis, and Polk's money with it.

As upset as anybody was Polk. The president called it "a mischievous & foolish amendment. . . . What connection slavery had with making peace with Mexico it is difficult to conceive." He believed that had time not run out, the Senate would have struck out the proviso and saved his $2 million and the House would have concurred. "Had the appropriation been passed," he grieved into his diary, "I am confident I should have made an honorable peace by which we should have acquired California, & such other territory as desired, before the end of October."[15]

The proviso was widely viewed as but the opening Northern move to block the spread of slavery and make all of the new territories free soil. It would in effect repeal the Missouri Compromise line and kill the idea that the Southern territories were open to slavery even if Northern territories were not. It would close them all to slavery, North and South. A reporter called it "the reddest rag that could have been waved in the face of the Southern Bull."[16] In Southern eyes it signaled "an entire revolution in the action of the government," a blocking out of the slaveholding South from the common country, "a revolution which could not occur without a total violation of the spirit and essence of the Constitution."[17] Southerners saw it as interference with a citizen's right to hold his property in territory common to all—and that was unconstitutional.

Southerners wished the hated proviso might "sleep the sleep of death."[18] But it had lived on, in vivid annoyance, being voted up in the House and down in the Senate in every session that had followed since. For three years it had "convulsed the Union."[19] It was

still there, convulsing the Union, ratcheting North-South antagonisms to a new height, and threatening dissolution on the eve of
1850.

~~⌒⌒ No Southern eye fixed on David Wilmot's handiwork in 1846
was more baleful than John C. Calhoun's. To that preeminent political theorist and philosopher of Southern rights—one critic called
him the "Southern Grand Llama [*sic*]"[20]—it was the ultimate in-
sult. But in a sense he welcomed it. It drew the line distinctly. He
saw in it a window of opportunity. "I am of the impression," he
told a friend, "that if the South act as it ought, the Wilmot proviso,
instead of proving to be the means of successfully assailing us and
our peculiar institution, may be made the occasion of [our] successfully asserting our equality and rights by enabling us to force
the issue on the North. Something of the kind was indispensable to
rouse and unite the South."[21]

Calhoun unleashed his trumpet call against the proviso on the
Senate floor on February 19, 1847, with a set of resolutions. His cry
was a clear and angry articulation of the South's grievance against
the North. The nonslaveholding states, Calhoun said, have "come
to a fixed and solid determination" on two propositions: no further slave states will be admitted into the Union, and slavery shall
not exist hereafter in any territories of the United States. These
propositions, Calhoun raged, give the nonslaveholding states "the
monopoly of the public domain, to the entire seclusion of the
slaveholding States."

"Sir," the aroused Southern giant protested, "there is no mis-
taking the signs of the times." What does it mean for the relative
strength of the South in the Union if the proviso prevails? "Sir," he
said, answering his own question, "already we are in the minority
. . . in the other House, in the electoral college . . . in every department of this government, except at present in the Senate of the
United States."

If the aggressive policy of the North prevails, Calhoun predicted, fourteen new nonslaveholding states will be added and not
one new slaveholding state. "How will we then stand?" he demanded. "The Government, sir, will be entirely in the hands of the
non-slaveholding States—overwhelmingly. . . . We shall be at [their]
entire mercy. . . . Can we look to their justice and regard for our
interests? Now, I ask, Can we rely on that? Ought we to trust our
safety and prosperity to their mercy and sense of justice?"

"Sir," he warned, "the day that the balance between the two sections of the country. . . is destroyed, is a day that will not be far removed from political revolution, anarchy, civil war, and widespread disaster." So be it, if that is what it comes to. "I say, for one, I would rather meet any extremity upon earth than give up one inch of our equality," Calhoun told the Senate. "What, acknowledge inferiority! The surrender of life is nothing to sinking down into acknowledged inferiority."[22]

So what did Calhoun want? He had always been against the North-South compromise line drawn in 1820, but, to preserve the Union, he would consider its extension in this case for the sake of union. "It has kept the peace for some time," he said.[23] This idea of extending the Missouri Compromise line all the way to the Pacific was now a common fallback position for most Southerners. They tolerated it because much of the land pried from Mexico lay south of the line. President Polk himself, after some indecision on the matter, had urged it as "the only practicable means of settling the agitation and excitement on the subject which existed in and out of Congress." He told his diary, "If the question can be thus settled harmony will be restored to the Union and the danger of forming geographical parties be avoided."[24] But Southern efforts to extend the line to the Mexican territories had twice been voted down by overwhelming majorities, and Northerners generally considered it useless as a vehicle for compromise. But it seemed the very least that Southern ultras would settle for. Senator Jefferson Davis of Mississippi was saying, "Never will I take less than the Missouri compromise line extended to the Pacific ocean."[25]

Calhoun was prepared to bend but little, and in only one direction. He laid down his resolutions: the territories are common property; Congress has no right to make any law that discriminates between the states and deprives any of its full and equal rights in all territories; any law that deprives any citizen from emigrating to any territory with his property violates the Constitution, erodes equality, and subverts the Union; people forming a government have the right to adopt any form they wish, only that it be republican, and the imposition of any other condition by Congress is unconstitutional.

Missouri Senator Thomas Hart Benton rose to call Calhoun's resolutions "a string of abstractions." Indeed, Benton, bluntly practical and fiercely pro-Union, considered Calhoun himself something of an abstraction. He hated him. Not only were his resolutions abstractions, Benton roared, but also "firebrands to set the world on fire." To which Calhoun replied, "The Senator does not at all comprehend me."[26]

Whether Benton comprehended Calhoun or not, whether Calhoun's resolutions were abstractions or not, the problem of slavery in the territories was firmly fixed and dominant in the political firmament by the end of 1849. Men had tried to disarm and neutralize it. In the presidential election campaign of 1848, won by Zachary Taylor, his opponent, Senator Cass, had jabbed at it with a theory he had developed called "popular sovereignty."

With his approach Cass was seeking a middle ground the country could stand on between the two extremes—the Northern free-soil formula, what Southerners were wont to call Wilmot Provisoism; and Southern demands for free slave access to the territories. He had first enunciated "popular sovereignty" in a letter in late 1847 when he was the likely Democratic candidate for president. Cass believed the subject of slavery in the territories "should be kept out of the National Legislature, and left to the people of the confederacy in their respective local governments." Congress, in short, should neither exclude it nor protect it. The government should leave the matter entirely to the people of the territory.[27]

Cass, a loyal Democrat and intense anglophobe who spoke fluent French, was approaching seventy years of age. The celebrated English writer, Harriet Martineau, seeing him for the first time, thought him "a shrewd, hard-looking man, the very concentration of American caution."[28] He was overweight, all "dewlap, jowls, dark-circled eyes and moplike wig," but blessed with robust health and deathless endurance, which he credited to never drinking alcohol or using tobacco. He wore suits of glossy black, had made a fortune from real estate investments in Detroit, and was given now in his fading years to "dismal droning" speeches.[29]

He struck four notes in his landmark letter to A. O. P. Nicholson of Tennessee on Christmas Eve, 1847. He doubtless hoped his thesis might be a Yuletide gift to the distracted Union. He believed that the Wilmot Proviso was unconstitutional, that it had no prayer of passing in the Senate; that slavery, having been abolished by the Mexican government long before we acquired it, did not then exist in the territory held by U.S. arms; that slavery would never go there, in any event, for natural and geographical reasons—it was not an apt environment for slaves; and that organized communities exercising the power of government in the territories alone had the right

to decide if they wanted slavery or not. Cass thought that the people
of the territories had the same right to govern themselves as had
the people of the states. Congress had no right under the Constitution to legislate on slavery one way or the other, as the Wilmot Proviso sought to do.[30]

Lewis Cass
U.S. Senate Historical Office

"Are not the people of the Territories competent to manage their
own internal affairs?" Cass demanded. "Are they not of us, and
with us?—bone of our bone, and flesh of our flesh? The same people
with the same views, habits, and intelligence; all, indeed which
constitutes national identity? . . . Cannot such people administer
their own government safely and wisely? Experience says they can."
And "where," asked Cass, whose own Michigan had been thirty-
two years a territory in training for statehood, "did the people of
the Territories get the right to legislate for themselves? . . . They

got it from Almighty God; from the same omnipotent and benefi-
cent Being who gave us our rights." It is "a right inherent in every
community—that of having a share in making the laws which are
to govern them, and of which nothing but despotic power can de-
prive them."[31]

What Cass's popular sovereignty theory did not say was
whether slaveholders had a right to take their slaves into any territory before the people there decided one way or the other, before
statehood. The South was saying that they did, the North that they
did not. That was the crux of the problem. For that reason Southerners were particularly wary of Cass's thesis. And at any rate, he
had lost the presidential election.

As December 3 approached, the day the new Thirty-first Congress was to convene in late 1849, the problem it faced was hydra-
headed. Five issues had to be compromised. All five were urgent,
all five Union-dividing.

There was the problem of California. It had ballooned to a population of 80,000 almost overnight, since January 1848, when the first
flakes of gold were panned from a mill canal at John A. Sutter's
fort in the Sacramento Valley. By 1849 a gold rush was in full cry.
Prospectors and gold seekers were swarming there from all over
the Union, gold pans in their packs, greed in their eyes, and weapons in their hands. Massachusetts Senator Daniel Webster marveled,
"There is within the history of mankind, within my knowledge, no
instance of such an extraordinary rush of people for private enter-
prise to one point on the earth's surface."[32] Gold had turned an
out-of-the-way frontier into an El Dorado. Now, wrested from
Mexico, thronged, virtually lawless, and needing a government in
a hurry, it had applied to Congress for admission as a state in early
1849.

This application worried Southerners. Slavery had been abolished in all territory wrested from Mexico by a Mexican edict twenty
years before. Every acre of land ceded to the United States beyond
the Rio Grande had come as free soil, and that law had not been
repealed or superseded by U.S. law. Most of the thousands of gold
seekers bloating much of California were free-soil Northerners.
When harried Californians applied for statehood in 1849, they had
drafted a constitution outlawing slavery. The South hadn't reck-
oned on that. California lay south of the Missouri Compromise line,
yet here it was, "overspread with abolitionists"[33] and pounding on
the door for admission as a free state. In Southern minds it was a

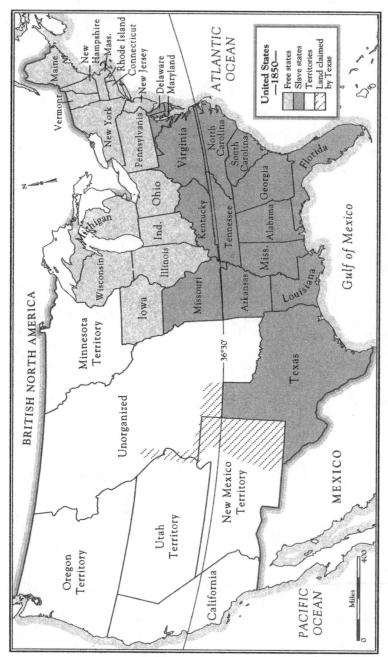

The United States in 1850
Map by Martha Tyzenhouse

crisis. Calhoun regarded California's admission as "worse than the Wilmot Proviso. What the latter proposes to do openly the former is intended to do covertly and fraudulently."[34] California as a state would throw the tenuous "geometry" of political balance between the North and South out of kilter.[35] There would then be sixteen free states and fifteen slave states. Southern control over the Senate, its last bastion of equality, would be lost—quite likely forever. Something had to be done.

Besides California, there was the problem of the rest of the land wrested from Mexico—New Mexico and Utah territory, also slave-free by Mexican law but not yet statehood-ready, by population or any other criterion. Would it also be lost to the slave-holding South? There was the odious Wilmot Proviso that would make it so. All of that land off limits to slaveholders and their property was seen as unendurable in the South. Many Southerners were not against admitting California per se, since its voters had already opted to be slave-free. But virtually all Southerners demanded that the question of keeping the rest of the territories open to them must first be adjusted. They resisted the California bill only to get a prior settlement of the Utah and New Mexico question on the basis of no congressional exclusion of slavery there until its residents decided the matter for themselves when applying for statehood. Something had to be done.

There was the problem of Texas. Already the biggest state in the Union, and a slave state, it wanted to be bigger yet. It was claiming—had claimed since it won its freedom from Mexico in 1836—four counties of New Mexico territory east of the Rio Grande now held by the federal government and considered free. When Texas became a state in 1845 it insisted that it also owned Santa Fe. That the disputed land should now be Texan and slave seemed reasonable to the South, unreasonable to the North. The Mexican War had been seen by many Northerners as simply a naked land grab to extend slavery in the first place. This Texas claim was also seen by many, including Henry Clay, as the Southern hope for "additional theater[s] for slavery."[36] Horace Greeley called it the "swindling claim of Texas."[37]

Texas had not yet tried to enforce the claim. But by 1849 it seemed ready to do so, by force of arms if necessary. New Mexicans, not willing to be gobbled up by Texas, seemed just as ready to resist, and they were appealing to the federal government for military protection. If there was a lit and sputtering fuse that might detonate civil war overnight, this was it. Something had to be done.

There was the problem of slavery and the slave trade in the District of Columbia. Both existed in the national capital "under the very eyes of Congress itself."[38] The North wanted them ended. Southerners saw their abolition as a mortal blow to slavery in their region, sufficient cause in many Southern minds for secession. Something had to be done.

Finally, there was the problem of fugitive slaves running away from their Southern owners, fleeing to the North, and not being returned. Indeed, they were sheltered and abetted in escape by Northern abolitionists. A Fugitive Slave Law mandating that runaways fleeing to the North must be returned to their Southern owners was written in 1793 and signed by President George Washington. Northerners had been violating it ever since. The South demanded that the law be tightened and vigorously reinforced. To Northern abolitionists it was the law of the devil. They wanted it repealed; and if it was not, they intended to continue to violate it. Something had to be done.

These five flaming issues were dividing North and South and threatening dissolution of the Union as the Thirty-first Congress was gathering in early December 1849. As Illinois Senator Stephen A. Douglas said, "It looks as though something would have to give."[39] Somebody would have to do something, and all eyes were turning to the soldier in the White House.

NOTES

1. Avery O. Craven, *The Coming of the Civil War* (New York, 1942), 221.
2. David M. Potter, *The Impending Crisis* (New York, 1976), 20.
3. This description of Wilmot owes much to his biographer, Charles Buxton Going, *David Wilmot, Free Soiler* (New York, 1924), 35–36, 128.
4. *Congressional Globe*, 29th Cong., 1st sess., 1214.
5. See excerpts from a Wilmot speech in O. C. Gardiner, *The Great Issue: or the Three Presidential Candidates* (New York, 1848), 57–62.
6. *Congressional Globe*, 31st Cong., 1st sess., Appendix, 389.
7. Benton, *Thirty Years' View*, 2:695.
8. Chaplain W. Morrison, *Democratic Politics and Sectionalism: The Wilmot Proviso Controversy* (Chapel Hill, NC, 1967), 36.
9. John C. Calhoun, "Correspondence of John C. Calhoun," ed. J. Franklin Jameson, in *Annual Report of the American Historical Association for the Year 1899*, vol. 2 (Washington, DC, 1900), 710.

10. Quoted in Potter, *The Impending Crisis*, 23. The image of a curtain rising on a sectional drama is also borrowed from Potter, page 18.

11. Going, *David Wilmot*, 98, 100.

12. Potter, *The Impending Crisis*, 54.

13. *Congressional Globe*, 30th Cong., 1st sess., Appendix, 1076.

14. My account of the origin of Wilmot's proviso, including quotes not otherwise cited, is woven from his own account in Gardiner, *The Great Issue*, 59.

15. James K. Polk, *The Diary of James K. Polk during His Presidency, 1845 to 1849*, 4 vols., ed. Milo Milton Quaife (Chicago, 1910), 2:75–77.

16. Dyer, *Great Senators*, 37.

17. Clingman, *Selections from Speeches and Writings*, 231.

18. Brooks, "Howell Cobb Papers" (September 1921), 43.

19. Benton, *Thirty Years' View*, 2:695.

20. William Ernest Smith, *The Francis Preston Blair Family in Politics*, 2 vols. (New York, 1933), 1:261.

21. John C. Calhoun to Percy Walker, October 26, 1847, in Morrison, *Democratic Politics and Sectionalism*, 38–39.

22. *Congressional Globe*, 29th Cong., 2d sess., 453–54.

23. Ibid., 454.

24. Polk, *Diary*, 3:501–2. Also see Potter, *The Impending Crisis*, 73.

25. *Congressional Globe*, 31st Cong., 1st sess., 249.

26. Calhoun's resolutions and Benton's retort are in ibid., 29th Cong., 2d sess., 455.

27. Greeley, *The American Conflict*, 190.

28. Harriet Martineau, *Retrospect of Western Travel*, 3 vols. (1838; reprint ed., New York, 1969), 1:49.

29. Holman Hamilton, *Prologue to Conflict: The Crisis and Compromise of 1850* (Lexington, KY, 1964), 28; idem, *Zachary Taylor: Soldier in the White House* (Indianapolis, 1951), 277; "Reminiscences of Washington," *Atlantic Monthly* 47 (February 1881): 244.

30. *Congressional Globe*, 31st Cong., 1st sess., 398.

31. Ibid., Appendix, 59, 73.

32. Smith, *The Francis Preston Blair Family in Politics*, 1:248.

33. Henry S. Foote, *Casket of Reminiscences* (1874; reprint ed., New York, 1968), 80.

34. Calhoun, "Correspondence of John C. Calhoun," 779.

35. This concept of an out-of-kilter "geometry" of balance is borrowed from Burns, *The Vineyard of Liberty*, 471–72.

36. Clay in *Congressional Globe*, 31st Cong., 1st sess., Appendix, 119.

37. Quoted in Nevins, *Ordeal of the Union*, 221 n.

38. *Congressional Globe*, 31st Cong., 1st sess., 250.

39. Frank E. Stevens, "Life of Stephen Arnold Douglas," *Journal of the Illinois State Historical Society* 16 (October 1923–January 1924): 401.

CHAPTER THREE

"OLD ROUGH AND READY"

MANY OF THE POLITICIANS converging on Washington believed that President Zachary Taylor was a very square peg jammed into a round hole.

He was a military man with a military mind, the hero of the U.S.-Mexican war. That fact had elected him president. Americans distrusted standing armies, but they were ready to raise hero-generals to the highest office in the land. They had elected Generals George Washington and Andrew Jackson and William Henry Harrison and, in 1848, Zachary Taylor. They had borne Taylor to his inaugural in March 1849 in a carriage drawn by four handsome grays followed by a procession of twelve military companies escorted by a hundred marshals, to salvos of booming artillery.[1]

Taylor was seen as "a perfect novice in politics."[2] No man in the history of the young country had come so far removed from politics to become president. Although now sixty-four years old, he had never voted. When a Whig politician first proposed that the old hero run for the presidency, Taylor had said, "Stop your nonsense and drink your whiskey!" When the improbable happened and he was nominated by the Whigs and the letter informing him of it hit the post office in Baton Rouge, it had come, as mail often did then, collect, and Taylor refused to accept it. It sat in the dead-letter office for a month before he learned it might have been of some importance and had it retrieved.[3]

Until he was nominated, Taylor had not been much of a Whig, the party he now led. He had confessed in a letter in 1848, when the clamor for his candidacy had reached a pitch he could not ignore, that he was "a Whig but not ultra Whig."[4] That meant, as he had also said, that he was "a Whig in principles" and had owned up to it "on all proper occasions."[5] It was believed that had he voted in 1844 he would have voted for the Whig, Henry Clay, against the Democrat, James Polk.[6] But he did not like to think of himself as a "party candidate." And if he had to be president, he didn't want to be thought of as a *partisan* president."[7] It was not unlikely that if he had been nominated by Democrats instead of Whigs—it had been distinctly possible in the jockeying that went on for his favor—he would just as readily have admitted he was a Democrat. As one contemporary wrote, "a nomination and election by the Democrats would have been just as acceptable to him as the same distinction conferred by the Whigs."[8]

Not only were Taylor's politics suspect, but also his capacity for the job. One observer was mirroring a common perception when he wrote of Taylor that he "was, of all the men who have filled the presidential chair by the choice of the people, the one least competent to perform its duties. He had been placed before his countrymen as a candidate, in spite of his repeated avowels of incapacity, inexperience, and repugnance to all civil duties."[9] Another wrote that the president "knew no more of statesmanship or the operations of government than a Comanche Indian."[10]

When his predecessor, James Polk, a Democrat, heard that Taylor had been elected he moaned into his diary, "it is deeply to be regretted. Without political information and without experience in civil life, he is wholly unqualified for the station. . . . Having no opinions or judgments of his own upon any one public subject, foreign or domestic, he will be compelled to rely upon the designing men of the Federal party who will cluster around him, and will be made to reverse, so far as the Executive can reverse, the whole policy of my administration. . . . The country will be the [loser] by his election." To Polk's utter astonishment on their ride together to the new president's inaugural, Taylor had said he believed that "California and Oregon were too distant to become members of the Union, and that it would be better for them to be an independent government." These, Polk told his diary, "are alarming opinions to be entertained by the President of the U.S." He thought Taylor was "no doubt, a well meaning old man" but "uneducated, exceedingly ignorant of public affairs, and, I should judge, of very ordinary capacity."[11]

Horace Greeley, editor of the *New York Tribune*, who had never met Taylor in person but who had an opinion about everything, said, "Old Zack is a good old soul but don't know himself from a side of sole leather in the way of statesmanship."[12] That was the common wisdom. Benjamin Brown French, a close observer of the Washington scene who knew Taylor well, called him "an honest, plain, unpretending old man, who, if left to his own course, would be as honest as it is possible for a man to be, but about as fit for

President of these United States as any New England Farmer that one might select out of a thousand, with his eyes shut."[13]

When another close Washington observer, George W. Julian, first met Taylor, he said, "I decidedly liked his kindly, honest, farmer-like face, and his old-fashioned simplicity of dress and manners.

Zachary Taylor
Library of Congress

His conversation was awkward and labored, and evinced a lack of self-possession; while his whole demeanor suggested his frontier life, and that he had reached a position for which he was singularly unfitted by training and experience, or by any natural aptitude."[14] "He really is a most simple-minded old man," Massachusetts

Congressman Horace Mann wrote after dining with him. "He has the least show or pretension about him of any man I ever saw; talks as artlessly as a child about affairs of State, and does not seem to pretend to a knowledge of any thing of which he is ignorant."[15]

Winfield Scott, the general in chief of the army, who was not particularly fond of him, called him as unlettered in literature as he was in politics, his literary knowledge extending not "much beyond good old Dilworth's Spelling Book." But Scott admitted that Taylor had "a good store of common sense," and that "few men have ever had a more comfortable, labor-saving contempt for learning of every kind. Yet this old soldier and neophyte states-man, had the true basis of a great character—pure, uncorrupted morals, combined with indomitable courage. Kind hearted, sincere, and hospitable in a plain way, he had no vice but prejudice, [with] many friends" and "not an enemy in the world."[16]

Taylor's oratory tended to be unfinished, halting, and wooden. George Julian noted that the president "frequently mispronounced his words, hesitated and stammered, and sometimes made a break-down in the middle of a sentence."[17] He was bereft of the gift of "colloquial accomplishments" and "narrative or descriptive talent," another Washingtonian observed.[18]

Few doubted that Taylor was in the presidency more from a sense of duty than preference. He would rather have been on the tented field leading armies—being what his devoted soldiers had called him, "Old Rough and Ready"—or on his plantation in Loui-siana. He admitted to Ethan Allen Hitchcock, one of his officers in the war with Mexico, that he wished he could "put the Presidency in somebody's hands and have nothing more to do with it."[19] But this strong sense of duty, honed by forty years in the army, had followed the reluctant Taylor to the presidency. It would be as strong there as it had been in the army. And if his detractors undervalued him, they also underestimated him.

Taylor had been a success in life from the start, and not just as a soldier. He was a Southerner, born in Virginia, and although it was difficult to tell by his rough demeanor and outward appear-ance, his own genealogy snaked back into the Virginia aristocracy. His mother was a cousin to President James Madison. He had mar-ried Margaret Mackall Smith, a wealthy planter's daughter, and had built a small inherited plantation in Louisiana into a fortune. He was an able manager and a gifted organizer, a fair-minded, humane owner of 145 slaves. For four decades he had been an outstanding, intelligent, and courageous soldier, unpossessed of pomp and ceremony but shrewd in battle. In the War of 1812 he had successfully defended Fort Harrison on the Wabash River in the Indiana territory, the first U.S. victory in that young war. He had won the first brevet commission—to major—ever awarded by the U.S. government. Later, on the frontier, he became known as an officer of compassion who protected the rights of Indians wherever he could, even as he fought them. And his spectacular victories in the war with Mexico against overweighted odds had won him the highest office in the land. He had good judgment, was independent minded, stubborn, proud, and sensitive with ample prejudices but absolutely truthful and honest. He was good humored, kind, cordial, fond of hominy, and dearly loved by his six children.[20]

So Taylor had been elected to the presidency against his own inclinations and to the utter regret of his wife. They reluctantly broke up housekeeping in Baton Rouge and left for the village-capital, bringing with them William Oldham, the faithful black who had been Taylor's body servant for years; Old Whitey, the general's famed Mexican War horse; and a favorite dog.[21] Taylor kept his hero-horse tethered on the White House lawn—unusual perhaps, but not so unusual as John Quincy Adams, who had kept an alligator and silkworms in the East Room.[22]

In Washington, Mrs. Taylor, who was frail and in ill health and preferring to be home in Louisiana, spent a good deal of her time shut up in her room on the second floor of the White House knitting and occasionally taking a drag on her pipe. She received only a few intimate friends and left the direction of White House social life and domestic affairs to their youngest daughter, twenty-five-year-old Betty Bliss.[23] Taylor also had with him his son-in-law, William S. Bliss, his right hand and most valued aide in Mexico, and known to many as "Perfect Bliss," one of the most skilled and scholarly officers in the army.[24]

Taylor was not the kind to change what he was just for an elevation in status and position, however lofty. Squat, thickset, and short legged, he and his dress would hardly pass fashionable muster. A visitor to the White House wrote, "He wore a shirt that was formerly white, but which then looked like the map of Mexico after the battle of Buena Vista . . . spotted and spattered with tobacco juice." The president had the aim of some of his cannoneers in firing tobacco juice toward a cuspidor, which he did constantly. The "flow" homed to its target with "unerring aim," never missing.[25]

Occasionally the president rode out on the wooded roads about Washington on Old Whitey. And often he could be seen in the city's streets on morning walks, his unbrushed gray hair, whiskers of military cut, and "weather-bronzed and care-furrowed" features standing out from under a high black silk hat angled on the back of his head. He generally wore a suit of black broadcloth that was much too large for him but styled, it is said, by his orders, for comfort.[26]

Southerners were delighted when the general was elected president. Indeed, he owed his election largely to the South. Southern Whigs, in particular, thought they were going to have a firm friend in the highest of places, a fellow Southerner and slaveholder who could be relied upon to protect their rights and block antislavery moves by the North—by veto, if necessary.[27] They had hoped to guide him in the interest of the South.

Taylor had made all the right preliminary moves. He had built a cabinet tilted to the South—four of its seven members were from slave states. Never mind that many observers viewed the cabinet as a collection of lightweights. Horace Greeley thought the cabinet mediocre at best: "Whenever any one of them shall drop out or be 'hove over,' he will sink like a stone and never be heard of again."[28]

But Taylor was not turning out the way Southerners expected. He had surprised Northerners and bewildered Southerners by transmuting into a "reverse doughface"—a Southern man with Northern principles.[29] Northerners, not Southerners, were now exulting over the new president. It was a Northerner, not a Southerner, who was saying of him now, "It is a fortunate circumstance that we have a man of pluck at the head of affairs in the present juncture. Whoever else may become alarmed, General Taylor will not. The country may repose in this conviction."[30]

Southern lawmakers returning to Washington were astonished and appalled to see installed at Taylor's right hand, whispering influentially in his ear, the new notoriously antislavery Whig senator from New York, William H. Seward. A strong Taylor supporter in the election campaign, Seward had ingratiated himself with the new president, who spoke of him as "the great Mr. Seeward, of New York."[31] It had been Seward and his political cohort, Thurlow Weed, a canny backroom operator with a sinister aura who spoke in hushed tones, not Taylor's New Yorker vice president, Millard Fillmore, whom the president had turned to for patronage advice in New York. And now Seward, as thoroughly lettered in politics

as Taylor was unlettered, was his most trusted adviser, the "direct-
ing spirit" of the new administration.[32] Seward saw the president
as "a sensible and sagacious man, but *uninformed about men. . . .* It
remains to be seen how far honesty and the very purest and most
exalted patriotism will cover the defect of political sagacity."[33]
Seward clearly intended to enstamp his own political sagacity on
the president's lack of it.

Aside from his reliance on Seward, Taylor had blocked out
Whigs in general from his inner circle. He had not sought their
friendship or advice in shaping his cabinet. Henry Clay, the party's
longtime leader, complained, "There is not, I believe, a prominent
Whig in either House that has any confidential intercourse with
the Executive."[34] Charles S. Morehead, a Whig congressman from
Kentucky, confessed, "I have never been able to converse one
minute with the President upon politics without his changing the
subject."[35]

It might have been different if Taylor had the Whig he really
wanted at his side. John J. Crittenden, former senator and now governor of Kentucky, had been the true mastermind of Taylor's presidential campaign, the man mainly responsible for launching and
guiding it. A widely respected lawyer, political leader, and former
U.S. senator, Crittenden was a lifelong friend of Henry Clay. But he
was also a lifelong friend of Taylor. Indeed, they were kinsmen;
Crittenden's first wife had been Taylor's cousin. So influential had
the governor been in the election campaign that Taylor had become
identified as Crittenden's candidate. It was generally thought that
Crittenden, a "calming, nonpartisan leader," would become the
"premier" in the new administration, its true guiding light. Indeed,
Taylor had wanted him for his secretary of state. But the Kentuck-
ian, who had resigned from the U.S. Senate to run for governor to
carry the state for Taylor, declined the appointment, staying in his
home state to fulfill his gubernatorial commitment.[36]

If Southerners were gravely disillusioned now with the president, he was equally disillusioned with them. Taylor had come to
believe, listening to Seward, that Southerners, not Northerners,
were behind all this trouble over slavery in the territories; that
Southerners, not Northerners, were being unreasonable. Whoever
was behind the trouble, whoever was being unreasonable, this turmoil over slavery in the territories threatened the Union and Taylor wanted it stilled. "In my judgment," he said, "dissolution [of
the Union] would be the greatest of calamities, and to avert that

should be the study of every American. Upon its preservation must depend our own happiness and that of countless generations to come. Whatever dangers may threaten it, I shall stand by it and maintain it in its integrity to the full extent of the obligations imposed and the powers conferred on me by the Constitution." Attachment to the Union, he believed, "should be habitually fostered in every American heart."[37]

Taylor had a plan. He would propose, when Congress convened, to admit California into the Union immediately. He saw California as fully qualified and ready. It would require an awkward bypassing of the traditional apprenticeship for statehood. But California was filling up at daunting speed, and Taylor, Seward said, "desired to substitute the rule of law and order there for the bowie-knife and revolvers."[38] The New Mexico territory would be urged to apply for statehood, when ready, either as free or as slave, whatever its citizens decided.

Taylor believed this proposal to be the logical and immediate solution to the slavery uproar. He believed it would diffuse the bomb by taking the issue out of the hands of Congress, which he thought had no business legislating on slavery in the new territory.[39] It would make the inflammatory Wilmot Proviso, which was anathema to the South, unnecessary. The plan, however, ignored the other three issues—the Texas-New Mexico boundary dispute (although Taylor had strong ideas about that one), slavery and the slave trade in the District of Columbia, and the fugitive slave problem.

After his inauguration in March, Taylor commissioned Thomas Butler King of Georgia as a special agent and sent him to California with instructions to promote the early formation of a state constitution and government that could then petition Congress for immediate admission. Taylor strictly instructed King that any measures Californians adopted must "originate solely with themselves . . . be the result of their own deliberate choice." Their constitution and plan of government "must originate with themselves, and without the interference of the Executive."[40] There was to be no strong-arming the would-be state into action.

King was something of a bizarre choice for the assignment that he knew would add a free state to the Union. He was a ten-year congressman and slaveholding member of the planter aristocracy in Georgia. It was an unlikely case of a Georgia slaveholder sent by a Louisiana slaveholder to create a nonslaveholding state. But King hurried away to California, arriving on June 4, 1849. There he found that Californians were already moving swiftly in the desired direction. Buoyed by further encouragement from the president, they moved ever faster. By the end of the year they had a constitution, ratified by the people, and elected officials in place. In December, Brigadier General Bennet Riley, the military governor, had passed his powers to his elected successor, and a state government had begun to function. All of this had been done outside of the usual channels, before statehood, and without the requisite congressional enabling act.

It raised two very big questions: How would this end run around its authority go down with the newly convening Congress, particularly with the Southerners? And what would it do to California's prospects in a highly charged and schismed Washington?

NOTES

1. For the inauguration ceremony see Lawrence A. Gobright, *Recollection of Men and Things in Washington during the Third of a Century* (Philadelphia, 1869), 97–98.

2. A. T. Burnley to John J. Crittenden, January 12, 1849, in William O. Lynch, "Zachary Taylor as President," *Journal of Southern History* 4 (August 1938): 282.

3. Benjamin Perley Poore, *Perley's Reminiscences of Sixty Years in the National Metropolis*, 2 vols. (Philadephia, 1886), 1:345–46.

4. Zachary Taylor to J. S. Allison, April 22, 1848, in Hamilton, *Zachary Taylor*, 80.

5. Thurlow Weed, *Autobiography of Thurlow Weed*, ed. Harriet A. Weed (1883, reprint ed.; New York, 1970), 580–81.

6. Smith, *The Presidencies of Zachary Taylor and Millard Fillmore*, 41.

7. Weed, *Autobiography of Thurlow Weed*, 582.

8. T. N. Parmelee, "Recollections of an Old Stager," *Harper's New Monthly Magazine* 47 (September 1873): 587.

9. "Reminiscences of Washington," 234.

10. Parmelee, "Recollections of an Old Stager," 588.

11. Polk, *Diary*, 4:184, 375–76.

12. Horace Greeley to Schuyler Colfax, March 17, 1849, in Nevins, *Ordeal of the Union*, 229.

13. Benjamin Brown French, *Witness to the Young Republic: A Yankee's Journal, 1828–1860*, ed. Donald B. Cole and John J. McDonough (Hanover, NH, 1989), 214.

14. George W. Julian, *Political Recollections, 1840 to 1872* (1883; reprint ed., Miami, FL, 1969), 82.

15. Mann, *Life of Horace Mann*, 292.

16. Winfield Scott, *Memoirs of Lieut.-General Scott, Written by Himself*, 2 vols. (New York, 1864), 2:382–83.

17. Julian, *Political Recollections*, 82.

18. Parmelee, "Recollections of an Old Stager," 588.

19. Ethan Allen Hitchcock, *Fifty Years in Camp and Field*, ed. W. A. Croffut (1909, reprint ed.; New York, 1971), 348.

20. I owe much in this brief description to John J. Farrell, ed., *Zachary Taylor, 1784–1850, Millard Fillmore, 1800–1874: Chronology, Documents, Bibliographical Aids* (Dobbs Ferry, NY, 1971), 2, 6; Smith, *The Presidencies of Zachary Taylor and Millard Fillmore*, 25, 27–33; Brainerd Dyer, *Zachary Taylor* (Baton Rouge, LA, 1946), 404; *American National Biography*, s.v. "Taylor, Zachary"; and H. Montgomery, *The Life of Major General Zachary Taylor* (Auburn, NY, 1849), 56.

21. "Reminiscences of Washington," 236.

22. Horse, alligator, and silkworm information are courtesy of the Presidential Pet Museum, Washington, DC.

23. "Reminiscences of Washington," 239; Dyer, *Zachary Taylor*, 399; Green, *Washington: Village and Capital*, 226.

24. Farrell, *Zachary Taylor, Millard Fillmore*, 7.

25. Richard M. Ketchum, "Faces from the Past: Zachary Taylor," *American Heritage* 14 (October 1963): 53.

26. "Reminiscences of Washington," 237, 239; Poore, *Perley's Reminiscences*, 1:357.

27. This expectation is nicely summarized in Cole, *The Whig Party in the South*, 127–28, 151.

28. Nevins, *Ordeal of the Union*, 230.

29. Fehrenbacher, *The South and Three Sectional Crises*, 39.

30. Pike, *First Blows of the Civil War*, 9.

31. Dyer, *Great Senators*, 108.

32. Rhodes, *History of the United States*, 1:102.

33. Seward, *Seward at Washington*, 101.

34. Henry Clay, *The Papers of Henry Clay*, ed. Melba Porter Hay et al., 10 vols. (Lexington, KY, 1991), 10:689.

35. Lynch, "Zachary Taylor as President," 290–91.

36. I have been guided in this discussion of Crittenden by Albert D. Kirwan, *John J. Crittenden: The Struggle for the Union* (Lexington, KY, 1962), 203, 225, 231, 233, 235, 238.

37. Richardson, *A Compilation of the Messages and Papers of the Presidents*, 5:24.

38. William H. Seward, *The Works of William Henry Seward*, ed. George E. Baker, 3 vols. (New York, 1853), 3:444.

39. Taylor had expressed this opinion to Ethan Allen Hitchcock in December 1848, before his inauguration. See Hitchcock, *Fifty Years in Camp and Field*, 348.

40. *Congressional Globe*, 31st Cong., 1st sess., Appendix, 315.

CHAPTER FOUR

DEADLOCK IN THE HOUSE

A FIERCE WINTER STORM pelted Washington on the night of December 2, 1849, laying down a sound-muting blanket of snow, followed by sleet and drizzle the next day as the members of the House of Representatives filed into their hall for the opening of the Thirty-first Congress.

If the world outside was muted, the world inside was not. The hall of the House was visually a model of architectural splendor and beauty, with a new carpet and new hangings replacing the faded ones of the previous Congress. But acoustically the hall was a nightmare. A smooth, rounded ceiling had made it into a Babel, where voices were followed by echoes that bounced jarringly off the walls. South Carolina Congressman Joseph A. Woodward called it an "unmannerly" room in which "order never could be maintained." "Look at it!" he growled. "A stranger would suppose that at the time it was constructed, there was not a man in the nation, from the President down, who knew that there was in nature such a science as acoustics, and that surfaces reflected sounds. It was not a hall—it was a cavern—a mammoth cave, in which men might speak in all parts, and be understood in none. . . . It was constructed with a view to concentrate the voice of the member on the Speaker's ear, leaving every one else deaf. Better that the members should be dumb too, unless a different Hall should be given to them." Many of them had been vainly trying to do so for twenty years.[1]

The members of the new Congress gathering in that acoustic horror to speak and try to be heard seemed to David Outlaw to be abnormally oversized. "The present House," he said, "contains an unusual number of large men. Perhaps their constituents supposed there might be a general melée in which physical power, might be as necessary as intellectual attainments."[2] The intellectual attainments appeared to run from near-genius to pedestrian. Robert Toombs of Georgia, a member nearer to fitting the first description than the second, was not impressed. "The present Congress," he thought, "furnishes the worst specimens of legislators I have ever seen here, especially from the North on both sides. There is a large infusion of successful jobbers, lucky serving-men, parishless parsons and itinerant lecturers among them who are not only without wisdom or knowledge but have bad manners, and therefore we can have but little hope of good legislation."[3]

Toombs's dim view might have been conditioned by his sectional frustration, for there were some glittering names with luminous talent gathering in this chamber of noise, bedlam, and confusion. Besides himself, there was his friend and fellow Georgia Whig, little Alexander H. Stephens, and yet another powerful Georgian, portly Democrat Howell Cobb. Together they gave that Southern state the most dynamic trio in the House, all three unhappy Southerners seeking compromise. Also filing in from the South were Henry W. Hilliard of Alabama, a noted educator; the handsome Linn Boyd, a former sheriff from Kentucky; Andrew Johnson, a former tailor from Tennessee; and Thomas L. Clingman of North Carolina, a particularly enigmatic specimen whom his fellow North Carolinian, David Outlaw, believed might be crazy, "some of the mental balance wheels necessary to regulate properly the machine, [being] either absent, or out of order." Outlaw noted that Clingman was "in the habit of talking to himself. His lips are generally moving."[4]

From the North, Massachusetts had again sent smooth, professorial, elegant-talking Robert C. Winthrop, Speaker of the Thirtieth Congress. Joining him was his fellow Bay Stater, Horace Mann, the famed educational reformer who was not given to temporizing with slavery. From Ohio came the radical, slavery-hating Joshua Giddings, who had no thought of temporizing, either. Illinois had sent two compromise-minded Democrats, John A. McClernand and William A. Richardson. New York sent a dynamic trio of its own in Preston King, James Brooks, and William Duer. And David Wilmot was back from Pennsylvania, active and watchful, still seeking interdiction of slavery in the territories.

Two hundred thirty representatives from the thirty states were filing into their seats in this famed echo chamber. Of the two major parties, the Democrats, with 112 members, only narrowly outnumbered the Whigs, with 105. Neither had a clear majority. There were thirteen Free-Soilers, a highly unlucky number for both of the major parties, for that slavery-loathing minority held in its few hands the power to decide whether the Whigs or the Democrats would control the House. The first act of the new Congress, indeed, was to decide who would command—who, from which party, from which section, could be elected Speaker. Until that happened the House could not do business. A look at the numbers and the paralyzing nature of the times clearly suggested that getting it done would not be easy.

The three parties went into caucus immediately and emerged with their candidates for Speaker. Neither of the two major parties had found the choice seamless. The Democrats, badly split between Northerners and Southerners, settled on the Georgian, Howell Cobb. The Whigs, just as schism-ridden along sectional lines, limped out of their caucus with Robert C. Winthrop. The Free-Soilers found their champion—with no chance of winning but only of causing havoc—in David Wilmot. Outlaw saw the prognosis as near-hopeless: "There is little probability of electing a Speaker from what I can see and hear for several days. My own impression is that the chance of electing a Whig at all is more than doubtful."[5]

As Speaker of the last Congress, Winthrop had been described as "the rising glory of the Whigs."[6] No great man in the Republic had roots running deeper into the American past. He was a direct sixth-generation descendant of John Winthrop, the first governor of the Massachusetts Bay Colony. Robert Winthrop was Harvard educated and had studied law in Daniel Webster's office. He was seen as "graceful, gallant, and accomplished," with "mental qualifications . . . of a very high order."[7] Gentility oozed naturally from his every pore. A forty-year-old Bostonian, eight years in Congress, he was a spare-framed man, thin faced and bespectacled, a powerful orator who seemed engineered by the gods for parliamentary debate. The well-known newspaper writer, James Pike, described his speaking style: "He declaimed with great animation in a highly finished style of elocution. His remarks were wire-woven. No broken threads or ravelled edges marred any portion." His mind, Pike believed, was "eminently methodical, his recollective faculties are strong, active, and in constant play, at the same time that he is in the full swing of extempore composition." His thoughts, Pike said, "are run in a mould, and his expressions daguerreotyped for the hearer. They are used like the pieces of a dissected map, and when his work is done, you see that every piece is put in its proper place and that the map is harmoniously and accurately complete."[8]

Winthrop had a "certain native hauteur," which, coupled with near-sightedness, often prevented him from recognizing persons of slight acquaintance. This shortcoming did not endear him to newspaper

reporters. He was opposed to the extension of slavery in the territories and deplored the very idea of sectional equilibrium anchored
to "sectional jealously, sectional fear, sectional hostility and hate."
But Winthrop was by nature a seeker of the middle ground in contentious, controversial deadlocks.[9]

Robert C. Winthrop
Library of Congress

He was at this hour the victim of a deadlock in his own party.
The Whigs were in a dissonant agony of sectional separation.
Winthrop had been elected Speaker in the last Congress by a uni-
fied phalanx of Northern and Southern Whigs. The phalanx this

time had shattered. A knot of six Southern Whigs, led by Robert Toombs and Alexander Stephens, had walked out of the caucus and abandoned him. While not disliking him personally, they said that they could not conscientiously support him in this controversy-ridden situation.[10]

Three-quarters of the Whigs in Congress were from the North. Nine of those had transmogrified into radical Free-Soilers who looked on their more conservative cohorts as "Silver grays" or "Snuff-takers." They had also abandoned Winthrop. They believed that he had not adequately recognized the antislavery sentiment in his committee appointments in the past, nor would he commit to recognizing them in the future.[11]

On the other side of the aisle, Howell Cobb had problems of his own. The owner of 1,000 slaves, the thirty-four-year-old Cobb was devoted to the peculiar institution and to Southern interests. Horace Mann called him "one of the fiercest, sternest, strongest proslavery men in all the South. He loves slavery. It is his politics and his patriotism, his political economy and his religion."[12] But as much as Cobb loved slavery, he loved the Union more. He had written, "This Union is the rock upon which the God of nations has built his political church, and we have been summoned to minister at its holy altars."[13] He had been one of the handful of Democrats who had voted against John C. Calhoun's "Southern Address," on grounds that it was Union-busting. He could be counted on to seek compromise until compromise was no longer attainable.

Already his uncompromising championship of compromise and Union was alienating him from his radical, secessionist-threatening fellow Southern Democrats. Cobb was formidable, a lifetime Georgian with a résumé packed with political experience that belied his youth. He had been not yet twenty-nine years old when elected to the Twenty-eighth Congress. He had been the minority leader in the Thirtieth Congress, a skilled debater intimate with parliamentary procedure and enormously popular personally. Physically he was a mountain of a man, round and jolly.[14]

Cobb was also a political realist. He had not been nominated by his party for the speakership a day before he was writing home to his wife, the former Mary Ann Lamar, whose ample dowry had given him some 200 slaves: "I have come to the conclusion that my election is *impossible*."[15] The first day's voting had convinced him of it. Four votes had been taken, and in all four Cobb had led Winthrop by six or seven votes, but each time short of the 111 necessary to elect. Six more ballots on the second day turned up the same result, with Winthrop creeping closer. Four more votes on the third day had the two men running neck and neck. To try to break the deadlock Andrew Johnson of Tennessee introduced a resolution to

Howell Cobb
Library of Congress

permit a plurality, instead of a majority, to elect the Speaker. But Abraham Venable of North Carolina bristled. He insisted that it would break "a time-honored rule," based on the Constitution, and that he "could never consent to let a Speaker be elected by a hand-ful of men."[16] The resolution was rejected.

By the fourteenth ballot, Winthrop had overtaken Cobb, but his ninety-nine votes were still shy of the number needed. By the sixteenth ballot on Thursday, December 6, Cobb had slipped to seventy-six votes. On Saturday the bottom fell out. By day's and week's end and the twenty-eighth ballot he could muster only five votes. But Winthrop had profited nothing by it. His vote was 101, still short of election. Democrat Emery Potter of Ohio had replaced Cobb with seventy-six votes.

When the House reconvened on Monday, December 10, and after the thirtieth ballot, Isaac Morse, a Louisiana Democrat, introduced a resolution "to terminate what was now beginning to be a ridiculous course of action on the part of this House." It was looking to him as if vote after futile vote would "forever prevent an organization of the House." His resolution might have been more ridiculous than the deadlock. It would put Cobb's and Winthrop's names in a box, one of them to be drawn out by one of the House pages, thus leaving the decision to dumb chance. Morse argued that "graver questions than this had been decided in the same way." It was Ohio's Joseph Root's turn to bristle. He regretted that they should be in "so unfortunate a predicament" as to be reduced to calling on "one of their little pages to intervene and help these two great parties out of the difficulty." Morse's resolution was resoundingly rejected.[17]

Before the thirty-second ballot, Potter, the rising new Democratic vote-getter, demurred. He said he was highly flattered by the vote but wanted his friends to drop the whole idea, so on the next ballot he got one vote. William J. Brown of Indiana, another unheralded Democratic name, climbed out of nowhere with fifty-six votes. Winthrop was still holding steady with 101. Cobb was mounting a modest comeback with ten. On the thirty-ninth ballot on December 11, Brown surged to 109 votes, only two shy of election. His momentum was making him look like a potential shoo-in.

Winthrop still had 101, but he had had enough. On December 11 he pulled his name, having wanted to do so for some time, thanked all of his friends and supporters, but urged them to "concentrate their efforts on some other candidate."[18] On the fortieth ballot on December 12 his vote shriveled to seventeen as his backers concentrated their votes on nobody, scattering them up and down the ballot. Cobb, with no votes, dropped completely out of sight.

Then a strange thing happened to William Brown. With the Speakership in his grasp, it was revealed that he had been doing some backroom bargaining, promising committee assignments in return for votes. Outlaw believed him to be "a violent Loco-Foco of the worst stripe."[19] But it was rumored that he was nesting with Free-Soilers of the Wilmot stamp, promising to place them prominently on committees. He admitted that there was a bargain, and he was done for. In fact, he said it himself, "I am done." From that day forward his delighted opponents would call him "Done Brown."[20]

Chaos followed. Edward Stanly, a North Carolina Whig, introduced a resolution to have a committee of three Democrats and three Whigs confer on the problem. He was "tired of this long-continued struggle" and believed every other member was tired of it too.[21] All day the House was in such disarray that it was difficult for the *Congressional Globe*'s reporter to render an accurate account of the proceedings and debates. Members left their seats to gather in large clumps around whoever held the floor. Finally the House adjourned in that state of confusion.

If it was hot inside, it was bone-chillingly cold outside and iced over. David Outlaw had "no doubt a wagon and horses could be driven across the Potomac."[22] On December 13, with tempers stretched and frayed and ready to snap, William Duer made the mistake in the heat of the hour inside of suggesting that there were disunionists in the House. Thomas H. Bayly of Virginia took exception. "There are no disunionists in this House," Bayly growled.

"I wish I could think so," Duer shot back, "but I fear there are."

"Who are they?" Bayly demanded. "Point them out."

"I believe there are some from your own State. I think I see one of them now," Duer said, pointing to Virginia Democrat Richard K. Meade.

"It is false," Meade shouted.

"You are a liar, Sir," Duer insisted.

"Quick as thought," the harried official reporter wrote in the *Globe*, Meade rushed toward Duer. Each man was "immediately surrounded by his friends. . . . Indescribable confusion followed, threats, violent gesticulations, calls to order, and demands for adjournment were mingled together. The House was like a heaving billow."

Every call was ignored until the sergeant at arms, Nathan Sargent, appeared with the mace, the emblem of the House's authority, which he held high above the bedlam. It had the effect of a cross thrust in the face of a vampire. Several cried, "Take away the Mace, it has no authority here." But the tempest was finally stilled and Duer was left to explain himself.[23] What next? Outlaw thought; "Meade will I suppose challenge him. Perhaps they may have a street fight." Outlaw, who feared a general mêlée would break out at any minute, had "almost come to the conclusion to vote for a democrat for Speaker, sooner than permit this thing to continue much longer."[24]

Amid the turmoil Robert Toombs, "his black, uncombed hair standing out from his massive head as if charged with electricity, his eyes glowing like coals of fire, and his sentences rattling forth like volleys of musketry," issued a Southern warning.[25] "I do not . . . hesitate to avow before this house and the country, and in the presence of the living God, that if by your legislation you seek to drive us from the territories of California and New Mexico, purchased by the common blood and treasure of the whole people, and to abolish slavery in this District, thereby attempting to fix a national degradation upon half the States of this Confederacy, *I am for disunion*; and if my physical courage be equal to the maintenance of my convictions of right and duty, I will devote all I am and all I have on earth to its consummation."[26]

This threat stunned the members of the House, including Toombs's friend Alexander Stephens, who said he "never expected to live to see the day when, upon this floor, [I] should be called upon to discuss the question of the union of these States."[27] Outlaw was now telling his wife that the House had degenerated into a "beer garden."[28]

On the forty-first ballot both Winthrop, with fifty-nine unasked-for votes, and Cobb, with forty, had climbed back into the race. Nobody was now remotely near a necessary majority. On the forty-second and forty-third ballots on December 14 both men slipped back. On the forty-fourth, Linn Boyd soared to the front with eighty-two votes. For the next three ballots nothing changed. On the forty-eighth, Boyd topped out at eighty-six votes, and the reluctant Winthrop was on the rise again with seventy. For the next three ballots there was no movement. On December 18, after ballots fifty-two through fifty-five, Winthrop was again in the high nineties and Boyd was slipping out of the race. By the fifty-ninth ballot two new alternatives had surfaced, John McClernand of Illinois and Edward Stanly of North Carolina. Winthrop had plunged down into apparent oblivion.

By Saturday, December 22, and the sixtieth ballot, Cobb had made a sudden comet-like return from two votes to ninety-five.

Winthrop was resurrected with ninety votes, with everybody else in the single digits. By the sixty-second ballot, Cobb and Winthrop were in a dead heat with ninety-seven votes each. They were back where they had all started three weeks before. It was painfully apparent in this long standoff that traditional party loyalties were in tatters. In place of partisanship there was now sectionalism.

A major deadlock-breaking difference had taken hold when Richard H. Stanton, a Kentucky Democrat, earlier revived the motion that if the next three votes were deadlocked, the subsequent vote would require only a plurality. This time it had carried. And with the sixty-second ballot that motion kicked in. On the sixty-third ballot, Cobb had 102 votes and Winthrop 99. Cobb was elected by a plurality and the deadlock was broken.[29]

"A slight murmur of approbation, not amounting to a distinct expression," the *Globe* reporter wrote, "passed over parts of the hall." Cobb took the Speaker's gavel and said, "It would be useless to disguise the fact that I feel deeply embarrassed in taking this chair under the circumstances attending my election," but he asked the members to "accept . . . my grateful acknowledgements for the honor you have conferred on me" anyhow.[30] "The agony is over," he wrote his wife that evening. "And now the question is whether it is most to be rejoiced over or regretted. . . . *I voted against the* [plurality] *rule throughout.* . . . I have done nothing to procure my election. Indeed all my personal efforts have been directed to my defeat for the last two weeks."[31]

The radical nonslavery men in the House mourned. "Now," Horace Mann lamented, "we shall have all proslavery committees. All the power of patronage of the Speaker, and it is great, will be on the wrong side."[32] But it was generally believed that in electing Cobb the House had come as near as it could to damping all the jarring elements. Cobb was popular with unionists, despite his addiction to slavery. They believed he would be fair in his appointments and in wielding his power.[33]

Whatever anybody believed, for better or for worse, the House was finally organized and President Taylor was informed that Congress at last was ready to receive any message he cared to send. The Senate, long since fully organized and marking time, was told that the House "is now ready to proceed to business."[34]

A message from the president arrived almost immediately, on Christmas Eve. It came in with the cold. By Christmas Day, Washington was in the grip of an extended bitter winter blast. On New

Year's Day it was 6 degrees Fahrenheit at seven o'clock in the morning with a sheet of snow covering the ground. But as Cobb wrote his wife, the first of the year was "a gala day in Washington." Despite the bitter weather, "all the world and his wife are out today in their best bib and tucker." But it was not gala enough for the new Speaker. He told his wife, "I have never felt more sick at heart with Washington than I now do, and never half so determined to retire from public life."[35]

Horace Mann
Library of Congress

The president's message also came in with a memorable malaprop: "We are at peace with all the nations of the world, and the rest of mankind."[36] The country might have been at peace with the world, plus some, but it was not at peace with itself. Taylor was aware of that, and his hope was that the plan he was proposing would avoid "all causes of uneasiness" and preserve "confidence and kind feeling" throughout the Union. To maintain "the harmony and tranquility so dear to all," he urged Congress, "we should abstain from the introduction of those exciting topics of a sectional character which have hitherto produced painful apprehensions in the public mind." He believed that his plan—admit California immediately as a free state and give favorable consideration for the New Mexico territory when it was ready, under whatever status it chose to enter the Union, slave or free—would settle the matter.[37]

Taylor's supporters were pleased. Winthrop, an ardent backer of California's immediate admission with its proposed constitution, believed the president's plan "wise and patriotic," the only one "which gives a triumph to neither side of this controversy. . . . It is a middle ground, on which both sides can meet without the abandonment of any principle, or the sacrifice of any point of honor."[38] Taylor's plan, another wrote, is "an easy settlement of this vexed question. . . . Nothing could be simpler than this, nothing easier or more natural, nothing less irritating."[39]

But violently irritated were most Southerners. To them the specter of a free California, with New Mexico likely to follow the same pattern, would never do. Two new free states to no new slave states, they knew, would irredeemably send the political equilibrium out of whack. And Taylor a Southerner, too! This was treachery! Rather than allaying sectionalism, the president had stirred "a volcano of wrath" in Congress.[40] Rather than silencing the contentious issue, he had triggered a clamorous uproar. It was made worse by the likelihood that he would veto any proposal from Congress that ran counter to his own. And plans that ran counter were flooding the legislative hopper. It was apparent that since the president's foes controlled both houses, he would have a difficult time with his two-part program. Instead of his plan to pacify the nation breezing through, he would have to fight off a host of others he did not want.

Taylor's plan addressed but two of the five Union-splitting issues when the situation cried for an all-embracing settlement. He was still silent on the Texas-New Mexico boundary problem, silent on the slave trade issue in the District of Columbia, silent on the urgent matter of a civil government to replace the military in New Mexico and Utah, silent on the fugitive slave question.

No Southerners were more alarmed by Taylor's plan and his general drift in the wrong direction than the two Georgia Whigs,

Robert Toombs and Alexander Stephens. No two men had been more enthusiastic backers of Taylor's run for president. In December 1846, Stephens had organized seven Whig congressmen into a Taylor club in the House that became known as the "Young Indians." They had worked tirelessly, elbow to elbow, with John Crittenden in the highest levels of Taylor's presidential campaign. Nobody short of Crittenden himself had played a larger role in winning Taylor the nomination and the presidency.

Toombs and Stephens were something of a political odd couple. Close friends, devoted to one another, constantly acting in consort, they could not have been more different. Toombs was a big, imposing, blustery, overbearing presence. Crittenden had recommended him as secretary of war, which one observer of the times said would have been "a piece of incomprehensible folly." With an obviously superior turn of mind, he was nonetheless "opinionated, arrogant, intractable, irascible, and would have been a disturbing force hardly endurable in any administration." Fortunately "for the harmony of the administration," this observer believed, Toombs declined the offer.[41]

Everybody agreed that Toombs was a man of superior intelligence. Varina Davis, Senator Jefferson Davis's insightful wife, believed that "one could scarcely imagine a wittier and more agreeable companion"—a "university man" who had "kept up his classics." She characterized Toombs's personal habits as those of "a fine gentleman . . . his diction was good, his wit keen, and his audacity made him equal to anything in the heat of debate." He stood over six feet tall with broad shoulders, and Varina was particularly taken with his "long, glossy black hair," which, when speaking, he tossed about like a mop on a handle. His teeth were "brilliantly white," his mouth "somewhat pendulous," his eyes "magnificent, dark and flashing," with "a certain lawless way of ranging about that was indicative of his character." His hands were "beautiful," Varina thought, "kept like those of a fashionable woman," and his voice was "like a trumpet."[42]

A friend said of Toombs that his "impulses were generous and noble, his faults were bluster and a vivid imagination not always hampered by facts." He was fiery, erratic, maverick minded, and impulsive, a forensic time bomb who was apt "in moments of commotion [to] explode in any direction." Howell Cobb believed he had the finest mind of his generation "but lacked balance." Another said of Toombs that he "disagrees with himself between meals."[43] He was given to rising at daylight to take French lessons with his daughters. The British minister recalled that he "loved books of the imagination, travels, anything that would help him to utter some of his brilliant paradoxes."[44]

Robert Toombs
Library of Congress

Toombs had made a fortune in slaves and real estate in Georgia and he had a gift for finance. He was an "aggressive defender of the South," a bitter foe of the Wilmot Proviso, damning it at every turn in his bugle voice and vowing to oppose it "even [to] the extent of a dissolution of the Union."[45] But for all of his sectional fervor, he was in his heart a strong unionist, seeking, despite his occasional secessionist rantings, some sort of compromise to hold it all together.

"Little Alec" Stephens, whom Varina Davis thought Toombs loved "with a tenderness that was almost pathetic,"[46] was physically everything Toombs was not. Indeed, Stephens came as close to being alive without a bona fide body as anyone had ever seen. He had been sickly from youth and was wracked in adulthood by an army of ailments. Rheumatoid arthritis kept his hands, arms, and legs in constant pain. He suffered remorseless pain in his face, neck, teeth, and abdomen as well as piercing migraine headaches, pruritis, colitis, and bladder stones. Although 5 feet 7 inches tall, he had never weighed more than 100 pounds in his life, and typically averaged between seventy and eighty pounds. Many of his dogs, which he dearly loved, easily outweighed him. He was "frail and thin to painful meagerness," easily mistaken for a child or some "boyish invalid escaped from some hospital," with the pallor of a corpse and the appearance of "a well-preserved mummy." He had a small head, outjutting oversized ears, incendiary black eyes, a thin tapered nose, pale lips down-sloping at the corners, and "long, bony fingers" that "looked like claws attached to the ends of broomstick arms." Stephens described himself as "a malformed ill-shaped half finished thing."[47]

But this wrecked shell of a body housed the steel-trap mind of a near genius. Toombs said of Stephens that he "carried more brains and more soul for the least flesh of any man God Almighty ever made."[48] A shrill, high-pitched, but musical voice screeched out from this pile of bones, giving ample evidence of his intelligence and startling everybody. He could orchestrate his voice "like a lyre," from low to loud, and shoot it at an audience "like bullets." The audience always had the sense, however, that "the cadaverous speaker might not live to finish the speech."[49]

Stephens was absolutely fearless when he knew he was right. And he had an acute sense of personal honor. At least five times in his life he had issued challenges to duels, sadly getting no takers. He had never married or even come close, and he was given to fits of deep melancholy. A man of principle, his first act on entering Congress in 1843 had been to protest his own election. He had been elected statewide, not from a district as the Constitution required. He was overruled and sworn in.

Washington journalist Benjamin Perley Poore said Stephens gave off the impression of a doomed man who "apparently had not a month to live, yet who rivaled Talleyrand in political intrigue."[50] Indeed, early in the new year he and his dear friend

Alexander H. Stephens
Library of Congress

Toombs, both worried to death over the Union and Southern rights, were ready to practice some political intrigue at the White House. Their audience with Taylor soon degenerated into a brouhaha. The two Georgians were there to urge Taylor to veto any enactment of the Wilmot Proviso or any like repugnancy. When the president suggested he would sign any constitutional bill passed by Congress and then see it executed, they suggested the possibility of Southern secession. Taylor interpreted that as a threat. It was as a red flag waved before the fevered eye of a bull.[51]

As Toombs and Stephens were coming out of the president's room—rather, driven out and nonplussed by the turn the interview had taken—they met Maine Senator Hannibal Hamlin coming in. They paid Hamlin, who in the House had helped draft the Wilmot Proviso, little attention in their chagrin, and he noted that those two "high priests in the inner councils of the slave power" seemed exceedingly agitated and angry. Entering Taylor's room Hamlin found the president even more so, "rushing around the room like a caged lion." His face was livid. Muttering fiercely to himself and shaking his fist at imaginary demons, Taylor was so worked up that he passed Hamlin three or four times without acknowledging his presence. When he did see him he stopped with a start and rushed up to him.

"Did you see those traitors?" Taylor asked. "They have been making demands concerning my administration, and threatened that unless they were acceded to the South would secede. But if there are any such treasonable demonstrations on the part of the Southern leaders, I will hang them. . . . I will hang them as high as I hung spies in Mexico, and I will put down any treasonable movement with the whole power of the government, if I have to put myself at the head of the army to do it." He vowed to Hamlin: "I am pained to learn that we have disunion men among us. Disunion is treason; and if the disunionists attempt to carry out their schemes while I am President, I will hang them."[52] He had said as much to Toombs and Stephens. When the New York politico, Thurlow Weed, followed Hamlin into the presidential chamber a few minutes later, after being similarly ignored by his friends Toombs and Stephens outside the White House, he found Taylor still fuming, still striding angrily to and fro.[53]

Instead of the lines of disagreement shortening, they were lengthening. Already in the House the president's plan was floundering in heavy shoal water. Southern opponents of compromise were delaying and filibustering, demanding roll call votes, freezing action. Admitting California as a separate measure, Taylor's avid hope, appeared doomed in the House. It seemed clear that if there was to be movement toward compromise it was going to have to start in the Senate. And even so, any kind of compromise fashioned in the divided and testy Senate would have to be delicately tailored to survive in the even more heavily schismed and gridlocked House.[54] Even if it did, would Taylor, with his new-stirred ire up, his heart set on his own plan, and his heels dug in, veto it?

NOTES

1. *Congressional Globe*, 31st Cong., 1st sess., 1425. Also see Allen, *History of the United States Capitol*, 180–81.

2. David Outlaw to Emily Outlaw, December 4, 1849, Outlaw Papers.

3. Phillips, "The Correspondence of Robert Toombs, Alexander H. Stephens, and Howell Cobb," 188.

4. David Outlaw to Emily Outlaw, December 17, 1849, Outlaw Papers.

5. Ibid., December 2, 1849.

6. Sarah Mytton Maury, *The Statesmen of America in 1846* (Philadelphia, 1847), 79.

7. Ibid., 79, 81.

8. Robert C. Winthrop Jr., *A Memoir of Robert C. Winthrop* (Boston, 1897), 108–9.

9. Ibid., 126, 121.

10. Ibid., 99 n.

11. Rhodes, *History of the United States*, 1:117. "Silver grays" and "Snufftakers" are from Parmelee, "Recollections of an Old Stager" (vol. 47, September 1873): 590.

12. Mann, *Life of Horace Mann*, 283.

13. Brooks, "Howell Cobb Papers," 52.

14. I am indebted for this brief rundown on Cobb to Robert P. Brooks, "Howell Cobb and the Crisis of 1850," *Mississippi Valley Historical Review* 4 (December 1917): 279–83; and Hamilton, *Zachary Taylor*, 245.

15. Phillips, "The Correspondence of Robert Toombs, Alexander H. Stephens, and Howell Cobb," 177.

16. *Congressional Globe*, 31st Cong., 1st sess., 6.

17. Ibid., 13.

18. Ibid., 17.

19. David Outlaw to Emily Outlaw, December 11, 1849, Outlaw Papers. The Locofocos were a radical group of New York Democrats who organized in 1835 to oppose the established party.

20. Hamilton, *Zachary Taylor*, 249–50; Brown's reaction and his new nickname are from a brief biographical sketch in *National Cyclopaedia of American Biography*, s.v. "Brown, William J."

21. *Congressional Globe*, 31st Cong., 1st sess., 18.

22. David Outlaw to Emily Outlaw, December 11, 1849, Outlaw Papers.

23. This explosive chain of events is recorded in *Congressional Globe*, 31st Cong., 1st sess., 27.

24. David Outlaw to Emily Outlaw, December 13, 1849, Outlaw Papers.

25. "Reminiscences of Washington," 240.

26. *Congressional Globe*, 31st Cong., 1st sess., 28.

27. Ibid., 29.

28. David Outlaw to Emily Outlaw, December (no date) 1849, Outlaw Papers.

29. The ballot-by-ballot account of the voting for Speaker is in the *Congressional Globe*, 31st Cong., 1st sess., 2–66.

30. Ibid., 66–67.

31. Phillips, "The Correspondence of Robert Toombs, Alexander H. Stephens, and Howell Cobb," 179–80.

32. Mann, *The Life of Horace Mann*, 284.

33. Brooks, "Howell Cobb and the Crisis of 1850," 284.

34. *Congressional Globe*, 31st Cong., 1st sess., 73.

35. Brooks, "Howell Cobb Papers," 35.

36. "Reminiscences of Washington," 241.

37. *Congressional Globe*, 31st Cong., 1st sess., 71.

38. Winthrop, *A Memoir of Robert C. Winthrop*, 123.

39. Pike, *First Blows of the Civil War*, 22.

40. Charles Eugene Hamlin, *The Life and Times of Hannibal Hamlin* (Cambridge, MA, 1899), 198.

41. Parmelee, "Recollections of an Old Stager," 586.

42. Varina Howell Davis, *Jefferson Davis, Ex-President of the Confederate States of America*, 2 vols. (1890; reprint ed., Freeport, NY, 1971), 1:409–10.

43. *American National Biography*, s.v. "Toombs, Robert Augustus"; William Y. Thompson, *Robert Toombs of Georgia* (Baton Rouge, LA, 1966), 66.

44. Davis, *Jefferson Davis, Ex-President*, 1:411.

45. Ulrich B. Phillips, *The Life of Robert Toombs* (New York, 1913), 54–55, 66.

46. Davis, *Jefferson Davis, Ex-President*, 1:410.

47. For this description of Stephens I have borrowed heavily from Thomas E. Schott, *Alexander H. Stephens of Georgia* (Baton Rouge, 1988), 19–21, 213. His love of dogs is from Henry Cleveland, *Alexander H. Stephens, in Public and Private* (Philadelphia, 1866), 236.

48. William P. Trent, *Southern Statesmen of the Old Regime* (New York, 1897), 231.

49. Schott, *Alexander H. Stephens of Georgia*, 29, 31, 56, 81.

50. Poore, *Perley's Reminiscences*, 1:317.

51. Thurlow Weed Barnes, *Memoir of Thurlow Weed* (1884; reprint ed., New York, 1970), 177.

52. This account is taken from Hamlin, *The Life and Times of Hannibal Hamlin*, 201–2.

53. Barnes, *Memoir of Thurlow Weed*, 176–77. Years after this supposed encounter of Toombs and Stephens with Taylor, both Georgia congressmen denied that it had ever taken place. Their position was aired in a running exchange with Thurlow Weed in the *New York Herald*, May 31, June 13 and 23, and August 8, 17, 21, and 24, 1876. I am persuaded that it did occur as reported by Weed and Hamlin.

54. This brief description of the situation owes much to National Archives, "Westward Expansion and the Compromise of 1850," 17–18.

CHAPTER FIVE

"THE STAR OF THE WEST"

THE SENATE CHAMBER in the Capitol was modeled on the theaters of ancient Greece. Like those stages and unlike its counterpart on the House side, this storied chamber had near-perfect acoustics. Also like its classical forerunners, it was thought of as a theater. "This noble theater," Henry Clay called it; this "splendid theater," Thomas Hart Benton said of it, "this elevated theater."[1] In a time when political oratory was considered prime entertainment, it was one of the most popular theaters in America.

It was semicircular and gracefully proportioned, with crimson carpets, crimson draperies, dark marble columns, and an air of "stately dignity." Around the chamber overlooking the floor ran a gallery for the public, the audience to the dramas performed there. Many of the sixty senators of the Thirty-first Congress from the thirty states of the Union had come wearing claw-hammer coats, or tailcoats—what passed in their times for the togas worn by the senators of ancient Rome.[2]

Henry Clay, the great Whig leader who dominated this chamber for so many years, believed that perennially it gave nothing away to the ancients for distinction and skill. When he left it for what he thought was the last time in 1842, he called the Senate "a body which may be compared, without disadvantage, to any of a similar character which has existed in ancient or modern times."[3] Those words might have been said of the senators of this new Thirty-first Congress in particular. Indeed, they later were. "No similar group of men," Clay's grandson would write, "were ever gathered together in any legislative hall upon this continent, before or since."[4]

Aging and somewhat worn, Henry Clay himself was there again, newly returned without a dissenting vote by the Kentucky legislature, which perhaps sensed that the country needed him once more in this time of trouble.[5] He was called "The Star of the West," and for forty years he had been a political power and talent without peer. But he was now nearly seventy-three years old and showing

"traces of advancing age." Daniel Webster of Massachusetts was
there, as he had often been, with Clay, for four decades one of the
most powerful and stirring orators of that or any other time. One
congressman believed, on seeing him, that Webster "had not lost
his old grandeur; the face, even in repose, expressing power, and
his whole bearing displaying dignity." John C. Calhoun of South
Carolina, a Senate giant in fame and talent equal to Clay and
Webster, was also there again, his tremendous intellect intact but
with "the touches of time now being visible in the outlines of his
face and in his form, which had lost something of its activity and
vigor." In fact, he was dying.[6] Together these three giants, all born
during the Revolution and now in the twilight of great careers, had
dominated American politics for nearly one-half century. "The great
trio,"[7] "a constellation of unrivalled splendor,"[8] they were together
once more in the time of the Union's greatest peril.

Thomas Hart Benton, a throwback to the Jacksonian years and
before, was also there in the evening of a storied career, only a cut
below the trio in esteem and as crusty, pugnacious, and hard-work-
ing as ever. He had been in the Senate for thirty uninterrupted years,
the longest continuous span in the nation's young history. Lewis
Cass, the recently defeated Democratic presidential nominee, another seasoned veteran of past political wars, was there. His "pro-
truding and superincumbent abdomen" and "sleepy-looking eyes"
were deceiving. He would not miss much that was about to be acted
out in this theater.[9]

The bearers of other names with strong claims to renown,
power, and skill were seated in the chamber: big, charming Willie P.
Mangum of North Carolina, Sam Houston of the new state of
Texas, independent-minded John M. Berrien of Georgia, Daniel
Dickinson of New York, the contentious and irritating Henry S.
Foote of Mississippi, Calhoun disciples R. M. T. Hunter and James
Mason of Virginia. Calhoun's South Carolina colleague Andrew P.
Butler, living in the great man's shadow, was present together with
the venerable William King of Alabama, former House Speaker John
Bell of Tennessee, Alabama radical Jeremiah Clemens, French trans-
plant Pierre Soulé of Louisiana, the witty and respected Thomas
Corwin of Ohio, New Jersey's dignified William Dayton, ardent
abolitionist John P. Hale of New Hampshire, the scholarly James
Pearce of Maryland, America's first Jewish senator David Yulee of
Florida, Henry Dodge of Wisconsin, and his son Augustus Dodge
of Iowa.

Relatively new to this claw hammer-suited body was a quartet of young freshmen senators who seemed marked for greatness, both by their own natures and by the nature of the times: Stephen A. Douglas, the "Little Giant" from Illinois, chairman of the pivotal Committee on the Territories; William Henry Seward, former governor of New York, the radical antislavery Whig who was whispering in Taylor's ear; Jefferson Davis of Mississippi, the Mexican War hero, Taylor's former son-in-law, and avid Southern rights champion, often thought of as the successor to the mantle of John C. Calhoun; and Salmon Portland Chase of Ohio, a slavery-hating former governor widely celebrated—or notorious—for lending a legal hand to runaway slaves.

Presiding over this luminous collection of political and forensic talent—peopled with thirty-three Democrats and twenty-seven Whigs and Free-Soilers, and seething with sectional anger—was the Whig vice president, Millard Fillmore. He had never presided over any legislative body. However, Fillmore's large stature and impressive appearance were matched by a dignified carriage, a generous, fair-minded spirit, and a deep and pleasing voice made for presiding in testy times. In truth, to many he looked more like a president of the country than the president himself.[10]

Henry Clay had returned to the Washington he knew so well and checked into his old quarters at the National Hotel, in rooms with a "good parlour and bedroom opening into each other" and costing $30 per week. His near co-tenants were the British minister Henry L. Bulwer and his wife, the niece of the Duke of Wellington, with whom Clay occasionally dined. He rarely went out at night, declining invitations to dinner whenever he could, keeping to his room playing cards, sipping on his bourbon, and going to bed regularly at ten o'clock.[11] Clay was alone, as he usually always was in the capital. His wife, the former Lucretia Hart of the Kentucky Blue Grass gentry, with whom he had just celebrated their golden wedding anniversary, hated Washington social life and no longer accompanied him there.

He and Lucretia had drunk far more than their portion from the cup of sorrow. She had borne him eleven children, six of them daughters, all of whom had "lived to win his heart and then to die." He was laughing and joking with friends when the letter from home arrived telling of the sudden death of his last and most beloved daughter, Anne Clay Irwin. One of these friends later said that when he opened and began to read the letter, he started up and then "fell as if shot."[12] Of their eleven children only four—all boys—still lived. He wrote Lucretia in his anguish: "if the thunderbolt of H[e]aven had fallen on me—unprepared as I fear I am—I would have submitted, cheerfully submitted, to a thousand deaths to have saved this dear child."[13]

For eight years he had been in what he had thought was permanent retirement from the Senate. He had since been defeated twice again in his three-decade-long quest for the presidency—as the Whig nominee in 1844 and as a rejected candidate in 1848. Clay was returning to this forum, which had been for so long his stage, without enthusiasm. When he left in 1842 he said he was seeking "that repose which is only to be found in the bosom of one's family—in private life—in one's home." Bidding his colleagues, "one and all, a long, a last, a friendly farewell," he had returned to Ashland, his 600-acre plantation in Lexington.[14]

When named by his state legislature to return to the Senate in early 1849, he said, "I go to Washington for the last time with reluctance, and against my wishes and judgment. My relations to the Whigs are wholly changed by the events of the past year [being denied the Whig nomination for president in favor of Taylor]. Whatever obligations I may have been under to the party are now discharged, and I shall take my seat in the Senate with little hope of rendering any service to the country, but solely to prevent my friends from being sacrificed by this piebald administration."[15]

"Ancient Henry," as some were calling him,[16] entered the Senate chamber on December 3, 1849 and took his old seat to a "thunderous ovation." It had been forty-three years since he had first sat there. He was looking much older than many remembered him, worn by the decades of public service. He was partially bald now, his fringe streaked with gray. He was dressed, as always, in black with a white shirt and a high-standing collar reaching to his ears. He was coughing—a great deal—and had been for months. The great man had tuberculosis.[17]

Clay was one of those men who could instantly outshine the brightest stars in any galaxy just by showing up. When he went to the House of Representatives as a newly elected freshman in 1811 he was immediately elected Speaker. Horace Greeley was known to have said that a person only needed to see Clay's back to know that it was the back of a distinguished man.[18] A correspondent of the *New York Express* believed "the very presence of the man is an influence."[19] "Henry Clay," a contemporary Washingtonian wrote, "is a political war cry that will at any time and in any part of this Union create more sensation among men of all parties than any other name that can be uttered."[20] Alexander Stephens believed "whole acres" of people would come to hear him speak.[21]

Henry Clay
Library of Congress

No distinguished man in America was so lionized. Clay was so celebrated a public figure, one contemporary said, that he could not travel in the usual way "but only make progresses. When he left his home the public seized him and bore him along over the land, the committee of one State passing him on to the committee of another, and the hurrahs of one town dying away as those of the next caught his ear."[22]

Clay reveled in this adulation. Thomas L. Clingman, the North Carolina congressman, "never knew a man who seemed to be more gratified by applause." Clingman added, "he probably made more personal friends than any man who ever lived."[23] Clay appeared to love crowds as much as they loved him. John Wentworth, an Illinois congressman and Clay's messmate at the National Hotel, recalled that while other great men such as Calhoun, Webster, and Benton "would cross the street to avoid one [a crowd], Clay would cross the street to meet one. . . . In his walks Clay would quicken or slacken his pace for company." He often visited the House, coming "on general account, to have a good, social chat with such members as he might meet."[24]

Despite the acclaim, and as hard as he tried, Clay could never translate that sway over the masses into a ride to the White House. Five times over nearly three decades he had been a candidate for the presidency—twice in conventions of the Whig Party and three times in canvasses. With each run "millions of hearts glowed with sanguine hopes of his election" and "bitterly lamented his and their discomfiture" when he lost.[25] His great rival, Webster, who had not been on good terms with him for years, nonetheless believed "he ought long ago to have been elected President."[26] Webster also believed that of himself.

One observer said Clay "can get more men to run after him to hear him speak and fewer to vote for him than any man in America." The great man did not disagree. After one of those repeated frustrations he said he was "always run by my friends when sure to be defeated, and . . . betrayed for a nomination when I, or anyone, would be sure of an election." Following his particularly galling defeat by Polk in the 1844 canvass, Lucretia took him in her arms and said, "My husband, this ungrateful people can never truly appreciate you while living."[27]

Clay was over six feet tall, "slender and loose-jointed."[28] Anybody looking at him saw a bold, self-confident, skillful, beguiling leader graceful in body and superendowed with charm, wit, and eloquence. It was said that he could take snuff, to which he was addicted, "more elegantly than any man of his time." In private he had an "easy familiarity," but in public he could assume a grandeur as unmatched as his elegance with snuff.[29] A friend, James D.

Harrison, described him as "delicately strung . . . the most emotional man I ever knew," of broad sympathies and "magnetic power."[30]

Ben Perley Poore, the Washington journalist, thought Clay's head was rather small for his body, and his eyes "peered forth less luminously than would have been expected in one possessing such eminent control of language. His nose was straight, his upper lip long, and his under jaw light. His mouth, of generous width, straight when he was silent, and curving upward at the corners as he spoke or smiled, was singularly graceful, indicating more than any other feature the elastic play of his mind."[31] Clay's mouth, in truth, was a cave. It was enormously broad-beamed, as if split open "with a broad-axe."[32] His mouth, someone said, "looked like the stone mouth of the great Sphinx."[33]

In early December when the House was locked in the fight for Speaker, Clay entered the hall and took a seat near Horace Mann. The celebrated educator had been sent by Massachusetts in April 1848 to take the seat left vacant by the death of John Quincy Adams—sent there, Mann said, by "strange events." Given to studying heads to illuminate character, Mann took to interpreting Clay's cranium as the great man sat nearby. "Manipulating it with the mind's fingers," Mann thought it a head "of very small dimensions." However, "benevolence is large; self-esteem and love of approbation are large," Mann mused.

> The intellect, for the size of the brain, is well developed. His benevolence prevents his self-esteem from being offensive; and his intellect controls the action of his love of approbation, and saves him from an excessive vanity. This vanity, however, has at some periods of his life, led him into follies. He derives his whole strength from his temperament, which is supremely nervous, but with just as much of the sanguine as it was possible to put into it. Considering the volume of the brain, or size of the head, it has the best adjusted faculties I have ever seen. The skull, after death, will give no idea of his power, as he derives the whole of it from his temperament.[34]

Clay oozed charm. Horace Greeley said of him that he was "by nature genial, cordial, courteous, gracious, magnetic, winning."[35] Thomas Clingman said of him, "No one could be more graceful and urbane in manner."[36] He seemed "born to be loved." And perhaps to love, for he enjoyed kissing all the pretty women. Even many men who could not abide his politics were won over. Calhoun admitted, "I don't like Clay. He is an impostor, a creature of wicked schemes. I won't speak to him—but by God, I love him."[37] When General Thomas Glascock of Georgia, a hero of the First Seminole War of 1817, took a seat in Congress in 1821, a mutual friend asked, "General, may I introduce you to Henry Clay?" "No, sir!" said the general. "I am his adversary, and choose not to subject myself to his fascination."[38]

"Nobody can look like Mr. Clay when he wishes to be persuasive," James Pike said. "Nobody has that sort of eyelid lift of his countenance that he has; no man can talk through and with his hands like Mr. Clay; nobody else has that speaking toss of the head from side to side, that brailing up and letting run of the mouth, that familiar jocularity of expression in looks as in language; no one can command that sudden shift from ease to severity of feature, that quick transformation from familiar tone to lordly manner; in a word, no other man possesses that *tout ensemble* of the agreeable and commanding phases of oratory in his own personal presence." Pike thought Clay a great actor: "If he had gone upon the stage, he would have driven the Keans and Kembles out of the field."[39] This genius for drama was converted by Clay at every turn into a genius for oratory—"the greatest *natural* orator, of the whole army of eloquent men," one writer believed.[40]

A reporter for the *National Intelligencer* wrote that when speaking, Clay's "whole body would become eloquent."[41] "He gesticulated all over," Ben Perley Poore recalled. "The nodding of his head, hung on a long neck, his arms, hands, fingers, feet, and even his spectacles, his snuff-box, and his pocket-handkerchief, aided him in debate. He stepped forward and backward, and from the right to the left, with effect. Every thought spoke; the whole body had its story to tell, and added to the attractions of his arguments."[42]

Another man who had studied him closely said, "Clay, of all men, relished a personal discussion—a duel with words for the weapons. He excelled in philippic and retort, and never flinched when he met an antagonist who could give as well as take. He was merciless in a skirmish of this kind, and had no hesitation in alluding to physical defects or natural infirmities of any description. He indulged frequently in coarse pleasantries and unsparing ridicule."[43] Moreover, Congressman Wentworth believed he had a particular knack for enduring interruptions. According to Wentworth, Clay excelled at counter argument with interrupting colleagues, which he handled without losing his main train of thought. Indeed, interruptions to deal with side issues were rather expected and welcomed. "Could the enemies of Mr. Clay have formed a combination never to interrupt him," Wentworth believed, "they would have deprived him of much of his senatorial glory. . . . As an impromptu, cut-and-thrust debater, always ready, never thrown from his guard, where is your equal of Henry Clay?"[44]

Perhaps it was his gambling nature. He loved the gaming table and he could dominate it as he could dominate the Senate floor. Gambling for high stakes had tailed off over the years. He could no longer play cards all night and debate all day as he once could. In the heyday of his gambling years a friend of Lucretia asked her, "Don't it distress you to have Mr. Clay gamble?" "No, my dear," she said, "he 'most always wins."[45]

His most mesmeric feature was his voice. "No orator's voice superior to his in quality, in compass and in management, has ever, we venture to say, been raised upon this continent. It touched every note in the whole gamut of human susceptibilities; it was sweet and soft, and lulling as a mother's to her babe. It could be made to float into the chambers of the ear, as gently as descending snowflakes on the sea; and again it shook the Senate, stormy, brain-shaking, filling the air with its absolute thunders."[46]

It was a voice of "majestic bass," full of "swelling cadences." "Who," an admirer asked, "ever heard one more melodious? There was a depth of tone in it, a volume, a compass, a rich and tender harmony, which invested all he said with majesty." Clay's voice "filled the room as the organ fills a great cathedral."[47] With this voice, "musical yet mighty," he could put "an amazing weight of expression on to the backbone of a single word," one admirer said, and he seemed always ready to limber up and fire away, like "a sort of flying-artillery."[48]

Ben Perley Poore described Clay's voice as "equally distinct and clear, whether at its highest key or lowest whisper—rich, musical, captivating."[49] It "fell upon the ear like the melody of enrapturing music," marveled his fellow senator from Kentucky, Joseph Underwood, and held crowded galleries spellbound, "as if enchanted by the lyre of Orpheus."[50] A reluctant admirer said of him, "I'm damned if I can listen to Mr. Clay speak and believe him to be wrong." It was difficult to believe that this greatest orator of the age had stammered in his youth.[51]

If harmony was in Clay's musical voice, it was also deeply ingrained in his political philosophy. In the midst of the disharmony of the times he was bound to be a seeker of compromise and accommodation. It was what he had always been, what he had always done, bending all of his heart, effort, and enormous prestige into twisting extremes into middle-ground solutions in national crises. According to Wentworth, "His loftiest flights of eloquence were when he was denouncing the projects of extremists upon all sides, and in laboring to reconcile antagonisms with which the boldest and most hopeful of men dared not meddle. He was a radical orator on the conservative side. His genius was the most transparent when soaring in the realms of peace."[52]

Clay had an ingrained affinity for "healing measure[s]."[53] He said of himself, "I go for honorable compromise whenever it can be made. Life itself is but a compromise between death and life, the struggle continuing throughout our whole existence. . . . All legislation, all government, all society, is formed upon the principle of mutual concession, politeness, comity, courtesy; upon these, every thing is based."[54] For thirty years he had been trying to compromise this distracting issue of slavery that had threatened to rend the Union. "I know no South, no North, no East, no West to which I owe any allegiance."[55]

What made Clay an ideal vessel for compromise was his virtually hypnotic power over people, his love of and allegiance to the Union, and his "parliamentary finesse."[56] He began turning those talents toward pacification of the slavery issue in the Missouri Compromise crisis in 1820. As Speaker of the House, he hastened committee action on an enabling bill for Maine statehood. When it reached the floor, he knew its fate depended on the unconditional co-admission of Missouri. Such a coupling had little hope in the House, but he also knew it would happen in the Senate. And when it did, he pushed for a conference committee of the two houses and stacked his side with conciliatory minds. When the compromise at last squeezed through both houses and went to President Monroe for signature, Clay's handprints were all over it. Then when Missouri, threatening to unravel the compromise, wrote a constitution barring free negroes and mulattoes from the state, Clay had once more stepped in to reconcile and pacify.[57]

Again in the early 1830s, when the Union appeared about to hit a wall of sectional separation over the tariff issue, in which one state, South Carolina, attempted to nullify the federal law and to secede if necessary, Clay had moved in. Calhoun, obsessed with the menace to Southern rights, had been behind this Union-threatening move, as he was behind the idea of disunion to save the South now. Clay engineered an accommodation that eventually defused it. South Carolina backed down and an infuriated President Jackson did not have to use force against the state, as he had threatened to do. Senator Corwin was to call Clay's compromise "the great measure of concord."[58]

These two major interventions on the side of compromise and concord had won Clay national acclaim and a reputation as the Great Pacificator and the Great Compromiser. Senator Butler of South Carolina called him "one of the high-priests officiating at the altar of the Union."[59] As a central actor in those two tense national dramas of potential disunion Clay had been in his element. Now returned to the Senate, he clearly saw the makings of an even more desperate situation needing a yet more skillful compromising hand. The House was deadlocked. President Taylor was impotent. What hope there was lay in the Senate. And what hope there was in the Senate could well lie with Clay, to whom men were now hopefully looking for an out.

Clay had hoped this would not be the case. Before returning to Washington to reclaim his seat in the Senate he had written a friend that he intended to lie low. "I shall not place myself in any leading position," he vowed. "But I shall seek to be a calm and quiet looker on, rarely speaking and when I do endeavoring to throw oil on the troubled waters."[60]

Soon after arriving in Washington, Clay discovered that it might not be that easy. He spoke of being compelled to "listen to the grating and doleful sounds of dissolution of the Union, treason, and war."[61] "Upon the whole," he wrote a friend, "there is a very uncomfortable state of things here both for the Whig party, and I fear for the Country. From both parties, or rather from individuals of both parties, strong expressions are made to me of hopes that I may be able to calm the raging elements. I wish I could, but fear I cannot, realize their hopes." He was finding "the feeling for disunion, among some intemperate Southern politicians, is stronger than I supposed it could be."[62]

Many men, knowing Clay, could agree with James Pike, who thought that he was about to play "another grand act in the drama of life . . . starring in it on a magnificent scale."[63] And indeed, as the House finally organized itself and as the new year rolled around, Clay was mulling over in his mind a package of compromise measures he hoped might still the national tempest.

By January 21 he had cobbled together the principal parts of his compromise. That evening it was bitter cold and he had a wracking cough. It was not a night or a time for him to be going out. But there was one man he had to talk with before he proceeded any further. He had not been on cordial terms with Daniel Webster for years, not since the early 1840s, and they were longtime rivals for the highest honors in the Whig Party and for the highest office in the country. As the presidential contest of 1848 had approached, Webster had said of Clay, "After all, what will Mr. Clay leave for future ages? His speeches contain nothing of permanent value, all relating to the temporary topics, and never discussing fundamental principles. He is not an instructed statesman, and he has always kept the Whig party subservient to his personal ambition."[64] But a visit with the great Massachusetts senator, who shared with him an abiding love of the Union and who was such a persuasive power in the Senate and the country, now struck Clay as necessary to the success of the "comprehensive scheme" of compromise that he had shaped.

Ordering his carriage he drove to Webster's house and knocked on his door unannounced at seven o'clock in the evening. He was cordially received, and for an hour the two men talked. To Webster, his old rival appeared very feeble and during their discussion became quite exhausted. While not committing himself totally until he had studied the measures closer, Webster, who was finding that the agitation over slavery in the territories was "mischievous, and creates heart burnings,"[65] assured Clay of his general support. As Clay departed into the fierce night, Webster turned to a friend who had sat in on part of the discussion and said he had no doubt of Clay's "anxious desire to accomplish something for the good of the country during the little time he had left upon earth." He thought that Clay's objectives were "great and highly patriotic," that perhaps Providence had designed his return to the Senate as a means of "averting a great evil from our country." Webster told his friend that his first impression was that he "could adopt the whole of it."[66]

It had been announced to the country beforehand that Clay was to appear in the Senate on January 29 to offer a set of resolutions. On that day the weather was bright and beautiful, and crowds hopeful of cramming into the Senate gallery began arriving early, long before the session opened. Alexander Stephens, who had gone to the Senate chamber with the mob, noted that "every aisle, nook and corner" was jammed. He estimated that when Clay rose to speak, "thousands were disappointed," unable to get within earshot of him.[67]

Clay stated that he was about to introduce eight resolutions covering the five festering issues. "Taken together, in combination," he said, "they propose an amicable arrangement of all questions in controversy between the free and the slave States, growing out of the subject of slavery." He called it "this great national scheme of compromise and harmony," which he ardently hoped might, and sincerely believed ought to, win the approval of the Senate. He ticked them off:

—California would be admitted as a state without restrictions for or against slavery—that is, free.
—All other territories acquired from Mexico where slavery did not exist by law and was not likely to be introduced would be organized without any restriction or condition as to slavery. He said this resolution declared two truths, one of law (slavery did not now exist there) and one of fact (it was likely never to be introduced, the conditions being unsuited to it).
—Texas was to relinquish its claim to the New Mexico territory.
—In return the federal government would assume Texas's public debt contracted prior to its annexation in 1845.
—Slavery would not be abolished in the District of Columbia.
—But the slave trade would be abolished in the District.
—Congress would have no power to prohibit or restrict slave trade in the states.
—The Fugitive Slave Law would be tightened.

His resolution package constituted "the whole scheme of arrangement and accommodation of these distracting questions" and contained "about an equal amount of concession and forbearance on both sides." Clay's compromise asked the North for more liberal and extensive concessions, because he believed the North was numerically more powerful. "You are in the point of numbers . . . greater," he told the Northern senators, "and greatness and magnanimity should ever be allied together," for the sake of "a sentiment of humanity and philanthropy . . . a sentiment without danger, a sentiment without hazard, without peril, without loss."

He held up a fragment from George Washington's coffin given him a few days before and said he saw it as "a warning voice coming from the grave to the Congress now in session to beware, to pause, to reflect before they lend themselves to any purposes which shall destroy that Union which was cemented by his exertions and example." Clay then revealed where his own heart lay on the distracting question: "I owe it to myself, I owe it to truth, I owe it to the subject, to say that no earthly power could induce me to vote for a specific measure for the introduction of slavery where it had not before existed." With that and with his resolutions now in the hopper, Clay asked that some convenient day in the following week be fixed for their full discussion.[68]

Most elements of Clay's compromise plan had already been introduced on the floor, most of them by Stephen Douglas, chairman of the Committee on the Territories, none of them by Clay himself. But now here they were, slightly revised, packaged, and presented by the ultimate packager of compromise. As Louisiana Senator Solomon W. Downs said, its power derived from the widespread belief that any prospective plan of compromise ought to come, very appropriately, from Clay, the acknowledged Great Pacificator. However, it became immediately apparent that Southern diehards, Downs among them, did not see Clay's resolutions as a compromise at all: they conceded the South nothing, and gave all to the North. By their preliminary remarks the Southerners promised that this was to be no easy sell, that Clay would be hearing from them.[69] One observer likened Clay's efforts to "undertaking to 'shingle a whirlwind.' "[70]

On February 5, fighting a cold and coughing violently but free of fever, Clay set out from his hotel to the Capitol to defend his resolutions, in the company of C. Cornell Van Arsdale. As they approached the steps to the Capitol, Clay turned to Van Arsdale and said, "Will you lend me your arm, my friend; for I find myself quite weak and exhausted this morning." They went around the back way, with Clay saying it was less fatiguing. He began to climb the steps with difficulty, stopping several times to catch his breath. Van Arsdale asked, "Mr. Clay, had you not better defer your speech? You are certainly too ill to exert yourself to-day." Clay replied, "My dear friend, I consider our country in danger, and if I can be the means in any measure of averting that danger, my health or life is of little consequence."[71]

Inside the Capitol, the Senate chamber was jam-packed again and had been for hours, pending the arrival of the great man. Nothing like it had been seen since Clay had given his farewell oration eight years before. The *New York Tribune* correspondent wrote, "What a squeeze! Benches, corners, desks, avenues, doors, windows, passages, galleries, every spot, into, upon, under, behind, or before, from which man or woman could see or hear the lion of the day, were filled, used, or occupied." The correspondent marveled, "Mr. Clay's unrivalled popularity has again secured him an audience such as no other statesman, no matter however able and respected, has ever before obtained here. To get within hearing of his voice I found to be impossible."[72] Congressman David Outlaw, fighting for a vantage point himself, saw several women faint and heard others so pressed by the crowd that they screamed.[73] Catherine Tuck, wife of Congressman Amos Tuck of New Hampshire, who could not inch into the gallery, climbed on a sofa in an anteroom. When the Senate opened and she tried to step down, she was swept away some distance before her feet touched the floor.[74]

At one o'clock, Clay rose from his seat and stretched to his full height. The chamber rocked with applause. Hearing it, the throng outside its doors took up the shout. The clamor rose to such a crescendo that the Chair ordered the entrances cleared as Clay waited for the tumult to subside.[75] He took the mandatory pinch of snuff, borrowed from Georgia Senator William Dawson, and began to speak, his voice faltering at first, then gathering its accustomed strength and grandeur.[76]

"I have never before arisen to address any assembly so oppressed, so appalled, so anxious," he began. The lobbies and passages outside the chamber erupted again in confusion and Clay paused until it had passed. He called the split in the country "a dreadful *crevasse*." In trying to bridge this *crevasse* it was the "passion, passion—party, party—and intemperance" that he most dreaded. He said his goal was "to calm the violence and rage of party—to still passion—to allow reason once more to resume its empire." At this moment in Congress and in the states, he continued, there were "twenty-odd furnaces in full blast . . . generating heat, and passion, and intemperance, and diffusing them throughout the whole extent of this broad land. . . . All now is uproar, confusion, menace to the existence of the Union and to the happiness and safety of this people."

He told his fellow senators that he had cut himself off from social life and confined himself exclusively, with very few exceptions, to his rooms. From the beginning of the session his thoughts had been "anxiously directed" to finding "some plan, of proposing some mode of accommodation, which should once more restore the blessings of concord, harmony, and peace to this great country." The result of his work was this "scheme of accommodation," this "scheme of arrangement and compromise," embodied in the resolutions he had introduced the week before.

"What do you want?" Clay demanded, "what do you want?— you who reside in the free States. Do you want that there shall be no slavery introduced into the territories acquired by the war with Mexico? Have you not your desire in California? And in all human probability you will have it in New Mexico also. What more do you want? You have got what is worth more than a thousand Wilmot provisos. You have nature on your side—facts upon your side— and this truth staring you in the face, that there is no slavery in those territories."

One by one he pulled up his resolutions and defended them, not finishing on February 5 but putting it over into the next day. On the 6th he was again on his feet continuing to try to persuade "this vast assemblage of beauty, grace, elegance, and intelligence," that his resolutions were the way to harmony and a just and equitable compromise.[77] Clay spoke for nearly five hours over the two-day span. He wrote Lucretia, "It has exhausted me very much."[78] It had been "an appeal to the North for concession and to the South for peace."[79] "What a singular spectacle . . . !" the editor of the *New York Herald* wrote.[80]

The first voices crying out after Clay's hours-long speech were Southern. Tall, argumentative Solomon Downs of Louisiana, "vehement and impressive in his manner,"[81] said again that it appeared all of the yielding was on the Southern side. He saw no concessions in the package to the South without undue compensation to the North. "These resolutions," he growled, "were held out to [the South] as bread, and are nothing but stone."[82]

Another voice was that of John Berrien, born in New Jersey and graduated from Princeton, who had been transplanted years before to Georgia and had been a senator from that state for a quarter of a century. He had been attorney general in Andrew Jackson's cabinet and was a major legal talent with a suave, mellow voice, impeccable manners, and an independent mind. He had opposed U.S. acquisition of Oregon, Texas, and the territories won from Mexico, fearing it would breed destructive sectionalism, as indeed it had.

But Berrien was strongly pro-slavery and states' rights and a vigorous foe of what he saw as Northern aggression, which he called "the fanaticism by which we are now assailed." He took the floor and warned Northern senators, "The people of the South are at length aroused to a sense of the danger to which they are exposed . . . you have awakened a feeling which can no longer be trifled with. . . . The South asserts, then, her right to participate in all of the territories which may be acquired by the United States. She asserts her right to emigrate to them, with her property of any description. That is the precise right which is denied by the North." But having said that, Berrien, describing himself as "always the advocate of moderate councils," said that "disunion is an idea which even in imagination I cannot fully realize. In moments of despondency, it floats before my mind, as a shapeless vision, to which I can give no distinct form, dimly exposing to my view in the background the horrors of anarchy and civil commotion."[83]

Next on his feet was young Jeremiah Clemens of Alabama, a deep-grained Southern radical. Aptly named, he delivered a jeremiad against Clay's compromise. "I have been all my life carrying on a warfare against his political measures," Clemens asserted, although he was but thirty-five years old. Clay, he said, "has been able to suggest no remedy which does not recognize the right of aggression on the one side, and demand unconditional submission on the other. He has submitted for our consideration a series of resolutions dignified with the name of a compromise, but which, like most other compromises between the weak and the strong, is little better than a cloak to hide from the public gaze a hideous wrong."

Clay, Clemens complained, long ago "made his choice between the North and the South." His compromise "concedes everything demanded by the North, and proposes nothing for the satisfaction of the South," except "rights already guaranteed and admitted." *Everything*, he said, underlining the word, "is conceded by the admission of California. . . . The North gets all she has ever asked." He finished his philippic, saying, "We want no compromise. A bond [the Constitution] has been executed, and we are willing to abide by its terms. If we are to go on compromising away provision after provision . . . it is better that it should be abrogated at once."[84]

Henry Foote, a Virginian by birth and now a Mississippi senator and as close to a gadfly as the Senate had ever seen, sprang to his feet. A gifted criminal lawyer, Foote rarely said anything that was not controversial, contentious, impetuous, flamboyant, provocative, vituperative, or combative. Reacting to Clay's proposals in a perfect distillation of his hyperbole, he told the Senate that "there is more in the sentiments and language of that speech [Clay's defense of his resolutions] to mortify southern sensibilities, to awaken dissatisfaction, and to provoke resentment too . . . than we find in any speech of professed Abolitionists."[85]

Clay was not indulging these assaults meekly, nor was he hiding his antipathy to slavery. He replied, "I have held, and I have said, from that day [when he first considered slavery] down to the present, again and again, and I shall go to the grave with the opinion, that it is an evil, a social and a political evil." He had this belief despite owning some forty slaves himself. He had long argued for removing the evil from these shores with compensated emancipation and African colonization of blacks. But now, arguing for his compromise, he said, "I intended, so help me God, to propose a plan of doing equal and impartial justice to the South and to the North, so far as I could comprehend it; and I think it does yet. But how has this effort been received by the ultraist? Why, at the North they cry out . . . 'It is all concession to the South.' And, sir, what is the language in the South? They say, 'It is all concession to the North.' "[86]

Jefferson Davis was nearly as irritating in his calm, dignified way as was his cohort Foote in his nervous, excitable way. Davis was ramrod straight in bearing with a demeanor born of a West Point education that reflected his way of thinking. He was cold, with a rigid self-control to match rigid opinions. Senator Isaac Walker of Wisconsin said of Davis that he "always speaks so positively, and with an air . . . which seems to say, 'Nothing more can be said'— 'I know it all'—'it must be as I think.' "[87] Davis had been chafing to leap on Clay's resolutions from the first moment he heard them on January 29. Indeed, he had argued with the old man on that very day, hounding him to discuss the resolutions then and there. Clay had demurred, saying, "I choose not to give way now." "And I say now," Davis insisted.[88]

It was not that Clay and Davis were natural antagonists. Indeed, Clay harbored a special affection for the young Mississippian, the hero of the Mexican War. Clay's son had been killed in the Battle of Buena Vista while fighting in Davis's Mississippi Rifles. Clay told Davis one day, "My poor boy, in writing home from

Jefferson Davis
U.S. Senate Historical Office

Mexico, usually occupied about one-half of his letters in praising you." He called Davis "my young friend," and had said to him, "Come, my young friend, join us in these measures of pacification. Let us rally Congress and the people to their support, and they will assure to the country thirty years of peace." Davis, a hot defender of Southern rights, refused.[89]

Davis's "now" to challenge Clay's resolutions finally came on February 13, and for two days he slammed the compromise. "Disappointed—grievously disappointed" by them, he called the resolutions "dangerous doctrines." Clay, he said, "has chosen to throw his influence into the scale of the preponderating aggressive majority," not "in the cause of the weak against the strong, the cause of the Constitution against its aggressors," whom Davis saw as the "large part of the non-slaveholding states [who] have declared war against the institution of slavery."

A plantation owner himself, noted for his kind treatment of his slaves, Davis said, "slavery being property . . . and so recognized by the Constitution, a slaveholder has the right to go with that property into any part of the United States where some sovereign power has not forbidden it. I deny, sir, that this Government has the sovereign power to prohibit it from the Territories. I deny that any territorial community, being a dependence of the United States, has that power, or can prohibit it." Davis argued that the Mexican law barring slavery in the territories died when they were transferred to the United States, that the sovereignty of Mexico was replaced by a sovereignty "to be measured by our Constitution, not by the policy of Mexico." He also denied that slavery was excluded from the territories by a geographical nature unfavorable to it—that, to the contrary, the new territories might be better adapted to slave labor than to any other kind.[90]

So played the Southern music. But that ultimate voice of the South, the true heavyweight among them, John Calhoun, had not yet been heard from. He was now about to weigh in.

NOTES

1. Benton, *Thirty Years' View*, 2:399, 401, 739.

2. Seward, *Seward at Washington*, 104; Hamlin, *The Life and Times of Hannibal Hamlin*, 183.

3. Benton, *Thirty Years' View*, 399.

4. Clay, *Henry Clay*, 345.

5. Gerald W. Johnson, *America's Silver Age: The Statecraft of Clay-Webster-Calhoun* (New York, 1939), 254.

6. The quotes in this brief description of Clay, Webster, and Calhoun are in Hilliard, *Politics and Pen Pictures*, 212–13.

7. Richard Malcolm Johnston and William Hand Browne, *The Life of Alexander H. Stephens* (Philadelphia, 1878), 243.

8. Hilliard, *Politics and Pen Pictures*, 213.

9. The description of Cass is by Stephens in Johnston and Browne, *The Life of Alexander H. Stephens*, 249.

10. Millard Fillmore, "The Millard Fillmore Papers," vol. 1, ed. Frank H. Severance, *Publications of the Buffalo Historical Society* 10 (1907): 287; Hilliard, *Politics and Pen Pictures*, 212; Fredrika Bremer, *The Homes of the New World; Impressions of America*, 3 vols. (London, 1853), 2:44.

11. Clay, *Papers*, 10:632, 638, 642, 650.

12. Holmes Alexander, *The Famous Five* (New York, 1958), 2, 41.

13. Clay, *Papers*, 8:808.

14. Benton, *Thirty Years' View*, 399, 403.

15. Parmelee, "Recollections of an Old Stager" (vol. 45, August 1872): 448.

16. Merrill D. Peterson, *The Great Triumvirate: Webster, Clay, and Calhoun* (New York, 1987), 450.

17. Robert V. Remini, *Henry Clay: Statesman for the Union* (New York, 1991), 726, 731.

18. James Parton, *Famous Americans of Recent Times* (Boston, 1867), 50–51.

19. *New York Express*, February 18, 1850, in George Rawlings Poage, *Henry Clay and the Whig Party* (Chapel Hill, NC, 1936), 203.

20. French, *Witness to the Young Republic*, 213.

21. Alexander, *The Famous Five*, 42.

22. Parton, *Famous Americans of Recent Times*, 4.

23. Clingman, *Selections from Speeches and Writings*, 2, 255.

24. John Wentworth, *Congressional Reminiscences: Adams, Benton, Clay, Calhoun, and Webster* (Chicago, 1882), 25.

25. Greeley, *Autobiography*, 168.

26. Parton, *Famous Americans of Recent Times*, 29 n.

27. Alexander, *The Famous Five*, 11, 1, 41.

28. Peterson, *The Great Triumvirate*, 10.

29. Neil MacNeil, " 'The House Shall Chuse Their Speaker . . .' " *American Heritage* 28 (February 1977): 29.

30. Clay, *Henry Clay*, 397.

31. Poore, *Perley's Reminiscences*, 1:34.

32. Edward G. Parker, *The Golden Age of American Oratory* (Boston, 1857), 36.

33. Edgar Dewitt Jones, *Lords of Speech: Portraits of Fifteen American Orators* (Chicago, 1937), 20.

34. Mann, *Life of Horace Mann*, 261, 282.

35. Greeley, *Autobiography*, 250.

36. Clingman, *Selections from Speeches and Writings*, 256.

37. Alexander, *The Famous Five*, 13, 2.

38. Greeley, *Autobiography*, 250.

39. Pike, *First Blows of the Civil War*, 7, 36. Edmund Kean and Fanny Kemble were among the greatest actors of the time.

40. Parker, *The Golden Age of American Oratory*, 16.

41. Dyer, *Great Senators*, 229.

42. Poore, *Perley's Reminiscences*, 1:143.

43. Parmelee, "Recollections of an Old Stager," 446.

44. Wentworth, *Congressional Reminiscences*, 27–28.

45. Parmelee, "Recollections of an Old Stager" (vol. 46, December 1872): 96.

46. Parker, *The Golden Age of American Oratory*, 38.

47. Parton, *Famous Americans of Recent Times*, 11.

48. Parker, *The Golden Age of American Oratory*, 38, 43, 46.

49. Poore, *Perley's Reminiscences*, 1:143.

50. U.S. Congress, *Obituary Addresses on the Occasion of the Death of the Hon. Henry Clay* (Washington, DC, 1852), 8.

51. Alexander, *The Famous Five*, 2, 13.

52. Wentworth, *Congressional Reminiscences*, 33.

53. Clay, *Henry Clay*, 344.

54. *American National Biography*, s.v. "Clay, Henry."

55. *Congressional Globe*, 31st Cong., 1st sess., 368.

56. Clay, *Henry Clay*, 105.

57. The handprints that are all over this brief summary of Clay's role are Merrill Peterson's, from his outstanding study of Webster, Clay, and Calhoun, *The Great Triumvirate*, 60–65.

58. Ibid., 232.

59. *Congressional Globe*, 31st Cong., 1st sess., Appendix, 1247.

60. Clay, *Papers*, 10:604.

61. Ibid., 682.

62. Ibid., 633, 635.

63. Pike, *First Blows of the Civil War*, 37.

64. "Reminiscences of Washington," 809.

65. Daniel Webster, *The Papers of Daniel Webster*, ed. Charles M. Wiltse and Michael J. Birkner, vol. 7 (Hanover, NH, 1986), 5.

66. Clay's visit to Webster is recounted in George Ticknor Curtis, *Life of Daniel Webster*, 2 vols. (New York, 1870), 2:397.

67. Alexander H. Stephens, *A Constitutional View of the Late War between the States*, 2 vols. (Philadelphia, 1870), 2:199.

68. Clay's resolutions and accompanying remarks are in *Congressional Globe*, 31st Cong, 1st sess., 244–49.

69. Ibid., 251.

70. Pike, *First Blows of the Civil War*, 6.

71. Calvin Colton, *The Last Seven Years of the Life of Henry Clay* (New York, 1856), 130.

72. Quoted in Peterson, *The Great Triumvirate*, 456–57; and Rhodes, *History of the United States*, 1:123–24 n.

73. David Outlaw to Emily Outlaw, February 6, 1850, Outlaw Papers.

74. French, *Growing Up on Capitol Hill*, 7.

75. Remini, *Henry Clay*, 735; Carl Schurz, *Life of Henry Clay*, 2 vols. (Boston, 1887), 2:335.

76. Peterson, *The Great Triumvirate*, 457; Schurz, *Henry Clay*, 2:335.

77. Clay's speech, from which this brief summary is distilled, is in *Congressional Globe*, 31st Cong., 1st sess., Appendix, 115–27.

78. Clay, *Papers*, 10:672.

79. Schurz, *Henry Clay*, 2:335.

80. Peterson, *The Great Triumvirate*, 458.

81. *National Cyclopaedia of American Biography*, s.v. "Downs, Solomon W."

82. *Congressional Globe*, 31st Cong., 1st sess., Appendix, 165, 170.

83. Berrien's retort is from ibid., 202–3, 205, 210.

84. *Congressional Globe*, 31st Cong, 1st sess., 395–97.

85. Ibid., 403.

86. Ibid., 404–5.

87. Ibid., Appendix, 280.

88. *Congressional Globe*, 31st Cong., 1st sess., 249.

89. John Warwick Daniel, ed., *Life and Reminiscences of Jefferson Davis by Distinguished Men of His Time* (n.p., 1890), 16.

90. Davis's speech on the resolutions is in *Congressional Globe*, 31st Cong., 1st sess., Appendix, 149–57.

CHAPTER SIX

THE PROPHET OF SOUTHERN ANGER

AT THE END of February 1850 the Washington correspondent of the *New York Herald* looked at Congress and editorially wrung his hands. "We are on the very eve of bloodshed in the capital," he warned.

> There is no telling when its crimson streaks may deluge the halls of Congress. Without a moment's warning, civil strife and massacre may commence. . . . There is a fearful and an alarming state of things here, and when or where it will end, God alone knows. It is impossible for those at a distance to realize that their delegates in Congress are preparing for such scenes as have never been witnessed in our heretofore peaceable civil contests. The Southern members are excited to the highest pitch. Men go armed, and are preparing for the contest and personal strife that will ensue before a week has passed. We are in the crisis so long and so justly dreaded.[1]

Into this desperate tableau on a breezy March 4 came John C. Calhoun. He had not been to the floor for several weeks. Now he appeared, entering the chamber supported on one side by his South Carolina Senate colleague, Andrew Butler, and on the other by Virginia Senator James Mason, his messmate and disciple. The gallery was packed, as it always was when one of "the great trio" was to speak.

Not only were the years telling on Calhoun—he was sixty-seven—but the aura of death was also about him. As everyone in the chamber and in the gallery knew, the senator was dying, "standing," John Wentworth said, "upon the brink of eternity."[2] Harriet Martineau, the English writer, had described Calhoun in his prime as "the cast-iron man, who looks as if he had never been born, and never could be extinguished."[3] But now he was haggard, frail, and feeble, riddled with tuberculosis and wracked by coughs. With his long magisterial hair hanging down the sides of his sunken face with its deep-socketed eyes, he seemed more a specter than a man. "He was so emaciated, pale, and cadaverous," one observer wrote, "like a fugitive from a grave."[4]

Calhoun had never presented less than a vivid image, but this Calhoun, on the floor in the twilight of his life, presented a far different one from "the young Hercules" of earlier days. He had been tall—6 feet 2 inches—stiff and earnest, stern in demeanor, unbending in temperament, with nothing resembling a sense of humor, and not given to wasting time. Daniel Webster, not a man to resist cracking a joke and descending to recreation and amusement now and then, said of Calhoun, "he had no recreations, and never seemed to feel the need of amusement."[5] There was a wisecrack going around that he had once started a poem, with the word "Whereas," and that was as far as he got. It is said he had read one novel in his life, and then only because a female friend from Charleston had sent it to him and asked his opinion of it.[6]

Calhoun's mind was devastating—lacking somewhat in imagination, perhaps, but powerful in thinking and reasoning. His was a gifted, "commanding intellect." The character that went with it was unspotted—he was not known to swear, smoke, or drink. He was "more Puritan than the Puritans" but of "engaging manners and brilliant conversation."[7]

Calhoun's striking figure had always invited description. "Tall, well-formed," Ben Perley Poore, the Washington journalist, wrote, "without an ounce of superfluous flesh, with a serious expression of countenance rarely brightened by a smile, and with his long. . . hair thrown back from his forehead, he looked like an arch-conspirator waiting for the time to come when he could strike the first blow."[8] Horatio Seymour, a New York politician, saw him as "tall and commanding in figure, very erect in his bearing, and in appearance coldly dignified," but in manner and in address, simple, affable, unassuming, frank, and open.[9]

Varina Davis, Senator Jefferson Davis's acutely aware wife, observed that Calhoun's forehead was "low, steep, and beetled squarely over the most glorious pair of yellow brown shining eyes, that seemed to have a light inherent in themselves." Those eyes riveted Varina's own. "They looked steadily out from under bushy eyebrows that made the deep sockets look still more sunken," she explained. "When excited, the pupils filled the iris and made his eyes seem black. He lowered them less than any one I have ever seen; they were steadily bent on the object with which he was engaged; indeed on some people they had an almost mesmeric power."[10] A friend said, "his face is all intellect, with eyes so dazzling, black, and piercing that few can stand their gaze."[11] As for his voice, Varina did not find it musical. "It was the voice of a professor of mathematics," she said, "and suited his didactic discourse admirably. He made few gestures, but those nervous, gentlemanly hands seemed to point the way to empire. He always appeared to me rather as a moral and mental abstraction than a politician."[12]

John C. Calhoun
Library of Congress

Another who knew him was also struck by the bushy eyebrows that "overshadowed deep blue eyes, which gleamed like stars; his furrowed forehead and gaunt cheeks" showing "great mental activity and care." His thin lips, that friend believed, gave him "the melancholy look seen in the portraits of Dante." Calhoun's long, coarse lion-like mane made a statement all its own. It had whitened over the years and he wore it as he always did, cascading back "in masses from his high forehead." One morning, sitting for a portrait, he said, "I have always endeavored to dress with a simplicity that would not attract notice, and I have succeeded, with the exception of my hair."[13]

What really attracted notice to this unique and unique-looking man, however, was his mind. One observer said that his style, "both as an orator and writer was terse and condensed to a degree rarely equaled." He had driven congressional reporters to distraction over the years by speaking "with extraordinary fluency and rapidity, at times uttering short, pregnant sentences that had the force of a round shot, and then running into a prolonged and involved sentence that required a sharp man to follow and comprehend."[14] Congressman Wentworth found him to be a man of "seductive language" who spoke "like a college professor demonstrating to his class." He was a well-oiled reasoning machine, Wentworth said, a man with a "perceptive, comprehensive, and analytic mind."[15] Harriet Martineau believed his theories of government, "almost the only subject on which his thoughts are employed," were "the squarest and compactest theories that ever were made."[16]

~ The son of a farmer, Calhoun had never thought of being anything but what his father had been until he was eighteen years old. But with that mind, which everybody recognized as extraordinary, he found himself at Yale, where he took everything seriously, joked not at all, and impressed everyone high and low with his brain power. He graduated and returned to the South with "the most complete confidence in the infallibility of his own mind."[17] He was, one friend and admirer thought, "the most unpersuadable of men."[18] Harriet Martineau, who came to know him well, believed his mind had "long lost all power of communicating with any other." She spoke of "his utter incapacity of modification by other minds." "I know no man," she wrote, "who lives in such utter intellectual solitude."[19]

Calhoun took his Yale education, his magnificent mind, and his rock-like confidence in himself almost directly into politics, where he quickly and predictably rose to the top—to a level in time short only of the presidency itself, which he had coveted but, like Clay and Webster, had never attained. James H. Hammond, one of his political lieutenants, would later say that Calhoun "sprang into the arena like Minerva from the head of Jove, fully grown and clothed in armor: a man every inch himself, and able to contend with any other man."[20] He had been secretary of war, vice president, and one of the acknowledged three greatest senators of the first half of the nineteenth century.

He had first come to Washington from South Carolina in the Twelfth Congress in 1811, when he was twenty-eight years old. There he had met Henry Clay. Over the years they became friends and political allies, then adversaries. But Calhoun knew quality when he saw it. And beneath his stern idea-driven nature there was a generous heart. One observer said of him that he was "appreciative in estimating the capacity of his contemporaries in public life. His judgment was not disabled by political differences or personal dislike." When he and Clay clashed in the Senate, it was said to be "a conflict of giants." They were wholly "unlike in the structure of their minds, and habits of thought and action," one observer said; "there was hardly a point in which they resembled each other." Calhoun was unequaled for careful incisive analysis, while Clay was a hipshooter, "intolerant and aggressive, delighting in gladitorial combats," mixing personal aspersions with argument, seeking to rout an antagonist with accusations and cutting intimations of unworthy motives. The two senators had been on the outs for six years by 1842. But when Clay made his farewell speech in the Senate that year to return to Kentucky for what he thought was forever, Calhoun "gave way to his feelings and shed tears like a woman."[21]

This spectral man, gaunt and gray now, had over the years changed from an ardent unionist to "the stern zealot,"[22] the "archdefender of the slave system,"[23] the "terse, vigorous, relentless"[24] champion of the extension of slavery, free trade, and state sovereignty—the paladin of the South. He had spearheaded South Carolina's nullification movement in the early 1830s, refined its theory and argued for it, and been called "the Great Nullifier."[25] He had never been timid about threatening secession if the South could not be protected in any other way. It has been suggested that what Calhoun really wanted was "not . . . to break up the Union but to dominate it."[26]

Here he was again, perhaps for the last time, making his way to his seat near the center of the chamber, come to defend Southern rights one more time. It was doubtful he was there to talk compromise. He deplored the word. He had said, "I hold concession or compromise to be fatal. If we concede an inch, our ranks will be so broken that effectual resistance would be impossible."[27] Clay had once described Calhoun as "looking as if he were dissecting the last and newest abstraction which sprung from some metaphysician's brain, and muttering to himself, in half uttered words, 'This is indeed a crisis!' "[28]

There was indeed a crisis on this fourth day of March 1850, the nation's and Calhoun's own personal one. As he took his seat, with the hushed chamber watching, he had come to believe that the moment for the South was "critical," that its fate was at stake, that never before had his section "been placed in so trying a situation, nor can it ever be placed in one more so." He had come to believe, much as he deplored it, that it was "difficult to see how two peoples so different and hostile can exist together in one common Union."[29]

After resting for a short time in his seat, Calhoun rose and in a feeble voice told the waiting chamber that he had prepared a speech which he had hoped to deliver. But he said that appeared to be impossible for him to do, so he proposed that Senator Mason be allowed to read it for him. The Senate, visiting Congressman Henry Hilliard later wrote, seemed "to be stilled, almost awed" by what was happening. As Mason began to read there was "an unbroken silence, and the attention of all present was riveted to the words."[30] Calhoun sat motionless in front of Mason, huddled in his seat, his cloak wrapped around his shoulders. Present and listening intently to every word were Henry Clay and Daniel Webster.[31]

Mason began reading in "a very haughty and defiant tone,"[32] Calhoun's take on "this all-engrossing subject." "I have . . . believed from the first," Calhoun spoke through Mason, "that the agitation of the subject of slavery could, if not prevented by some timely and effective measure, end in disunion." He had seen that agitation mount with almost no attempt to stem it, until it can "no longer be disguised or denied that the Union is in danger."

The South, said the man who had spoken for it so ardently for so long, is in a state of "almost universal discontent . . . wide and deep," which he insisted began with the agitation on the slavery question and had been quickening ever since. Its cause, Calhoun argued, was the belief in the South—"as prevalent as the discontent itself"—that the section could no longer remain in the Union "consistently with honor and safety." He blamed this widespread feeling on the North's "long-continued" agitation of the slave question and its "many aggressions" against the South, which he insisted had destroyed the equilibrium between the two sections.

Calhoun saw Northern predominance surging in every part of the government. Before the end of the decade, he predicted, the Senate, the last bastion of balance, would be stacked against the South: forty Northern senators to only twenty-four Southern. The imbalance in the House would continue to build on the Northern side, with a steady deterioration of the South's share in the electoral college. The balance, Calhoun said, was being "irretrievably" destroyed. If that had been the natural operation of time, he would have no complaint, but with the added interference of government it had become unbearable.

The government's interference had come in three forms in his view—acts of legislation excluding the South from the common territory; an unfair burden of taxation imposed on Southern states; and a system of political measures that had radically changed the character of the government. The measures he cited that had thus deprived the South began with the Ordinance of 1787, which excluded the South entirely from "that vast and fertile" region between the Ohio and Mississippi rivers, now embracing five states and one territory. The next undermining measure was the Missouri Compromise, which excluded the South from Louisiana Purchase territory north of 36° 30'. And now there was this third deprivation—the lands wrested from Mexico, which the North was trying to claim entirely for its own, "excluding the South from every foot of it." All of this part of America lost to slavery or about to be lost, Calhoun continued, constituted 2,373,046 square miles. And the Northern system of revenue and disbursement of public money, he argued, laid an unfair tax burden on the South. That had added to the wealth of the North while depriving the South, mushroomed the population of the North, and stagnated the South. All of these factors, Calhoun said, have worked together to destroy the political equilibrium of the sections and threaten the Union.

Driving all of this, Calhoun complained, was a changing government that had assumed full control over all of the powers of the system and that was now under the absolute control of the North—to the deadly disadvantage of the South. Moreover, the "fanatical zeal" in the North to abolish slavery gave impulse to the agitation and left the South and its social organizations in peril. "Unless something decisive is done . . . what is to stop this agitation, before the great and final object at which it aims—the abolition of slavery in the States—is consummated?" Calhoun demanded. "Is it, then, not certain that if something decisive is not now done to arrest it, the South will be forced to choose between abolition and secession?"

How, then to save the Union? The only way, Calhoun argued, was for the North to abstain from violating the constitutional guarantees for slavery, on the one hand, and to repel, on the other, all attempts to violate them. However, the opposite was now happening. President Taylor's plan, Calhoun argued, could in no way satisfy the South that it could remain in the Union with safety and honor. It was but "a modification of the Wilmot Proviso." Indeed, he called the plan the "Executive Proviso." It excluded the South from the territory "as effectually" as would Wilmot's resolution. The only difference was that the Wilmot Proviso did it "directly and openly," while the president's plan did it "indirectly and covertly." Both were equilibrium destroyers in Calhoun's view. He saw the president's course as monstrously unconstitutional, "revolutionary and rebellious in its character." The Constitution, Calhoun argued, held that territories must first be organized by Congress, not by the inhabitants of the territory, egged on by the Executive. Application of its inhabitants to form a constitution and apply for statehood must follow in its appointed time and place—under congressional aegis. The Executive-inspired course followed in California, Calhoun believed, violated all of those procedures.

As he did in early 1847, Calhoun argued that the Union could not be saved by a compromise—Clay's or any other—but only by a return to the Constitution. There is "no compromise to offer but the Constitution," Calhoun said, "and no concession or surrender to make." Indeed, the solution was simple. The North must merely concede to the South an equal right in the acquired territory, rigorously enforce the Fugitive Slave Law, cease the agitation of the slave question, and restore the lost equilibrium and parity between the sections. "The responsibility for saving the Union rests on the North," Calhoun charged, "and not on the South."

None of this was new to the Calhoun canon. But what he said next was. He proposed a constitutional amendment guaranteeing equilibrium. California, he said, was to be the test. If California were admitted under the conditions proposed, Calhoun warned Northern senators, then the South would infer that they meant "to exclude us from the whole of the acquired territories, with the intention of destroying irretrievably the equilibrium between the two sections." With this final warning, Calhoun then said, "Having faithfully done my duty to the best of my ability, both to the Union and my section throughout this agitation, I shall have the consolation, let what will come, that I am free from all responsibility."[33]

There it was, Congressman Hilliard concluded—the distillation of the Southern viewpoint by its preeminent champion. Basically it said that in view of the hostile attitude of the North and the measures to exclude the South from its full rights in the government, the section ought not to remain at the sacrifice of both its honor and safety. The central question, as Hilliard saw it, was whether the North would "admit the equal right of the slave-holding section to occupy the new Territory, and thus restore and preserve the political equilibrium of the Union."[34]

The basic message, as another saw it, was that aggression by the government and the North against the rights of the South had reached a point that unless something was done to stop it immediately and decisively—and that something guaranteed and enforced by the government, indeed by the Constitution—the South would secede. Calhoun had bluntly indicated that nearly every cord that held the Union together had already been severed.[35]

Throughout Mason's reading of his speech, Calhoun sat motionless in his seat. "Not a change passed over his face," one observer wrote. "With eyes partly closed and head never wavering," he waited for "the last word before he exchanged a glance with . . . friends around."[36] There were then immediate reactions around. A reporter called the speech "a sort of memento mori for the Union."[37] Senator Lewis Cass noted that "a somber hue pervaded his whole speech," prepared as it was "in the recesses of a sick chamber."[38]

The *memento mori* aspect of Calhoun's speech worried everybody who was remotely compromise-minded, North or South. One Southerner deeply frowning was Mississippi's Henry Foote, who called it "most alarming."[39] The proposed constitutional amendment bothered him in particular. He saw it as "an additional obstruction to the immediate settlement of the questions now pending." If insisted on, Foote maintained, it will "so procrastinate settlement as . . . will make *disunion almost inevitable*." He believed that the Constitution as it now stood was more than sufficient if adhered to.[40]

Foote usually did not balk at offending anybody, but no Southerner wanted to be critical of the greatest Southerner, now dying. But why had Calhoun not consulted other Southern senators before making this address? "To speak plainly," Foote said, "I almost

felt that a noose was put around my neck, while asleep, and without having antecedingly obtained my consent." He saw the as-yet
imprecisely known constitutional amendment as a new roadblock
thrown before the country in the midst of "this contest between
the free and slave states of the Union" that was "waxing still warmer
and more warm." Not only was Calhoun "obstructing all compromise," Foote complained, but he was "heard to denounce the very
name of compromise." Calhoun brushed Foote's objections aside.
"Well, sir," he was to say some ten days later, "I never did consult
any man upon any speech I ever made. I make my speeches for
myself."[41]

Having made this one for himself but unable to read it, Calhoun
returned to his sick chamber. More reaction, much of it vehement,
seemed certain to follow him there.

NOTES

1. *New York Herald*, February 28, 1850, in National Archives, "Westward Expansion and the Compromise of 1850," 42.

2. Wentworth, *Congressional Reminiscences*, 23.

3. Martineau, *Retrospect of Western Travel*, 1:243.

4. The quote is from Sargent, *Public Men and Events*, 2:363. The accompanying description in the paragraph is drawn largely from Sargent, 363–
65, and Hamilton, *Zachary Taylor*, 302.

5. Peterson, *The Great Triumvirate*, 18; Poore, *Perley's Reminiscences*,
1:137.

6. Richard Hofstadter, "John C. Calhoun: The Marx of the Master
Class," in *The American Political Tradition and the Men Who Made It* (New
York, 1973), 92; Foote, *Casket of Reminiscences*, 78.

7. Peterson, *The Great Triumvirate*, 24, 27.

8. Poore, *Perley's Reminiscences*, 1:64.

9. Howard Carroll, *Twelve Americans: Their Lives and Times* (1883; reprint ed., Freeport, NY, 1971), 6–7.

10. Davis, *Jefferson Davis, Ex-President*, 1:209–10.

11. Maury, *The Statesmen of America*, 181.

12. Davis, *Jefferson Davis, Ex-President*, 1:210.

13. "Reminiscences of Washington," 800.

14. Parmelee, "Recollections of an Old Stager" (vol. 47, October 1873):
757.

15. Wentworth, *Congressional Reminiscences*, 20–22.

16. Martineau, *Retrospect of Western Travel*, 1:243.

17. Parton, *Famous Americans of Recent Times*, 119, 121, 122.

18. Maury, *The Statesmen of America*, 182, 184.

19. Martineau, *Retrospect of Western Travel*, 1:244.

20. Hofstadter, *The American Political Tradition*, 93.

21. This Calhoun-Clay material and comparison are drawn from
Parmelee, "Recollections of an Old Stager," 758–59.

22. Davis, *Jefferson Davis, Ex-President*, 1:209.

23. Morrison, *Democratic Politics and Sectionalism*, 5.

24. Greeley, *Autobiography*, 251.

25. Hamlin, *The Life and Times of Hannibal Hamlin*, 198.

26. William E. Dodd, *Statesmen of the Old South; or From Radicalism to Conservative Revolt* (New York, 1911), 134.

27. Alexander, *The Famous Five*, 92.

28. Poore, *Perley's Reminiscences*, 1:273.

29. John C. Calhoun, "Correspondence of John C. Calhoun," ed. J. Franklin Jameson, *Annual Report of the American Historical Association for the Year 1899*, vol. 2 (Washington, DC, 1900), 775, 782, 784.

30. Hilliard, *Politics and Pen Pictures*, 220.

31. Hamilton, *Zachary Taylor*, 303; Peterson, *The Great Triumvirate*, 461.

32. So said John Wentworth in *Congressional Reminiscences*, 23.

33. Calhoun's speech is in *Congressional Globe*, 31st Cong., 1st sess., 451–55.

34. Hilliard, *Politics and Pen Pictures*, 220.

35. This brief summary leans heavily on Sargent, *Public Men and Events*, 2:363.

36. Charles A. Dana, quoted in Hamilton, *Zachary Taylor*, 304. However, Ben Perley Poore reported that Calhoun sat throughout, his eyes "glowing with meteor-like brilliancy as he glanced at Senators upon whom he desired to have certain passages make an impression." (Poore, *Perley's Reminiscences*, 1:366). Nathan Sargent also reported that Calhoun's eye flashed in "its deep socket as he cast it around on Senators when certain passages were read, as if to arrest their attention and enforce his words with its wonted fire." Either way, as Sargent said, it was "a most unique, impressive, and dramatic scene." (Sargent, *Public Men and Events*, 2:365).

37. Quoted in Peterson, *The Great Triumvirate*, 461.

38. *Congressional Globe*, 31st Cong., 1st sess., 517.

39. Foote, *Casket of Reminiscences*, 81.

40. *Congressional Globe*, 31st Cong., 1st sess., 462.

41. This exchange between Foote and Calhoun is in ibid., 519–20.

CHAPTER SEVEN

WEBSTER AND
THE SEVENTH OF MARCH

THE DAY AFTER Calhoun's speech, Northern senatorial guns began to bark—two skirmishers at first, then advance vedettes in what looked to be the start of a pitched sectional battle.

First on his feet was Senator Hannibal Hamlin of Maine, a Democrat with an antislavery, Free-Soil mind, riding shotgun for immediate admission of California, doing what Calhoun warned was a test of Northern intransigence. California had met all of the necessary criteria, Hamlin argued. "We should admit her, and admit her at the earliest day possible; and the earlier the day the better, not only for her, but for the whole country."[1]

The next day, March 6, Isaac P. Walker, a Wisconsin Democrat, rose to cry for slave-free status for the rest of the territory won from Mexico. Slavery was prohibited in those territories now by Mexican law, Walker argued, and that law was right and ought to remain in force. Southern senators interrupted Walker with counter thrusts as he delivered his set speech, and they continued to lash out at him after he was finished.

"I did not think that any speech from one so humble as myself could kick up such a 'bobbery' as this," Walker said. He fired back with a shot at Senator Andrew Butler of South Carolina, who had sharply challenged his remarks. "I will say to the honorable Senator from South Carolina, that he is mistaken from beginning to end," Walker told the Senate, "and I will prove it."[2]

Walker still held the floor on March 7. But the circumstances were different from the day before. On this second day the Senate was teeming with listeners. It was high noon and the chamber was packed. Every seat on the floor and in the gallery was occupied, every space where a human being could stand was filled. Walker looked around the chamber and into the gallery and said, "Mr. President, this vast audience has not assembled to hear me, and there is but one man, in my opinion, who can assemble such an audience.

They expect to hear him, and I feel it to be my duty, as well as my pleasure, to give the floor to [him]."[3]

Walker sat down and Daniel Webster began to rise. The sight of Webster rising on the floor of the Senate was one of the most riveting images in American politics. One observer explained, "the getting up of Daniel Webster was not a mere act; it was a process. ... The beholder saw the most wonderful head that his vision ever rested on rising slowly in the air; he saw a lionlike countenance, with great, deep-set, luminous eyes, gazing at him with solemn majesty; in short, he saw the godlike Daniel getting on his feet, and his heart thrilled at the thought of what might be coming."[4]

It had always been so. From the beginning, Daniel Webster had been heavy artillery booming out majestic oratory and making unforgettable risings. Born in New Hampshire in January 1782, two months before John Calhoun was born in South Carolina, Webster described himself in his younger days as "long, slender, pale, and all eyes." And when he entered politics at age thirty from the platform of a brilliant law career, he started at the top. Never having served or run for any office, he was elected to the Thirteenth Congress in 1813, bypassing all the usual lower stops. There in that Congress he met Clay and Calhoun, and "the great trio" was together for the first time.[5]

Ben Perley Poore said of Webster that he was "one of the few to whom Divinity has accorded a royal share of the Promethean fire of genius."[6] Indeed, Nature, another said, had "richly endowed" him with "enormous physical magnetism." He was, according to that observer, "a whole species in himself."[7] Another recalled, "when I first put eye upon him . . . I was as much awe-stricken as if I had been gazing on Bunker Hill Monument."[8]

Part of it was simply how he looked. The New England essayist, Ralph Waldo Emerson, said, "he alone of all men did not disappoint the eye and the ear, but was a fit figure in the landscape."[9] His dark, swarthy complexion, "which burnt gunpowder will not change," was inherited from his grandmother, Susannah Bachelder, and had won him the epithet, "Black Dan." Webster was not a very tall man, but "his shoulders were very broad and his chest was very full"[10]—a "military chest" to go with his "imperious bearing" and "erect gait."[11] He appeared to the English wit, Sydney Smith, to be "a steam engine in trousers."[12] One admirer said, "I have seen men taller than Webster; I have seen men larger; but I never saw anyone who *looked* so large and grand as he did when he was aroused in debate." He broke the mold for personal magnetism. "The head, the face, the whole presence of Webster was kingly, majestic, godlike."[13]

Daniel Webster
Library of Congress

His hair, once raven black against his bronze complexion, was now "a rich iron gray," topping a head absolutely "phenomenal in size."[14] Leonine was the word often used to describe his head. It was known to be a fact that as he was approaching his full powers, his hat size had to be enlarged from year to year for several years.[15] That was presumably to accommodate his outsized brain, said to be one-third larger than the average.[16] Indeed, Horace Greeley said, "Webster's intellect is the greatest emanation from the Almighty Mind now embodied."[17]

"His lips," one contemporary remarked, "were of chiseled iron, closing on teeth regular as art and white as ivory."[18] Moving upward one found an enormous outcropping of brows, overhanging the most unforgettable pair of eyes in the Union. They were black as pitch, "living coals," Thomas Carlyle, the English writer, said, "like dull anthracite furnaces needing only to be blown."[19] They were likened by another to "great burning lamps set deep in the mouths of caves."[20]

Matching these otherworldly eyes was an otherworldly voice— deep, melodious, theatrical, operatic. Horatio Seymour, the New Yorker, called it "a voice of great power and depth—a voice full of magnetism, a voice such as is heard only once in a lifetime."[21] And few men have ever taken such a voice to such oratorical heights. When Webster spoke, he was "the Great Expounder," launching thunder.[22] When he was aroused, one writer said, his speech was something akin to heavy cannonading: "Vesuvius . . . in full blast. . . . No Gothic language has ever been pounded into more compact, cannon-ball sentences."[23] During his speeches Webster, assumed "his favorite attitude, with his left hand under his coat-tail, and the right in full action."[24] He reminded Congressman Robert C. Schenck of Ohio "of a man who was placing stone after stone in position until the whole of a wonderful structure was finally erected."[25]

The great man had a gift for mimicry and could imitate broken dialects to perfection.[26] He was also "full of racy anecdote," a friend said, which he told "in the most captivating manner."[27] And he dressed to fit his uniqueness—in a blue claw-hammer coat with brass buttons, ruffled shirt bosom, buff waistcoat, black trousers, white cravat, high soft collar, and a tall hat. Sydney Smith called Webster "a small cathedral."[28] Another said, "He must be an impostor, for no man can be so great as he looked."[29]

The look of him tended to overwhelm strangers. Jenny Lind, the renowned "Swedish Nightingale," with her rich soprano voice of "placid sweetness" and "slender figure full of grace," took concert halls by storm, as Webster took political chambers and courtrooms by storm.[30] Connoisseur George Templeton Strong in New York believed she had "in her vocal apparatus a fortune of mil-

lions."[31] To hear her sing cost Washingtonians $30: $14 for two tick-
ets, $4 to hire a hack, and $12 for the clothes the occasion demanded.[32] Her first concert in New York had raked in nearly $30,000,
"an enormous sum to be given in one city to hear a singer one
night."[33] On first meeting Webster this bowler-over of men was
herself bowled over. "I have seen a man!" she exclaimed.[34]

The man was not without his idiosyncracies and faults. In many
ways Webster was a flawed wonder—"a wonderful mixture of clay
and iron," one admirer said.[35] He appeared stern, haughty, aloof,
cold, and uncaring. When perturbed or otherwise uncomfortable
he was "as unapproachable as a porcupine."[36] Yet within this spiny
exterior was a heart that yearned inordinately for love, friendship,
and admiration, with a monumental knack for inspiring it.[37]

In 1850, Webster was not well. He was suffering from insomnia
and was often drugged. For years he had been a hard drinker, driven
there, some believed, by personal tragedy and sorrow. In 1828 his
wife, whom he dearly loved, died. The next year he lost a brother
whom he loved perhaps even more. His son, Major Edward Webster,
died in the U.S.-Mexican war. And on the very day his coffin was
brought home for burial, Webster's daughter, Julia, died of tuberculosis. As Julia was dying, Webster threw himself on a sofa and
"wept and wept, as if his heart would break."[38] He planted two
weeping willows, "brother and sister,"[39] on his estate in Marshfield,
Massachusetts, and then took to the bottle. He became careless
about financial matters and piled up debts he could not pay.

Like Clay and Calhoun, Webster had hungered to be president.
He grieved that he was not better liked beyond his native New
England, particularly by Southerners. He is reported to have said,
smiling, "I do not know why Southerners should not like me, for I
am as fond of good eating and drinking as [they] are, and they say
that I am rather careless about my debts."[40] Like many Southerners
he was a gifted angler; and he loved to hunt with his two expen-
sive shotguns, which he called "Mrs. Patrick" and "Wilmot Proviso."[41] He also shared with Southerners a profound contempt for
abolitionists, despite the fact that he was antislavery and despite
the fact that many of his constituents in Massachusetts were rabid
abolitionists and Free-Soilers.

He bitterly feared that the abolitionist movement was threatening the very life of the Union. And above all, Webster loved the
Union. He was perhaps one of the most patriotic Americans who

ever lived. What had made him widely known in New Hampshire, before he removed himself to Massachusetts, were his brilliant Fourth of July orations—five of them in eleven years.[42]

He was, as one observer said, "emphatically the child and mouthpiece of America." He was a brilliant lawyer who divided his time between serving in the Senate and arguing cases for clients before the U.S. Supreme Court. But, this same observer believed, his true client was his country: "Every speech of his bears the stamp of America." Because of it, "the hold that Henry Clay had upon the heart of his countrymen, Webster had upon the American mind."[43] Emerson thought that the people looked at Webster "as the representative of the American Continent."[44] Another of his contemporaries viewed him as "a kind of invisible presence in thousands of homes where his face was never seen."[45] Senator Thomas Hart Benton described him as "the colossal figure, bearing the constitutional ark of his country's safety upon his Atlantean shoulders."[46]

Was he going to be bearing the country's safety on those shoulders as he began the process of rising on the Senate floor on this early afternoon on March 7? Nobody knew for sure what Webster was going to say, how he was going to come down on the crisis threatening his beloved Union. He had taken little part in the proceedings up to then, being absent most of the time to appear before the Supreme Court. Two weeks earlier he had written his son Fletcher, "I am nearly broken down with labor and anxiety. I know not how to meet the present emergency or with what weapons to beat down the Northern and Southern follies now raging in equal extremes."[47]

His abolitionist constituents in New England assumed he was with them against the spread of slavery in the territories, against compromising with the South. But Clay had visited him in the bitter January cold to urge his support for his compromise package. Southerners feared that whatever he said would have tremendous impact on the country and perhaps make all the difference in this difficult time. Whatever he said was likely to be worthy. As James Pike noted, "Mr. Webster cannot speak without making an able speech."[48] And nobody doubted he would be arguing for his client, the country. Less than a month earlier he had written a friend blasting slavery "as a great moral & political evil . . . unjust, repugnant to the natural equality of mankind." But he had also said, "I cannot co-operate in breaking up social & political systems, on the warmth

. . . of a hope that in such convulsion, the cause of emancipation may be promoted."[49]

Just as both his presence and his country were immense, Webster was partial to mountains, overspreading elm trees, mighty oaks, ponderous bulls and oxen, wide fields, oceans, and "all things of magnitude."[50] It had been noticed that he not only liked huge things but required "a mighty theme" to be at his best.[51] As he processed to his feet on March 7, the times had thrown up a mighty theme.

A writer for the *National Intelligencer* had said of him in 1830, "He seizes the subject, turns it to the light, and however difficult, soon makes it familiar; however intricate, plain; and with a sort of supernatural power, he possesses his hearers, and controls their opinions."[52] Could he do that now—in 1850, in this time? "Mr. President," the deep, melodic voice boomed out into the chamber, "I wish to speak to-day, not as a Massachusetts man, nor as a Northern man, but as an American."

"The imprisoned winds are let loose," Webster began. "The East, the West, the North, and the stormy South, all combine to throw the whole ocean into commotion, to toss its billows to the skies, and to disclose its profoundest depths." In "this combat of the political elements," he said, "I speak to-day for the preservation of the Union. 'Hear me for my cause.' I speak to-day, out of a solicitous and anxious heart, for the restoration to the country of that quiet and that harmony which make the blessings of this Union so rich and so dear to us all."

Disorder outside the chamber halted Webster for a moment. Eventually as he soared along he came around to the subject of Texas—"this immense territory, over which a bird can not fly in a week"—and then of California and the New Mexico territory. "I hold slavery to be excluded from those territories by a law even superior to that [of men] which admits and sanctions it in Texas— I mean the law of nature—of physical geography—the law of the formation of the earth. That law settles forever, with a strength beyond all terms of human enactment, that slavery cannot exist in California or New Mexico." They are "Asiatic in their formation and scenery," composed of vast mountain ridges of enormous height, with broken ridges and deep valleys and slopes "entirely barren" and capped by perennial snow, a country "fixed for freedom" by an "irrepealable law."

No Wilmot Proviso was necessary there, Webster argued, no man-made prohibition whatsoever. "What is there in New Mexico that could by any possibility induce any body to go there with slaves?" he demanded. He would therefore not vote for the Wilmot Proviso or for any such prohibition, because it would only wound the pride of the South, to the endangerment of the Union. He said that although he had long been unwilling to do anything to extend African slavery in the continent, he would do nothing now either to favor or encourage its further extension.

But, he said, neither would he do anything to unnecessarily wound the feelings of the South. He would enforce the law to return fugitive slaves to their Southern owners, a constitutional requirement. On that issue, Webster said, "the South is right, and the North is wrong." Northern states were bound by oath to return runaway slaves, and he would support the resolution enforcing it. He then turned on the abolitionist societies, charging them with doing a disservice to the country. Over the past twenty years, he said, they have "produced nothing good or valuable." What they have done has been "not to enlarge, but to restrain, not to set free, but to bind faster, the slave population of the South."

Webster then assaulted the notion of secession. "I hear with pain, and anguish, and distress, the word secession. . . . Secession! Peaceable Secession! Sir, your eyes and mine are never destined to see that miracle. The dismemberment of this vast country without convulsion! The breaking up of the fountains of the great deep without ruffling the surface! . . . There can be no such thing. . . . Peaceable secession is an utter impossibility. Is the great Constitution under which we live here—covering this whole country—is it to be thawed and melted away by secession, as the snows on the mountains melt under the influence of a vernal sun, disappear almost unobserved, and die off? No, sir! no, sir!"

For Webster peaceable secession was not only politically unattainable but also morally impossible: "I would rather hear of natural blasts and mildews, war, pestilence, and famine, than to hear gentlemen talk of secession." Instead of "dwelling in these caverns of darkness, instead of groping with those ideas so full of all that is horrid and horrible, let us come out into the light of day; let us enjoy the fresh air of liberty and union."[53]

The Saturday before his speech, Webster, feeling compelled to test the mood of the South, just as Clay had felt compelled to visit him in January, called on his old friend, rival, and fellow Senate giant, John C. Calhoun. The two talked for over two hours in Calhoun's rooms. Webster left feeling that a healing speech by such an influential Northerner as he would be welcomed in the South.[54]

Shortly after Webster began speaking on March 7, the gaunt, dying Calhoun, wrapped in a long black cloak, entered the chamber through the lobby behind the vice president's chair with slow, feeble steps and took his seat on the opposite side. Not seeing him enter, Webster, in the course of his speech, deeply regretted that Calhoun was ill and absent. In a frail, hollow voice, Calhoun said, "The Senator from South Carolina is in his seat." Webster turned toward him with a start, saw his old friend, and "for a moment betrayed visible signs of deep emotion." Acknowledging Calhoun with a bow and "a smile of profound satisfaction," Webster went on with his speech.[55]

When he finished, Calhoun rose slowly to his feet and said, among other things, "Am I to understand him, that no degree of oppression, no outrage, no broken faith, can produce the destruction of this Union? . . . No, sir! the Union can be broken. Great moral causes will break it, if they go on; and it can only be preserved by justice, good faith, and a rigid adherence to the Constitution." His distance from Calhoun's seat and the crowded state of the chamber prevented Webster from hearing all that the old man said. But he had heard those last words. Calhoun, Webster insisted, was speaking of revolution, not peaceable secession—and that possibility, he admitted, did exist as an ultimate right, much as he would deplore it.[56]

Webster had spoken for three hours, proceeding slowly, with long pauses, laboriously at times, sweat standing out on his craggy brow.[57] There was no question that Webster's constituency in Massachusetts as well as antislavery and anticompromise men everywhere had heard, with horror, all he had said. Return runaway slaves? The South is right, the North is wrong? Abolitionists have done a disservice to the country? Northern extremists could hardly believe their ears.

"With such noble intrepidity," Tennessee Senator John Bell thought, he "has breasted the torrent of fanaticism at the North."[58] A New Englander said of the speech that it "fell on the foes of slavery expansion like a clap of thunder from the clear sky." They received it as "a recantation of principle, the ruin of a noble career, and the turning back of the hands on the clock of time."[59] The cry of outrage from abolitionists in the North was swift and bitter.

Throughout New England, Webster was vilified. The abolitionist theologian, Theodore Parker, roared, "I know no deed in American history done by a son of New England to which I can compare this but the act of Benedict Arnold."[60]

Nobody was more angry than Webster's fellow Bay Stater, the rigorously slave-hating Horace Mann. Webster, he cried, "is a fallen star!—Lucifer descending from heaven! . . . He has disappointed us all . . . given a vile catastrophe to [his life's] closing pages . . . played false to the North." Mann called it a "dreadful" defection. "Indeed, the more I think of the speech, the worse I think of it," he raged.[61] Robert C. Winthrop, a Massachusetts man like Mann and Webster, called these vicious outpourings "the rhapsodies of Horace Mann."[62]

The New England abolitionist editor and writer, John Greenleaf Whittier, wrote Webster off with verse:

> From those great eyes
> The soul has fled:
> When faith is lost, when honor dies,
> The man is dead![63]

"My poor speech is launched forth," Webster confessed, "and is a good deal tossed upon the waves. . . . There is one comfort, and that is, that if its fate should be to go to the bottom, it has no cargo of value, and only one passenger to be drowned."[64] Whatever the abolitionists thought, pragmatic Northerners, the main base of his support back home, approved of his speech. Business interests, hating the idea of commerce-disrupting disunion, particularly liked it. Between 600 and 800 New York businessmen sent Webster a letter and a gold watch thanking him. Nearly 1,000 leading Bostonians published their names in the *Boston Courier* under a letter of support. More than 3,000 turned up at Faneuil Hall in Boston to support the compromise.[65] And doubtless Webster had the gratitude of Henry Clay.

In many parts of the country, Webster was hailed for his courageous statesmanship. His speech was widely seen as giving a strong push for compromise, perhaps marking a turning point, certainly bringing new support for accommodation. It appeared to be a body blow to the Wilmot Proviso and to any extension of the Missouri Compromise line to the Pacific. It was also seen as poison for the scheduled meeting of Southern separatists in Nashville in June.

Winthrop said, "Webster's speech has knocked the Nashville convention into a cocked hat."[66] "The necessity of the Convention," the *Virginia Free Press* wrote, "if it ever existed is now at an end. . . . Since the delivery of Mr. Webster's speech the great body of the people feel a confidence that the agitating and exciting question of the day will be amicably settled and the clouds which lately lowered so darkly over the Union will be dispelled."[67]

Webster, the *Baltimore Sun* reported, "has this day exhibited a higher degree of moral courage than ever graced a great captain on the battle field. This speech is Webster's apotheosis."[68] Alexander C. Bullitt, writing in the Taylor administration's newspaper, *The Republic*, said, "The triumph of the statesman was never more complete, or more conspicuous. It could be seen everywhere. . . . It was acknowledged that a blow had been struck for the Union. It was regarded as though the crisis had been passed; that the tempest tossed and billow beaten bark had come safe to harbor."[69] The *Journal of Commerce* in New York was to suggest, in hindsight, that Webster "did more than any other man in the whole country, and at greater hazard of personal popularity, to stem and roll back the torrent of sectionalism which in 1850 threatened to overthrow the pillars of the Constitution and the Union."[70]

Whatever else Webster's speech, one of the most telling of his career, had done, it uncorked a deluge of letters. His friend, George Ticknor, wrote from Washington, "The number of letters he receives about it is *prodigious*; and the flood still comes in, as if none had flowed before."[71]

What Webster's Seventh of March speech could not do, however, was to staunch the flow of rhetoric on the slavery issue on the floors of the Senate and the House. That would rage on to an even greater crescendo.

NOTES

1. *Congressional Globe*, 31st Cong., 1st sess., Appendix, 248.
2. Ibid., 289.
3. *Congressional Globe*, 31st Cong., 1st sess., 476.
4. Dyer, *Great Senators*, 288–89.
5. Peterson, *The Great Triumvirate*, 27, 32, 37.
6. Poore, *Perley's Reminiscences*, 1:79.
7. Parton, *Famous Americans of Recent Times*, 57, 98.
8. Theodore Ledyard Cuyler, *Recollections of a Long Life: An Autobiography* (New York, 1902), 125.

9. Ralph Waldo Emerson, "The Fugitive Slave Law," in *The Complete Essays and Other Writings of Ralph Waldo Emerson*, ed. Brooks Atkinson (New York, 1940), 863.

10. Poore, *Perley's Reminiscences*, 1:79.

11. "Military chest" and "imperious bearing" are from Alexander, *The Famous Five*, 56; "erect gait" from Wentworth, *Congressional Reminiscences*, 34.

12. Jones, *Lords of Speech*, 37.

13. Dyer, *Great Senators*, 251–53.

14. Ibid., 252–53.

15. Parker, *The Golden Age of American Oratory*, 62.

16. Parton, *Famous Americans of Recent Times*, 110.

17. Dyer, *Great Senators*, 284.

18. Jones, *Lords of Speech*, 37.

19. Poore, *Perley's Reminiscences*, 1:288; Peterson, *The Great Triumvirate*, 223.

20. Dyer, *Great Senators*, 252.

21. Carroll, *Twelve Americans*, 7.

22. Hamlin, *The Life and Times of Hannibal Hamlin*, 213.

23. Parker, *The Golden Age of American Oratory*, 93, 113.

24. Martineau, *Retrospect of Western Travel*, 1:290.

25. Carroll, *Twelve Americans*, 234.

26. Parmelee, "Recollections of an Old Stager" (vol. 45, October 1872): 750.

27. *Obituary Addresses on the Occasion of the Death of the Hon. Daniel Webster. . . .* (Washington, DC, 1853), 69.

28. Alexander, *The Famous Five*, 53.

29. Parker, *The Golden Age of American Oratory*, 49–50.

30. This description of Jenny Lind is from Hilliard, *Politics and Pen Pictures*, 239–43.

31. Strong, *Diary*, 18.

32. Green, *Washington: Village and Capital*, 224.

33. David Outlaw to Emily Outlaw, September 11, 1850, Outlaw Papers.

34. Poore, *Perley's Reminiscences*, 1:79.

35. Cuyler, *Recollections of a Long Life*, 129.

36. Parmelee, "Recollections of an Old Stager," 750.

37. Peterson, *The Great Triumvirate*, 37.

38. Walker Lewis, ed., *Speak for Yourself, Daniel: A Life of Webster in His Own Words* (Boston, 1969), 369–70.

39. Alexander, *The Famous Five*, 48.

40. Clingman, *Selections from Speeches and Writings*, 258.

41. Alexander, *The Famous Five*, 49.

42. Parton, *Famous Americans of Recent Times*, 80.

43. Parker, *The Golden Age of Oratory*, 55–56, 68, 83, 84.

44. Emerson, "The Fugitive Slave Law," 863.

45. Edwin P. Whipple, ed., *The Great Speeches and Orations of Daniel Webster with an Essay on Daniel Webster as a Master of English Style* (Boston, 1919), xiv.

46. Dyer, *Great Senators*, 297–98.

47. Daniel Webster to Fletcher Webster, February 24, 1850, in Daniel Webster, *The Letters of Daniel Webster*, ed. C. H. Van Tyne (1902; reprint ed., New York, 1968), 393.

48. Pike, *First Blows of the Civil War*, 17.

49. Webster, *Papers*, 11.

50. Parton, *Famous Americans of Recent Times*, 110.

51. Jones, *Lords of Speech*, 39.

52. Peterson, *The Great Triumvirate*, 223.

53. Webster's Seventh of March speech is in *Congressional Globe*, 31st Cong., 1st sess., 476–83.

54. Charles M. Wiltse, *John C. Calhoun, Sectionalist, 1840–1850* (Indianapolis, 1951), 459–60.

55. This moment on the floor is captured by Peter Harvey, *Reminiscences and Anecdotes of Daniel Webster* (Boston, 1877), 220–22.

56. This exchange is in *Congressional Globe*, 31st Cong., 1st sess., 483.

57. Peterson, *The Great Triumvirate*, 464.

58. *Congressional Globe*, 31st Cong., 1st sess., Appendix, 1088.

59. Hamlin, *The Life and Times of Hannibal Hamlin*, 213.

60. Rhodes, *History of the United States*, 1:155.

61. Mann, *Life of Horace Mann*, 293, 294, 296, 299.

62. Winthrop, *A Memoir of Robert C. Winthrop*, 125.

63. John Greenleaf Whittier, "Ichabod," in *The Complete Poetical Works of John Greenleaf Whittier* (Boston, 1910), 187.

64. Daniel Webster, *The Private Correspondence of Daniel Webster*, ed. Fletcher Webster, 2 vols. (Boston, 1857), 2:359.

65. Paul Arnston and Craig R. Smith, "The Seventh of March Address: A Mediating Influence," *Southern Speech Communication Journal* 40 (Spring 1975): 292, 299.

66. Foster, "Webster's Seventh of March Speech and the Secession Movement, 1850," 255.

67. Quoted in Herman V. Ames, "John C. Calhoun and the Secession Movement of 1850," American Antiquarian Society *Proceedings*, New Series 28 (April 1918): 41.

68. Peterson, *The Great Triumvirate*, 464.

69. Lynch, "Zachary Taylor as President," 288–89.

70. Nevins, *Ordeal of the Union*, 297.

71. George Ticknor, *Life, Letters and Journals of George Ticknor*, 6th ed., 2 vols. (Boston, 1876), 2:264.

CHAPTER EIGHT

THE HIGHER LAW

WILLIAM HENRY SEWARD of New York was tousle-headed, with straw-colored hair tinged with red. His eyes were blue-gray, his nose a "high sharp beak" outjutting over a chin in a state of recession. This thatch of bird's-nest hair and "jay-bird" countenance topped a slight frame with sloping shoulders. He regularly carried a silver snuffbox and an unlit cigar. He was forty-eight years old.[1]

But beneath this antic veneer lurked a quick-minded political sagacity difficult to match. He had been a two-term governor of New York—an excellent one. And now he was a freshman senator, with a distaste for the extension of slavery in the territories also hard to match. Of all the Northern Whig senators, he was the most fervently radical and extreme. One Southern critic called him "a very striking and peculiar character . . . cold and unexcitable."[2] On March 11 he seized the floor of the Senate to deliver his maiden speech on the slavery issue. It was widely believed by many hopeful Northerners that he would deliver the no-compromise, no-concession to slavery speech that Webster ought to have delivered four days before but did not.

Oratory was not Seward's strong suit. His voice was slow-moving and metallic—"guttural and uncultivated," one of his friends thought, "which probably arises from an absence of all pleasure in music; confessedly he cannot distinguish a chant from a jig."[3] It was said of him that when responding to serenades he threw out sentences "like clanging oracles into the night."[4]

Twenty minutes into his speech on March 11, the gallery had virtually emptied. This was no Clay mesmerizing them with his music, Calhoun threatening hot secession, or Webster paralyzing them with his thunder. However, all three of "the great trio" were there throughout, listening closely to everything Seward was saying. For they knew that he spoke for the most powerful state in the Union and, more important, that he had some kind of hold on Zachary Taylor.

William H. Seward
Library of Congress

"Yes; let California come in," Seward said, "in her robes of free-dom gorgeously inlaid with gold." He assailed the South's objec-tions to California's entrance. Southerners had argued that it sought to come without the preliminary consent of Congress and there-fore "by usurpation." They argued that California had drawn its own boundaries without the authority of Congress, that it was too large for one state, that no census had been taken, and that no laws had been enacted for the qualification of suffrage and apportion-ment of representatives before its constitutional convention was held. They argued that it sought to come in under the infamous influence of the president himself.

Seward scorned all of those arguments. "They have no foundation in the law of nature and of nations," he argued, "nor are they
founded in the Constitution." California, he insisted, "is already a
State—a complete and fully appointed State." He lashed out against
compromise: "I am opposed to any such compromise, in any and
all forms in which it has been proposed." He was particularly
against linking the admission of California to a compromise on the
other questions arising out of the slavery issue. "I think all legislative compromises radically wrong and essentially vicious," he said.
"I shall vote for the admission of California directly, without conditions, without qualification, and without compromise."

He was ironwilled against the Fugitive Slave Law. He saw the
recapture and return to bondage of runaway slaves as "unjust, unconstitutional, and immoral." Moreover, "the law of nations dis-
avows such compacts. The law of nature, written on the hearts and
consciences of freemen, repudiates them." He would outlaw slavery in the District of Columbia and in all the territories: "I shall
vote to admit no more slave states unless under circumstances absolutely compulsory." He found "no authority for the position that
climate prevents slavery anywhere. It is the indolence of mankind,
in any climate, and not the natural necessity, that introduces slavery in any climate." Therefore, the Wilmot Proviso was necessary.

One thing he said riveted everybody remaining in the near-
empty hall and would echo like a cannon shot around the country.
"There is a higher law than the Constitution" governing this issue,
he announced. For many that was a bombshell of a theory, new,
startling, and repugnant.

What Seward said, then, could be neatly summarized: no compromises, no concessions, no yielding to the South. A higher law
than the Constitution forbade it.[5]

In the process, he had ripped into all three of "the great trio,"
and all three of them assailed his speech. Clay dismissed it entirely.
He scorned its "wild, reckless and abominable theories, which strike
at the foundations of all property, and threaten to crush in ruins
the fabric of civilized society." He believed the speech had eradi-
cated any respect the freshman senator might have enjoyed.[6]
Webster sneered, and it was not difficult to know what Calhoun
thought of it.[7] "Seward's '*Execrable*,' " Virginia Senator Robert M. T.
Hunter labeled it, rather summing up what the South in general
thought.[8] Senator Lewis Cass, appalled, called the speech "one of
the most disingenuous . . . I have ever heard." If Seward supported

the Constitution, as he said he did, Cass growled, "he has a very strange way of showing it."[9]

Willie Mangum was a raw-boned, national-minded, just, and patriotic senator from North Carolina with a reputation for sound judgment and convincing argument. He was refined, genial, hearty, fun-loving, always at the service of his friends, and a first-rate story teller, "beloved by every body." He was, one observer said, "independent and high-toned," "above the reach of all sinister influences."[10] He was also a mover and shaker in Whig Party counsels, one of the founders of the party in North Carolina in the 1830s, and a warm personal friend of both Clay and his compromise. And he was livid.

After Seward's speech, he stormed into Zachary Taylor's office in the White House denouncing what he saw as "monstrous declarations," telling the president that "if such were the doctrines of the administration, I was its decided opponent henceforth, and if those were Whig doctrines, I was a Loco-foco." Taylor hurried in alarm to see A. C. Bullitt, the editor of the *Republic*, and stammered, "A-aleck, this is a nice mess Governor Seward has got us into. Mangum swears he'll turn Democrat if Seward is the mouthpiece of my administration. The speech must be disclaimed at once, authoritatively and decidedly. Don't be mealy-mouthed about it, but use no harsh language. We can't stand for a moment on such principles. The Constitution is not worth one straw if every man is to be his own interpreter, disregarding the exposition of the Supreme Court." So Bullitt wrote in the *Republic*, "When a Senator rises in his place, and proclaims that he holds his credentials from Almighty God, authorizing him to reject all human enactments"—and went on from there.[11]

By March 13, Henry Clay was in a glum mood. "We are still in the Woods here, on the Slavery questions," he wrote his son, "and I don't know when we shall get out of them."[12] Stephen A. Douglas had an idea how. On the same day Clay was writing his letter, Douglas was taking the floor to have his say on the national distraction. The squat Democratic senator from Illinois was a tall player in this troubled tableau. Only a second-year freshman, Douglas was the chairman of the important Committee on the Territories, the incubator of most of the territorial legislation making its way to the floor. And he was growing more and more irritated.

Douglas was Cass's alter ego on the matter of "popular sovereignty" and believed it was *the* solution to the problem of slavery in the territories. If Cass had been elected in 1848 instead of Zachary Taylor, the slavery question would have been settled by now, he thought. "Upon the principle of non-interference, by the action of the people themselves," he was now reminding his fellow senators,

> California, with her free constitution, would have been received into the Union as a State long ago, and the usual territorial government would have been established for the residue of the country. The whole country would have remained free, as it is now, by the existing laws of the land, by the will of the people who inhabit it, and by the laws of nature, climate, and production. The adjustment would have been effected quietly, peaceably, and satisfactorily. No offense would have been given to any portion of the Union. We would have had none of this irritating agitation— experienced none of this painful excitement. We would have heard not a word of southern rights and northern aggressions, much less the harsh and discordant sounds of disunion.

Believing strongly in popular sovereignty as the national panacea, Douglas stood against the Wilmot Proviso: "I could never have voted for the Wilmot proviso under any emergency or conceivable state of facts." With that made perfectly clear, he went on next to speak to "those very interesting questions called 'southern rights' and 'northern aggression.' " He lit into Calhoun's thesis that the South had been deprived of its rightful share of the territories, slamming what he called the South Carolinian's "one great fundamental error—the error of supposing that his particular section has a right to a 'due share of the territories' set apart and assigned to it."

Douglas reminded Southern senators that they themselves had voted for the acts of Northern "aggression" that Calhoun had listed in his speech on March 4. He reminded them that the people themselves in the states carved from the territory northwest of the Ohio barred slavery, not the government. As to the Missouri Compromise, Southerners voted for it as well, and many of them now clamored for that line to be extended to the Pacific. In the Oregon territory, there too the people themselves excluded slavery, not Northern aggression. He argued that this was the way it should be, "that it is wiser and better to leave each community to determine and regulate its own local and domestic affairs in its own way," as was the case in California.

Douglas called Calhoun's proposed constitutional amendment to ensure a slave-state equilibrium with the free states for all time to come "a moral and physical impossibility." In the first place, he assured senators, the people in the free states would never agree to it. And even if they did, it would be impossible to carry out. He cited the compulsion over time for slave states themselves to become free. When the Constitution was adopted, there were twelve slaveholding states and only one free. Of the twelve, six had since abolished slavery. Douglas predicted that others would follow their lead over time. It was likely, he said, that the vast territory from the Mississippi to the Pacific would produce seventeen new free states. Where, he asked, is there to be found slave territory to balance these seventeen, or even one of them? "There is none," he said, "none at all." Worse, in Douglas's view, any such arrangement for the sake of balance would "destroy the great principle of popular equality"—his beloved popular sovereignty. "It would be a retrograde movement," he insisted, "in an age of progress that would astonish the world."

By the end of the day on March 13, Douglas had not finished. The next day he still held the floor, to speak to the Mexican prohibition of slavery in the territories. It remained in effect, he said, by virtue of the treaty and the laws of nations unless repealed by competent authority. As for admitting California immediately as a free state, he asked, "Sir, why should we not do it?" He argued that Congress for two years had refused to pass a law to permit Californians to organize a government, form a constitution, apply for statehood, and enter the Union. So they organized without a law. That was irregular, perhaps, but understandable. "The people of California were entitled to a government," Douglas said, "ought to have had one, and it is not their fault that one was not given to them." Moreover, he said, "I hold that the people of California had a right to do what they have done—yea, that they had a moral, political, and legal right to do all they have done."

More than a year before, in December 1848, Douglas had introduced the bill to authorize California to form a constitution and state government and to come into the Union. He had pressed for its passage from the first week of that session to the last day. His first proposition had been to bring not only California, but also the whole of the country acquired from Mexico, into the Union as one state, reserving the right later to subdivide all of it east of the Sierra Nevadas into as many states as Congress should determine—and all by popular sovereignty. Well knowing that all of those states would likely be free, Southern senators would not hear of it. In defeating it, Douglas now argued, the measure for an adjustment to the slavery issue was prevented, the people of the territories were deprived of governments, the question remained open, and the agitation continued, producing the present impasse.[13]

When Douglas finally finished on March 14, Cass lumbered to his feet to put an amen to what his young ally had said about North-South equilibrium. "In the days of Solomon," Cass rumbled, "it was said that there was nothing new under the sun; but I confess, that a perfect equilibrium, for all time and for all interests, be these interests greater or smaller, would be something new." Mississippi Senator Henry Foote, still fuming over Seward, rose to scour the New Yorker's higher-law speech, charging that Seward had been "especially active . . . in stirring up the embers of discord, and in reawakening that fell spirit of contention which has been already productive of so much mischief."[14]

George E. Badger, a North Carolina Whig, was as upset over Seward as Foote was. Badger was a man worth listening to. A powerful speaker, he was capable of clear, forceful argument, with a keen grasp of the law, a sharp intellect, a fun-loving nature, and a gift for repartee. He also had a quick temper given to dishing out biting satire and ridicule. He had been secretary of the navy in the short administration of William Henry Harrison in 1841. He had resigned, with most other Whigs, when John Tyler succeeded to the presidency and proved unfaithful to Whig policies. Badger had been a relentless foe of the war with Mexico and of the acquisition of Mexican territory, fearing that it would bring what indeed it had: slavery's reentry into the political arena. A talented political organizer and strategist, he had long been one of the leaders of the Whig Party in North Carolina. He was a friend of Henry Clay, and strongly procompromise.

Now he had the floor to rail against the higher-law thesis of his fellow Whig, William Seward, and to deplore the paralyzed state of the Congress. Seward's hypothesis, Badger insisted, rendered it impossible to count upon the execution of any manmade law. Then he said, "It cannot be—I will not believe it—nothing but demonstration, nothing but the accomplished fact shall satisfy me—that we have so degenerated from our sires of the Revolution as not to be able to adjust the questions before us."[15]

Henry Clay was in an even gloomier mood by March 16. He was disgusted with Zachary Taylor. "I have never before seen such an Administration," he complained in a letter to a friend. "There is very little cooperation or concord between the two ends of the avenue. There is not, I believe, a prominent Whig in either House that has any confidential intercourse with the Executive," not even Seward anymore since his speech, which Clay assumed had cut him off from Taylor. "I shall continue to act according to my convictions of duty," Clay vowed, "co-operating where I can with the President, and opposing where I must."[16]

John P. Hale
Library of Congress

Only temporarily, to hear out Douglas, had Northern ire toward Calhoun been put on hold. On March 19 it burst out again when New Hampshire's droll senator, John P. Hale, the ardent Free-

Soiler with a talent for hyperbole, took possession of the floor. Hale had been the first man elected to the Senate on an undiluted anti-slavery issue. He was clever, witty, combative, and eloquent, a strong impromptu debater who was not much for backing down from any argument. His resonating voice soared into a speech laced with long, excerpted quotes from an army of sources aimed at proving that nothing Calhoun had said was true. He suggested that Calhoun's address was "more like the romance than the truth of history," assuming the form of "a regular catechism." As Hale rattled along for parts of two days, Southern senators fired countersalvos. Hale's philippic soared to a climax with the news that he envisioned a day "when the word 'slavery' shall be a word without meaning." Then, he said, "shall the united and universal shout of a regenerated people go up in one strong, swelling chorus to the throne of the Most High, unmingled with the groans or prayers of the victims of oppression living under any human form of government."[17]

Over in the House chamber, the same sort of give-and-take North and South had been playing out. Robert Toombs, assessing it all on March 22, wrote Alexander Stephens's brother in Georgia, "we have been in a whirlwind of excitement a good deal of the time here."[18]

On March 25, Robert Hunter, the Virginia Democrat, held the floor in the Senate. He was a Calhoun disciple, but he also had a conciliatory nature. He had entered the Senate in 1847 and had been troubled ever since. "Live together, sir, we cannot," he told his colleagues, "unless something is done to settle these differences and compose this strife which seems to be growing daily in intensity and bitterness. The cords which bind this Union together will fret asunder from the mere force of agitation, unless something can be done to quiet it." Particularly troubling to Hunter was the "war" that the North—its government and its abolitionists—had been waging "against the rights of property of the slaveholding states." Echoing Calhoun, he spoke of the urgent necessity of preserving the South's "political weight" in the country, a matter "to us of the highest possible political importance," what the South needed "to protect herself within the Constitution and the Union." There was one thing Hunter, despite his wont to be conciliatory, would never do. "I will not sacrifice those rights which are necessary to protect the liberties of my native State, be the consequences of that refusal what they may."[19]

When Salmon Portland Chase, the Free-Soiler from Ohio, took the floor the next day, it was fire answering fire. Chase, a mint-fresh senator, had become so notorious for legally defending run-away slaves in his home state that neighboring Kentucky called him the "attorney-general for runaway negroes."[20] He had moved to Ohio from the East in 1830 seeking "Fame's proud temple." It was said of him by his political enemies that he was as "ambitious as Julius Caesar."[21]

Chase began his maiden oration in the Senate by laying out the ground rules for fighting slavery. "We have no power to legislate on the subject of slavery in the States," he said, but we have the power—and the duty—to prohibit its extension into the national territories. All that day he spooled out an exhaustive review of the history of slavery in America back to 1619, when the first blacks were brought to the New World. Still holding the floor on March 27, he said, "There can be no foundation whatever for the doctrine . . . that an equilibrium between the slaveholding and non-slaveholding sections of our country has been, is, and ought to be, an approved feature of our political system. No such equilibrium, nothing look-ing towards such an equilibrium, can be found in the Constitution, nor in any early action under it. It was not thought of by anybody."

Chase believed it untrue that every right derived from state law—slavery, for one—could be carried beyond the state into the territories or elsewhere, or that just because a state permitted it, that Congress must therefore authorize it in the territories. He thought that Clay's compromise will "hardly prove comprehen-sive enough." California, Chase predicted, was bound to come in. But he was not for connecting its admission to the slavery ques-tion or tying it to a territorial bill for the New Mexico and Utah territories.

On the Texas-New Mexico boundary squabble, Chase was hard-line. "Let Texas keep her lands and her debt," he said, but keep hands off New Mexico. On abolishing slavery in the District of Columbia, he was just as calcified. It ought to be abolished, he de-clared, along with the abominable slave trade. He would go even farther. He would see slave trade abolished among the states them-selves. As for the Fugitive Slave Law, he had violated it often enough and would violate it again, for he would never vote for any law that returned slaves to slavery. But that was because he considered that odious law not a constitutional requirement, but only a treaty stipulation to be carried out by the states. Whether to abide by it should be up to the individual state governments to decide.

Chase was very much for the Wilmot Proviso, a positive outlawing of slavery in the territories. He called it "the Proviso of Freedom." He would not trust to nature, soil, climate, geology, or

Salmon P. Chase
U.S. Senate Historical Office

latitude or longitude to exclude it. Nor would he leave it to Mexican law. Slavery "can be barred from the territories," he believed, only by "positive law." Otherwise there was no guarantee that it would be excluded anywhere. "The power [of Congress] to prohibit

slavery in the territories is, in my judgment, clear and indisput-
able; and the duty of exercising it is imperative and sacred."

As for the cry of disunion in the South, he did not believe a
word of it. It was an old cry, he said, an old ploy that had been
wielded by Southerners since 1774 to get their way. "And now, sir,"
he continued, "we have the last republication of this old story. Now
we are threatened with dissolution of the Union unless we will consent to what no republican Government ever did consent to; what
is in direct opposition to the principles and spirit of our institutions, and is condemned by the earliest and best precedents of our
history; namely the extension of slavery into the territories now
free! Shall we yield to this outcry? For one, I say, never!"[22] Chase
had just said everything the Northern Free-Soilers and abolitionists believed and everything the South detested.

Good Friday followed his speech, and the Senate voted to adjourn for a long weekend. Hale said: "I shall vote to adjourn over,
not because it is Good Friday, for I would rather be inclined to sit
on that day, but I shall vote to adjourn over upon the general ground
that the world is governed too much, and the longer the period of
adjournment, and the oftener we adjourn, the better."[23]

NOTES

1. I owe much in this description to Murat Halstead, *Three against Lincoln: Murat Halstead Reports the Caucuses of 1860*, ed. William B. Hesseltine
(Baton Rouge, LA, 1960), 119; and Hamilton, *Zachary Taylor*, 316.

2. Foote, *Casket of Reminiscences*, 123, 125.

3. Maury, *The Statesmen of America*, 32.

4. John Russell Young, *Men and Memories: Personal Reminiscences*, ed.
Mary D. Russell Young, 2d ed. (New York, 1901), 60.

5. This summary of the essential points of Seward's speech is culled
from *Congressional Globe*, 31st Cong., 1st sess., Appendix, 260–69.

6. Ibid., 572; Clay, *Papers*, 10:689.

7. Rhodes, *History of the United States*, 1:166.

8. Robert M. T. Hunter, "Correspondence of Robert M. T. Hunter, 1826–
1876," ed. Charles H. Ambler, in *Annual Report of the American Historical
Association for the Year 1916*, vol. 2 (Washington, DC, 1918), 112.

9. *Congressional Globe*, 31st Cong., 1st sess., 518.

10. Parmelee, "Recollections of an Old Stager" (vol. 49, June 1874):
117.

11. Ibid. (vol. 47, September 1873): 589.

12. Clay, *Papers*, 10:687.

13. This account of Douglas's speech is taken from the *Congressional
Globe*, 31st Cong., 1st sess., Appendix, 367–74.

14. *Congressional Globe*, 31st Cong., 1st sess., 529, 533.

15. Ibid., Appendix, 387, 391.

16. Clay, *Papers*, 10:689.

17. *Congressional Globe*, 31st Cong., 1st sess., Appendix, 1054, 1065.

18. Phillips, "Correspondence of Robert Toombs, Alexander H. Stephens, Howell Cobb," 188.

19. *Congressional Globe*, 31st Cong., 1st sess., Appendix, 375–76, 378, 382.

20. J. W. Schuckers, *The Life and Public Services of Salmon Portland Chase* (New York, 1874), 52.

21. The two quoted phrases are from Stephen T. Maizlish's biographical sketch of Chase in *American National Biography*, s.v. "Chase, Salmon Portland."

22. Chase's positions are culled from the *Congressional Globe*, 31st Cong., 1st sess., Appendix, 468–79.

23. *Congressional Globe*, 31st Cong., 1st sess., 617.

CHAPTER NINE

PULLING IT ALL TOGETHER

NO SENATOR WAS more irritatingly present on the floor these days than Henry Foote. Every day, it seemed, sometimes at every turn, the Mississippian was on his feet, butting in, saying something, and often something that offended somebody.

He himself confessed that he was of "a very impulsive nature."[1] Others would put it far stronger than that. David Outlaw called Foote "that talking machine," given to quoting "Greek, Latin, the Bible, Shakespeare, Vattel, and heaven knows what else."[2]

Foote was forty-six years old, slight, short, bald, mettlesome, talkative, and pugnacious. His tempestuous tongue and his attitude had already pitched him into four duels and several fistfights. He had been shot three times in his duels, twice—on two different occasions—by the same opponent, the first time by one of Andrew Jackson's dueling pistols borrowed for the occasion. He had squared off in a brawl with his fellow Mississippi senator, Jefferson Davis, on Christmas Day 1847, and on the final night of the 1848 session he and Simon Cameron of Pennsylvania had grappled and rolled down the Senate aisle. He had been whacked out on a Washington street not long since by Arkansas Senator Solon Borland. One observer called him a "most restless statesman . . . afflicted with a sort of patriotic form of the dance St. Vitus. . . . How he ever stood long enough to be shot at, is a mystery to me; and how any man could look into such a funny face and fire is another."[3]

In the last Congress, Foote had vowed on the Senate floor that if John Hale of New Hampshire, equally irritating, ever came to Mississippi, he would be hanged to "one of the tallest trees of the forest" and that he, Foote, would himself "assist in the operation." Ever since then he had been called "Hangman Foote."[4] He later regretted this intemperate outburst, admitting it was "one of the most fumy, rabid, and insulting speeches that has ever dishonored a grave and dignified parliamentary body."[5]

Oddly, Foote considered himself "a lover of concord."[6] It was true he wanted concord in the Union. Although he often sounded like a firebrand, he was at heart a Southern moderate seeking compromise. He said of himself that he was "a man anxious, above all things, to revive the reign of good feeling here, and in the country, and secure the final adjustment of all pending questions on terms of equality and honor."[7]

Henry S. Foote
Library of Congress

The state of things in the country distressed him. By late February, Foote was forecasting doom by the weekend if the Senate did not do something. "Sir," he cried, "every day that we have sat here—deliberating as we call it—agitating the question of slavery in this hall, we have placed the Union in still greater peril. It is possible, in my opinion, to dissolve this Union by agitation within the halls of Congress." He predicted on Monday, February 25, that by Saturday, if something was not done within the week besides making speeches, which he believed only increased the agitation, the country would divide.[8] That brought out the wags, who said, "Therefore . . . disunion will positively take place on Saturday next at one o'clock, P.M., and that there will be no postponement on account of the weather."[9]

Foote had plowed all of his nervous energy into bundling Henry Clay's compromise resolutions into a single comprehensive package covering the whole ground of the controversy, which he believed was the only way to get the compromise passed in the House of Representatives and veto-proofed at the White House. He said, "I want all the questions settled together." He feared that Clay's measures, taken separately, particularly admitting California separately, would strengthen the North at the expense of the South. He warned that "if California is dragged into the Union in the mode now proposed [smuggled in, he called it], the southern States of the Confederacy will feel that all hope of fraternal compromise has become extinct," and Northern oppression so intolerable as "to justify, nay, to demand secession from the Union," to save themselves from "evils still worse than disunion itself."[10]

Clay had called his resolutions a scheme of compromise, but he had not intended for them all to be stuffed into a single package. His idea had been to parcel them out one at a time, separately. He thought they had a better chance that way, fearing that, bound together, the combination would unite its enemies and make passage more difficult. He had favored carefully constructed single-issue legislation adding up to a comprehensive compromise in the end. Stephen Douglas, the chairman of the Committee on the Territories, felt the same way—and felt it strongly.[11]

Foote was not only badgering Clay to bind them all together, but he had entered a resolution to form a committee of thirteen senators: six from the slave states, six from the free states, and one chosen by the other twelve "to procure a compromise embracing all the questions now rising out of the institution of slavery."[12] Many senators thought this move premature. Andrew Butler, John C. Calhoun's colleague from South Carolina, stating his opinion and mirroring Calhoun's, thought so. He wanted Clay's resolutions debated first. New Jersey's William L. Dayton, 180 degrees removed from Butler ideologically, agreed. It was too soon. "Why not tarry a little?" he suggested. "Let us wait a little; let us have the light of the minds of other gentlemen who are disposed to give us their opinions upon this question. . . . Let us hear what they have to say to us."[13] But Foote had his mind made up. He introduced his resolution just after Daniel Webster's Seventh of March speech.

Clay, who found Foote "a gentleman of fine imagination and of great fancy," was not "sanguine" that the product of such a committee could command a majority vote in the Senate. Still, he said, he would "make the experiment, and I would make experiments day after day, and night after night, if necessary, to accomplish the great and patriotic object" he sought.

Webster was dubious. He saw no benefit "likely to arise from any attempt to draw up a series of resolutions for the settlement of all the questions now in agitation. I see no hope that such a series of resolutions would pass the two Houses of Congress." He was prepared to vote to admit California but thought the measure should be kept separate. However, he would not oppose Foote's resolution "if anybody thinks it necessary, or would be useful."

Lewis Cass did not see much good coming of it either, but he would vote "for almost any proposition that had the appearance of bringing this country into harmony upon this perplexing question," this "fearful controversy." Cass was disgusted in general. "We have been three months here," he complained, "and what have we done? Nothing. We have not passed a single law of the least national importance." He was certain of two things, however: "No Wilmot proviso can be passed through this Congress. That measure is dead." He hoped that it was the last time they tried "to interfere with the right of self-government within the limits of this Republic"—to interfere with popular sovereignty. He also maintained that an extension of the Missouri Compromise line to the Pacific could not pass. He saw it as no "proper settlement" of the question either. It would also frustrate popular sovereignty.[14]

And so it went, as the debate cranked along on the Senate floor.

⁓ On Saturday evening, March 30, Calhoun had his mail read to him, commented on some of the letters, and ordered his table cleared, as he did every night. He knew his time was swiftly running out. If he regretted anything, it was probably the regret of unfinished work. Not long before, contemplating his end, he had said, "The South! The poor South! God knows what will become of her."[15] Her fate would no longer be on his shoulders. At 7:30 the next morning he was dead. In the night his body servant, who had waited on him for thirty years, also died.

On Monday, April 1, the Senate reconvened from its long weekend and Butler rose "to discharge a mournful duty." He officially announced Calhoun's death and said that "one of the brightest luminaries has been extinguished from the political firmament."[16] A "profound silence" settled on the chamber. At length, Webster turned toward Clay and stared at him with his cavernous eyes. Clay slowly rose and began speaking quietly. "None shone more bright and brilliant than the star which is now set," he said. "I was his senior, Mr. President, in years—in nothing else." Clay gazed for a moment at Calhoun's vacant seat and, gesturing toward it, asked, "And when, Mr. President, will that great vacancy . . . be filled by an equal amount of ability, patriotism, and devotion, to what he conceived to be the best interests of his country?"[17] Webster processed to his feet when Clay had finished and said of Calhoun, "when he last addressed us from his seat in the Senate—his form still erect, with a voice . . . with clear tones, and an impressive, and I may say, an imposing manner—who did not feel that he might imagine that we saw before us a Senator of Rome, when Rome survived."[18]

Jefferson Davis, who stood to be Calhoun's successor as the defender of Southern rights, thought him the champion who "was taken away from us like a summer-dried fountain, when our need was the sorest."[19] Thomas Hart Benton, who despised Calhoun for his disunionism, declined to offer a eulogy but told Webster, "He is not dead, sir—he is not dead. There may be no vitality in his body, but there is in his doctrines.The last thing I did before leaving home was to denounce him and his treasonable sentiments, and I shall do the same thing when I return home. . . . Calhoun died with treason in his heart and on his lips. . . . Whilst I am discharging my duty here, his disciples are disseminating his poison all over my State."[20] Benton feared that Calhoun's disunionist doctrines were "hallowed by the grave."[21] Senator Foote, who despised Benton, agreed with him, however, on that last point—to a point. "In the tomb," Foote was to say, Calhoun "is as high authority—yea, higher than he was in life," his "character and sage teachings come to us now, as it were, canonized from the tomb."[22]

Robert C. Winthrop of Massachusetts shared few of Calhoun's beliefs, from wherever they came, but he was a compassionate man. He told the House, "a star of the first magnitude has been struck

from our political firmament. Let us hope that it has only been transferred to a higher and purer sphere, where it may shine with un-
dimmed brilliancy forever." Standing beside Calhoun's coffin at
his lodgings, where the great senator appeared "full as striking a
figure as he had ever been in his seat in the Senate," Winthrop
turned to his son, who had accompanied him there, and said, "here
was a truly great man, if there ever was one."[23]

The funeral obsequies for Calhoun were performed the next
day in the Senate chamber. It was a beautiful day. Washington was
in the first flush of springtime renewal. David Outlaw wrote his
wife Emily that the trees were "rapidly putting forth their buds,
and the grass in the public grounds is green and beautiful."[24] The
gallery was packed, and hundreds of mourners had been turned
away. The members of the House of Representatives entered, the
justices of the Supreme Court followed. Zachary Taylor and his
cabinet filed in, and the president took a seat at the right of the vice
president. The diplomatic corps, high-ranking officers of the army
and navy, and distinguished visitors occupied the sofas in the lobbies. At 12:30 the coffin was brought in. At the end of the ceremo-
nies a mourning cortege followed the body to a receiving vault in
the Congressional Burying Ground, where it would await removal
to South Carolina. Clay and Webster were pallbearers, with Senators Cass, Willie Mangum, William King, and John Berrien. The
funeral procession was said by one young Washington resident to
be "a good deal more than a mile long I think. I never saw such a
one before."[25] Afterward, a friend asked Senator Benton, "I suppose, Colonel, you won't pursue Calhoun beyond the grave?" Despite his vow to Webster that he would denounce Calhoun and his
"treasonable sentiments" when he returned to Missouri, Benton
said, "No, sir. When God Almighty lays his hand upon a man, sir, I
take mine off."[26]

≈ Two days after Calhoun was laid in the vault, restless, hyper
Henry Foote was back on the floor plugging for his committee of
thirteen to bundle the compromise. But Webster was growing impatient. "I think it my duty," Webster said, "to remind the Senate
that we have now gone through the first four months of the session," have done virtually nothing, and "should proceed to some
action." He wanted to "take up these subjects beginning at the beginning," the beginning being the admission of California, then the
territorial bills and all the rest "step by step."

But Foote, clinging leech-like to his bundling approach, rose to disagree with Webster. The beginning, he believed, began properly with the territorial question, not California. To Foote, that question was the far more important and dangerous issue. California, he argued, was easier and more certain of passage than solving the other, more difficult issue. He argued that if the California bill were passed first, the territorial question would not be resolved in this session. Webster reminded Foote of his earlier dark prediction that the Union would be doomed by the next Saturday: "The day went over, and no pillar of the Constitution was shaken—no bond of the Union was severed. The sun rose in the morning, we all enjoyed a very agreeable day, and we all went to bed at night conscious of the integrity of the Government still subsisting."

James Shields, a hero of the Mexican War, Douglas's Senate colleague from Illinois, and a newcomer who emphatically favored admitting California, predicted that "at the rate you dispatch business here, California may stand some chance of admission at some indefinite time between now and the millennium." He added, "Sir, you might as well undertake to plant orange groves in Siberia as establish slavery in California or New Mexico."

Virginia's James Mason seized the floor to say he emphatically favored a solution of the territorial problem before admitting California, as most Southerners did. Also like other Southern senators, Mason saw no law of nature that necessarily excluded slavery from the territories. Indeed, he agreed with Davis that slave labor might be needed and more desirable there than anywhere. Butler entered the debate at this point. "You would force California upon us," he said to the Northerners, "and then put into the territorial bills the Wilmot proviso, or what is equivalent to it." And that, in Butler's view, would spell disaster.

Clay was not well. He was present, on watch, although his health, he told the Senate, "scarcely justifies" his being there at all. He was only there, he said, because of "the deep inextinguishable anxiety I feel on this subject." Clay had now come around to Foote's point of view. At first wanting to admit California immediately and then move on to the other parts of his compromise, he now believed that California would not happen unless it was combined with the territorial issue. It turned out now, in his view, because of circumstances, to be the quickest way to get California into the Union. He was now willing to lump kindred parts of the compromise into one bill.

Senator Benton weighed in on April 8, occupying a position far removed from Clay's, whose apparent caving in to the Foote approach had the effect, Benton said, "of starting me from my tranquil seat." No senator more strongly disagreed with Foote's approach or was more unshakably for keeping the California issue disentangled from the rest of the issues than Benton. He told the Senate that he was "opposed to this mixing of subjects which have no affinities. . . . I am against it in the lump." In his view this was no way to treat California. It was not right, he said, "it is an indignity."

Senator Douglas, who had introduced the California bill in the first place, agreed. He saw no virtue—no necessity—for naming a committee to take bills already before the Senate, consider them, and feed them back again in a package. He moved to table Foote's resolution and to proceed to the bill to admit California. His motion failed.

Douglas's popular sovereignty soul mate, Lewis Cass, was more impatient than ever. Not only had they been in session from four to five months and accomplished practically nothing, but "we have been going on from worse to worse." He was ready, with Clay, to hand the lump to a committee and get past this impasse. What was the harm in lumping them? he asked. After the committee reports, "we shall be just as free to act as we are now; not at all bound by anything they may do."

Truman Smith, an antislavery Whig from Connecticut with a reputation for being generally agreeable but also quite direct, was not convinced. Smith had been his party's national chairman in the 1848 presidential campaign and had turned down Taylor's offer to be secretary of the interior and had been elected to the Senate instead. A compromise committee, he asked, "to be sent out to do what? What, in the name of Heaven, are they to do?" So they come back with everything packaged. Favoring some parts of the compromise and not others," he demanded to know how he was supposed to vote. "I venture to predict here now that the whole thing will fail. . . . We ought not to have things mixed up so that no human being on earth can tell whether to say yes or no when the question is put to him. I regard this as a disreputable mode of proceeding."

That remark clearly riled Foote. He called Smith a shill for the administration's "non-action policy," which he thought "the most absurd, the most ridiculous, the most unstatesmanlike, yea, the most contemptible in all respects that was ever attempted to be advocated by any Administration or any legislative body in Christendom." Foote's insults, laced with exaggeration and hyperbole, were illegal under Senate rules. Millard Fillmore, presiding, ruled him out of order.

On April 11, Benton was back crusading relentlessly to keep the California issue separate. He cited sixty years in which seventeen states had been admitted and in not one of those was the legislation mixed with other matters, not even his Missouri. He repeated that it was an indignity to California. Clay looked at him quizzically and asked, So where is the indignity in it?

William Dayton, the antislavery Whig from New Jersey, sided with Benton. "They [the committee] will take the question of [California's] admission into consideration, and connect it with other matters, making the whole bill obnoxious to us, as would be any bill of such a character, whereby we are compelled to vote against California. It is not only unjust to California, but unjust to the members of this body who are disposed to vote for her admission standing alone." This statement brought veteran Democratic Senator William King, who had represented Alabama in the Senate since its admission to the Union in 1819, up from his seat. "Sir," he said, "I suspect that the Senator from New Jersey would not be so exceedingly desirous of admitting California instantly, promptly, and without a moment's delay, had there not been a clause in her constitution prohibiting slavery."

Webster, who was not against a committee, was nonetheless offended by the wording that set it up. It said that the committee was to mature "a scheme" of compromise for the adjustment of all pending questions growing out of the slavery issue. That phrase seemed to Webster to imply that "something is to be compromised away." He was ready to vote for California now, separately, and, if there was to be a committee, to keep the California issue out of it.

A war of amendments to Foote's resolution broke out by April 11, and on the 12th, Clay was deploring it, regretting the delay, and calling the effort to avoid a committee "nothing but a great and useless waste of time." He suggested that the committee be raised and make its report without meanwhile arresting discussion of the measure before the Senate. In effect, give us a committee and then talk all you want while it deliberates. Benton would soon leave his tranquil seat again to object to that. "It is nothing more or less," he grumbled, "than that a jury should go out with the case, and after the jury has gone out with it, the counsel and advocates may proceed

to argue it." By April 16, Foote had been reduced to quoting popular verse backing his cause. From a public meeting in New York
had come this:

> Disputed questions in one bill
> Should pass without delay;
> Quit party strife for their country's good—
> So all the people say.

Still seeing no need of a committee, but believing something
had to be decided one way or the other at once, Douglas moved
that if the committee resolution failed, then the Senate should take
up the California bill immediately. Clay agreed. Seldom in the habit
of calling for yeas and nays, he called for them now. It was agreed
to take up Foote's resolution again on a special order of the day at
half past twelve on the next day, April 17.

One of the most notorious of the amenders had been Benton.
He had offered a multipronged, four-part amendment detailing
what the committee, if formed, could not consider. It could not consider abolition of slavery in the states. It could not consider sup-
pressing slave trade between the states. It could not consider
abolishing slavery in the forts, arsenals, dockyards, and navy yards
of the United States. And it could not consider abolishing slavery
in the District of Columbia. Further, it could not take up any questions relating to domestic slavery that had not been specifically
referred to it by the order of the Senate.

Clay moved to amend that last requirement in Benton's amendment to say that it would not be necessary to give any instructions
in advance to the committee. In short, Clay explained, Benton's
amendment "proposes to give such and such instruction to the committee. My amendment [to his amendment] says that the Senate
will give none." That, Benton objected, was "a new method of applying the gag—a thing never done in this body. It is a new way of
stultifying the whole body of Senators, except those who go out on
the committee." We would "sit here in Egyptian darkness, until
the committee comes in and illuminates the Chamber."

Clay countered. The committee, he argued, must be "left free
as air, to explore through the whole region of patriotic intellect" to
settle the unhappy question—as his Committee of Twenty-three did
in the Missouri crises. Clay's amendment to Benton's amendment
was passed. The committee, when and if it ever got formed, would

be uninstructed. Then Benton rebounded with yet another amendment of not just four, but fourteen, points, which the committee was not to consider. "I understand that the Senate declines to give instructions to this committee," he growled, "but I have a parliamentary right to offer them; and, when they are offered, there is no way to get rid of them but by a vote upon them."[27]

Clay was losing his patience. His face, usually serene and composed, darkened, one observer thought, like the face of a lake in a storm, "with black clouds lying closely down upon it . . . with its foaming ripples torn up by fierce gusts." His "iron-gray hair hung loose like a roused lion's mane well shaken. . . . His small, aristocratic-looking hands quivered with agitation. His face spoke a thousand emotions. . . . He tossed his head, flashed fire from his eyes, scowled fiercely, stamped convulsively upon the floor, shook thunders from his tongue, and terrors from his countenance." Both Clay and Benton, the observer said, were "alike intolerant, alike intrepid, alike imperious, alike unbending and indomitable."[28]

Foote, who, that same observer noted, "had held in all day, got nervous on his empty stomach at about five o'clock, and rose to reply in his hectoring manner to some remarks that Benton had just finished." Foote had "gone on but a few minutes, made about half a dozen fierce gesticulations, and stamped his feet but two or three times, and indulged in but one or two of his vocal roars . . . when he alluded in significant language to the senator from Missouri in person."[29]

There was no man Foote detested more than Thomas Benton. It had been so for a long time. "Ten years ago," Foote admitted, "I expressed my opinion of him. . . . His opinion is with me a matter of absolute indifference." He had resumed insulting Benton early in the session. In January he had spoken of an "absurd and unfounded idea" that was gaining entrance to Benton's "cranium." He had called Benton a plagiarist and accused him of being "more responsible, in my judgment, than any man living or dead, for the unhappy condition in which the republic is involved." Foote compared Benton to "that degenerate Roman Senator," Catiline. Later he had knocked Benton's "insidious *tactics*."[30]

On March 26, Foote had called Benton "this Napoleon of parliamentary strife—this more than *lieutenant-general* upon the arena of political warfare," bringing "all of his thunderbolts of vengeance and of perdition . . . all the artillery of his logic, his sarcasm, and his self-idolizing rhetoric, into our very midst." He went on to cite "certain stains which have most hideously blemished the character of the honorable Senator from Missouri."

To all this Benton had asked, "Can I take a cudgel to him here?" Several alarmed senators had shouted, "Order, order." "Is a Senator to be blackguarded here in the discharge of his duty, and the culprit go unpunished?" Benton had demanded. "Is language to be used here which would not be permitted to be used in the lowest pot-house, tavern, or oyster cellar, and for the use of which he would be turned out of any tavern by a decent landlord?"

On the next day, March 27, Benton was still raging. "If this Senate permits language to be used here which cannot be used in the filthiest brothel . . . if they permit such language to be used here, and to be used here with respect to me, I mean from this time forth to protect myself, cost what it may."[31] That sort of talk from Benton was not to be taken lightly. In the world of brawling, dueling, and fistfighting, the delicate Foote was a pale amateur compared to the hulking Benton, who had excelled with firearms and fists at the highest levels, having fought Andrew Jackson in a sword-and-pistol brawl, seriously wounding Old Hickory. Benton looked, sounded, and acted the part. "An iron looking man,"[32] he was commanding, and his dominating appearance was coupled to a fearsomely stentorian voice. Nobody ever heard him whisper from his chair. What came out boomed into the remotest corner of the chamber.[33]

Ben Perley Poore described him as large and heavily framed, with curly hair. He "wore the high, black-silk neck-stock and the double-breasted frock coat . . . varying with the season the materials of which his pantaloons were made, but never the fashion in which they were cut. When in debate, outraging every customary propriety of language, he would rush forward with blind fury upon every obstacle, like the huge, wild buffaloes then ranging the prairies of his adopted State." Though headlong and headstrong, Benton was not a popular speaker. When he took the floor, the gallery generally began to clear and many senators "devoted themselves to their correspondence."[34]

One contemporary agreed that Benton, exceedingly popular in Missouri—he had been one of its first two U.S. senators—did not always use elegant language. He said "bamboozle" on the floor one day, and a fellow senator called it inappropriate and vulgar. The next morning, Benton appeared in the chamber followed by several pages with armfuls of books—dictionaries, mostly—and piled them on his table. He spent half an hour opening them to vindicate his use of the word.[35]

Thomas Hart Benton
Library of Congress

John Wentworth, the Illinois congressman, said that while Calhoun was distinguished for his logic, Webster for his arguments, and Clay for his eloquence, Benton was distinguished for his research.[36] Harriet Martineau, observing him on the floor, wrote that he "sat swelling amidst his piles of papers and books."[37] He was,

Wentworth believed, a mixture of "indomitable industry, and an iron constitution, and an undying memory." He had "no use for poetry, nor fiction, nor fancy, nor any of the flowers of rhetoric." Among his favorite expressions were, "What are the facts? Give us the facts." He was the merciless "foe of all diplomacy, intrigue, casuistry, or craft." Benton believed, said Wentworth, that "what was morally wrong, could never be made politically right."[38]

One writer has stated, "It is doubtful if we ever had a man in public life, in America, equal to Colonel Benton in physical strength, endurance and courage, in toughness and elasticity of constitution, and in mental and moral fortitude." An eight-hour speech was a cakewalk for Benton. He was widely know as "Old Bullion" for his uncompromising support of hard money in the past. Since the nickname itself suggested toughness and solidity, it was apt. The same writer called him "a Roman gladiator in body and temper." Benton was haughty, belligerent, overbearing, tactless, and without fear. A senator once accused him of being involved in "a quarrel." Benton took exception. "Mr. President, sir," he objected, "the senator is mistaken, sir. I never *quarrel*, sir; but I sometimes fight, sir; and whenever I fight, sir, a funeral follows."[39]

It was perhaps a funeral Benton had in mind when, on April 17, in the train of his latest set of crippling amendments to the resolution for a committee of thirteen, a very livid Foote rose and began to excoriate him. Standing at his desk near the main aisle, Foote lapsed into an ever deeper, cutting, and personal attack as he railed along.

Benton had soon heard enough. He rose from his own seat "with every appearance of intense passion," hurled his chair aside, and rushed toward Foote. Foote retreated—"advanced backward," as he later put it, "gliding" down the main aisle toward the vice president's chair, drawing and cocking a five-chambered revolver as he backpedaled, "intending," he later explained, "to take a defensive attitude, and then await any assault which might be made." In an instant every senator was on his feet, many calling for order. Several clustered around Foote. Two of Benton's closest friends, the unique senatorial father and son pair—Henry Dodge of Wisconsin and Augustus Dodge of Iowa—attempted to restrain him. With the vice president's gavel pounding and Foote now having glided to the desk of the secretary with his drawn pistol, Benton, with several senators now hanging onto him, proceeded around the lobby to cut Foote off at the opposite side of the chamber. Tear-ing away from his hangers-on he threw open his shirtfront and shouted, "Stand out of the way! I have no pistols. Stand out of the way! Let me pass! Let the assassin fire! I scorn to go armed. Only cowards go armed."

Vice President Fillmore continued to pound his gavel violently and call for order. New York's Daniel S. Dickinson gingerly took the pistol from Foote, uncocked it, and locked it in his own desk. "It was cheerfully surrendered," Foote later explained, "on application being made for it, and upon seeing that I was no longer in danger of being assaulted."

Dickinson, attempting to get things back on a normal track, asked the chair, "Mr. President, what is the question before the Senate?"

"The question is on the appeal from the decision of the chair," the vice president answered.

"I should like to hear the question again stated," Dickinson said, "as I do not remember precisely what it was." Neither did anybody else.

Benton by now had been wrestled back to his seat, roaring, "We are not going to get off in this way. A pistol has been brought here to assassinate me. The scoundrel had no reason to think I was armed, for I carry nothing of the kind, sir."

"I brought it to defend myself," Foote retorted.

"Nothing of the kind, sir. It is a false imputation. I carry nothing of the kind, and no assassin has a right to draw a pistol on me."

"Order!" several senators shouted, "order!"

Order was eventually restored, and Benton demanded that the Senate take immediate notice that a pistol was brought to the floor to assassinate him. "Will the Senate notice it, or shall I myself, for it shall not pass. I will not be satisfied here."

"I have nothing of the assassin about me," Foote protested. "I have never worn arms at all in the Senate, except when menaced, as I was the other day in the Senate with a cudgel. My friends urged upon me that, being diminutive in size and quite feeble in health, I should at least wear arms for my own defence."

Willie Mangum introduced a resolution for a seven-senator committee to investigate the disorder and report to the Senate. It was adopted. Then nobody wanted to serve on it. The vice president named the seven, and several of those tried to pull out. Only Henry Dodge succeeded in doing so, on a plea of his long and close friendship with Benton.[40]

One observer said he had never before seen such an uproar in a legislative body.[41] The investigating committee, when it reported three months later, had "searched the precedents, and [found] that no similar scene has ever been witnessed in the Senate of the United States."[42] Webster, who had not been present when the incident occurred, heard an account of it in sad silence and then, ever the patriot, said, "I'm sorry for my country."[43] Foote later vowed to write a very small book in which Benton would play a major role. Benton vowed to write a very large one in which Foote would have no part whatever.[44]

On the next day, April 18, Benton, somewhat calmer but no less opposed to Foote's committee-of-thirteen idea, demanded that all previous orders be postponed and called for the yeas and nays on admitting California. It was laid on the table by a 27-to-24 vote on a mainly North-South split. And consideration of Foote's resolution for a committee of thirteen continued.

Foote announced that for the benefit of everybody and "out of consideration to the exigencies of the hour," he intended "saying not another word; I only ask for an early vote." Mangum greeted that news with pleasure and said that he hoped nobody would say another word unless it be yea or nay. Even Benton agreed, after a fashion. "Votes and no words," he said, and spoke briefly on the virtues of a "dumb" legislature, one that should vote and not speak. He then moved, in a parting shot, that Foote's resolution be laid on the table so they could vote on California before the afternoon ended. The motion was voted down.

However, before it could vote on Foote's resolutions, the Senate still had somehow to get rid of Benton's fourteen-point amendment, point by point. All fourteen were speedily rejected in order. Another round of amendments was proposed, including one that would require the various petitions to abolish slavery, which had been cascading in from the North and been laid on the table, to be resurrected and referred to the committee of thirteen when and if it was formed. Alabama's Jeremiah Clemens said in that case he intended to submit a petition he had received from New York urging "the absolute necessity of establishing a United States lunatic asylum for the immediate treatment of some of the worthy Senators and Representatives in Washington," particularly the abolition members, who should be at once "placed in confinement, so that they may not injure themselves, their friends, or their country." The amendment to refer petitions was ruled out of order.

Then, with the amendment-strewn path finally cleared, the slavery issue in all of its particulars was referred at last to a select Committee of Thirteen, by a 30-to-22 vote—one-quarter of a year after Foote had first proposed it. On the next day, Friday, April 19, members of the committee were selected by ballot. Joining Clay as chairman would be six slave state senators—William King, James Mason, Solomon Downs, Willie Mangum, John Bell, and John Berrien. Balancing them were six free state senators—Lewis Cass, Daniel Dickinson, Jesse Bright (Indiana), Samuel Phelps (Vermont), James Cooper (Pennsylvania), and Daniel Webster.[45]

It was Friday, and an exhausted Senate adjourned for the weekend. For the next two and one-half weeks the compromise and all of its attendant issues would be put on hold while the committee hammered out an all-encompassing bill. That, however, did not deter Benton on the following Monday from launching into a speech against tacking bills together that covered nine tight-packed columns in the *Congressional Globe*.

NOTES

1. *Congressional Globe*, 31st Cong., 1st sess., 951.
2. David Outlaw to Emily Outlaw, January 31 and January 9, 1850, Outlaw Papers.
3. Smith, *The Presidencies of Zachary Taylor and Millard Fillmore*, 109, 164–65.
4. Julian, *Political Recollections*, 92 n.
5. Foote, *Casket of Reminiscences*, 76.
6. *Congressional Globe*, 31st Cong., 1st sess., Appendix, 267.
7. *Congressional Globe*, 31st Cong., 1st sess., 603.
8. Ibid., 418–19.
9. Pike, *First Blows of the Civil War*, 14.
10. *Congressional Globe*, 31st Cong., 1st sess., 365–67.
11. The thinking of Clay, Douglas, and other supporters of this single-bill approach is succinctly summarized in National Archives, "Westward Expansion and the Compromise of 1850," 19.
12. *Congressional Globe*, 31st Cong., 1st sess., 416–17.
13. Ibid., 418, 421.
14. These views of Clay, Webster, and Cass of Foote's Committee of Thirteen resolution are in ibid., 367, 510, 517–18.
15. "Reminiscences of Washington," 243; Alexander, *The Famous Five*, 88.
16. *Congressional Globe*, 31st Cong., 1st sess., 623–24.
17. Ibid., 624; Parker, *The Golden Age of American Oratory*, 17–18.
18. *Congressional Globe*, 31st Cong., 1st sess., 625.
19. Ibid., Appendix, 995.
20. Wentworth, *Congressional Reminiscences*, 23–24.

21. Peterson, *The Great Triumvirate*, 468.

22. *Congressional Globe*, 31st Cong., 1st sess., Appendix, 580, 582.

23. Winthrop, *A Memoir of Robert C. Winthrop*, 115–16.

24. David Outlaw to Emily Outlaw, April 2, 1850, Outlaw Papers.

25. French, *Growing Up on Capitol Hill*, 10.

26. Dyer, *Great Senators*, 213.

27. All of this debate in the Senate in this section thus far is distilled from the *Congressional Globe*, 31st Cong., 1st sess., 640–42, 648, 651–52, 656, 659, 662–64, 704–8, 722, 747–48, 751–52, 755–56, 761–62.

28. Pike, *First Blows of the Civil War*, 28–29.

29. Ibid., 29.

30. *Congressional Globe*, 31st Cong., 1st sess., 610, 167–68, 402.

31. Ibid., 603–4, 609.

32. Parker, *The Golden Age of American Oratory*, 17.

33. O. H. Smith, *Early Indiana Trials and Sketches* (Cincinnati, 1858), 188.

34. Poore, *Perley's Reminiscences*, 1:66.

35. Gobright, *Recollection of Men and Things in Washington*, 410–11.

36. Wentworth, *Congressional Reminiscences*, 20.

37. Martineau, *Retrospect of Western Travel*, 1:300.

38. Wentworth, *Congressional Reminiscences*, 46.

39. Dyer, *Great Senators*, 198, 200–202.

40. This recounting of this notorious incident is stitched together from reports in the *Congressional Globe*, 31st Cong., 1st sess., 762–64, 769; Sargent, *Public Men and Events*, 2:361; Julian, *Political Recollections*, 91–92; "Reminiscences of Washington," 242; and Gobright, *Recollection of Men and Things in Washington*, 114.

41. Julian, *Political Recollections*, 92.

42. Rhodes, *The History of the United States*, 1:171.

43. Parker, *The Golden Age of American Oratory*, 83.

44. Elbert B. Smith, *Magnificent Missourian: The Life of Thomas Hart Benton* (Philadelphia, 1958), 272.

45. Events in the Senate from the Foote-Benton clash to the adoption of the resolution for and naming of a Committee of Thirteen are covered in the *Congressional Globe*, 31st Cong., 1st sess., 769–74, 780.

CHAPTER TEN

THE OMNIBUS

FOR HENRY CLAY it had been "a most disagreeable April—cold, damp, and rainy," not the best weather for his chronic cough.[1] So he was looking forward to doing what he always did when there was a big job to do or a major speech to make.

Leaving Washington on April 26, he piled his books into a carriage and with his servant drove out to Riversdale, the home of Charles B. Calvert near Bladensburg, Maryland. There, in that tranquil setting, he would write the report for the Committee of Thirteen. Calvert was Clay's friend, one of the wealthiest men in his state and one of its leading agriculturalists. A direct descendant of Lord Baltimore, he also owned the National Hotel in Washington where Clay boarded. The room where Clay worked at Riversdale, a thousand-acre tobacco plantation, was on the ground floor at the back of the mansion, opening onto a large portico that overlooked stunning scenery. There he sat in his easy chair in his dressing gown and slippers and turned his attention to the task at hand.[2]

Besides Clay's compromise resolutions, the committee had considered an alternative proposal introduced on the last day of February by Tennessee's John Bell. A man of humble beginnings, the son of a farmer and blacksmith, Bell was now a wealthy slaveholder and related to Clay by marriage. He had been secretary of war under William Henry Harrison and was a former Speaker of the House of Representatives. A loyal Whig, he considered the acquisition of New Mexico and California a "curse."[3] He had been an early backer of Zachary Taylor, and in the Senate he had worked to disarm North-South tensions. He was not a ready debater because he was too thin-skinned for ego-pounding give-and-take, but he was good at set speeches and was a skilled politician.

Bell was a stiff, glum-natured man, "dignified even to the point of aloofness," able to muster a smile on occasion but never a laugh. He was large-framed with a "calm and cautious visage" and believed that "life, public and private, was a serious business." This attitude made him appear older than his years. As the leader of moderate middle-of-the-road Southerners on the slavery question, he had sounded the opinions of "at least a dozen honorable Senators," who shared his disapproval of parts of Clay's package, to shape his own proposal.[4]

Bell's package tied the admission of California to several concessions for the South. The main piece of his compromise was a proposal to carve four new states from the slave state of Texas, to be organized with or without slavery. The possibility of such a subdividing had been envisioned when Texas entered the Union in 1845. Bell proposed that it be implemented now as part of an overall compromise. He had hoped his proposal would be referred to the Committee on the Territories. Instead, it landed in the Committee of Thirteen.

Clay worked on the report at Riversdale and returned to Washington to present it to the Senate on Wednesday, May 8. Since it was laced with erasures, edits, and alterations, he read it to the waiting senators himself. He began by saying that debate on the matter referred to the committee had been "singular for its elaborateness and its duration." The report offered a network of proposals and recommendations "as would accomplish a general adjustment of all those questions." He left out Bell's proposal that Congress hew four new states out of Texas, saying the committee believed that if that was done, it ought to be done not by Congress but by Texans. If Texans decided to create such states, Clay believed, then Congress must admit them to the Union. Any such move by Texans, however, was a forlorn hope.

Clay then presented the committee's package accompanied by bills to implement it:

> —California was to be admitted as a free state.
> —Governments were to be established for the rest of the territory won from Mexico, brought "within the pale of the Federal authority," and made into territories suiting their conditions. Two pieces of geography were involved: New Mexico and Utah. The committee recommended incorporating this important bill into the bill for the admission of California and adopting them as a unit. There was nothing in the bill to prohibit slavery in the territories—no Wilmot Proviso. Neither was there anything engineered to encourage, protect, or sanc-

tion slavery in the territories. The people themselves would decide between free or slave when they applied for statehood.

—Texas was to relinquish its claim to the New Mexico territory, and in return the United States would pick up its debts. This bill also was to be folded into the California-territories package. With the passage of this three-headed combination the committee hoped that "every question of difficulty and division which has arisen out of the territorial acquisitions from Mexico will . . . be adjusted, or placed in a train of satisfactory adjustment."

—The Fugitive Slave Law was to be tightened.

—Slavery would not be abolished in the District of Columbia, but the slave trade would be.[5]

Clay's report covered thirteen printed columns in the *Congressional Globe* and was basically a restating and reordering into a single package of his original resolutions. It was instantly tagged the Omnibus Bill, coined into the political lexicon for the occasion after the multipassenger omnibus, a new form of urban transport unusual for carrying passengers from all social classes and both sexes.[6] The bill for California's admission led the package.

The dissents, caveats, and waffling began instantly. Out of the chute, five of the committee members—two from the North, three from the South—hastened to say they did not agree with all of the recommendations or the reasoning behind them. However, Willie Mangum, a committee member and strong supporter of the report, found it a "matter of surprise to me that we have agreed so well." Despite Magnum's surprise, it was apparent that any agreement Senate-wide was going to come hard. Jeremiah Clemens of Alabama, a Southern hardliner who had not been on the committee, made it clear he intended to vote against the package. God knows, he said, why the committee was ever created in the first place. "I expected it to result as it has resulted." He saw not "a solitary deviation" from Clay's original resolutions "in any vital point."

Southern senators in general appeared unmoved by the committee's work. David Levy Yulee of Florida said flatly, "the measures . . . proposed by the committee . . . cannot obtain my support or vote." Solon Borland of Arkansas labelled them "the same propositions now presented to us in the new dress of this report." If compelled to have voted for them in the old dress, he said he would have voted against them, "from beginning to end." He saw nothing in this new incarnation to change that intention.

Northern hardliners were no happier. Senator John Hale complained, "This bill turns the whole of the territories into a slave pasture, and offers no obstruction to the spread of slavery over every inch of it." Newspaper columnist James Pike, writing in the *New York Tribune*, perhaps spoke for most Northern Whigs when he said, "The Omnibus Bill is not only the great scheme to give triumph not only to the Loco Foco party, but to that aristocratic, perverse, Slavery-loving, intolerant, bitter, uncompromising portion of it, that finds its head in the South and its tail in the North. . . . The dynasty which is to float into power on this rising tide of the Omnibus Bill, is to be built up of the rotten timbers and worm-eaten planks of the condemned hulk of Slavery Democracy. . . . I protest in earnest that no Whig should so stultify himself as to lend a hand to this scheme, fatal alike to his party and to the Administration of his choice, and full of perils to the cause of Liberty and Humanity."

In the face of this onslaught, Clay was Horatio at the bridge. "I stand here," he said, "and I mean to stand, to vindicate what has been done, and to vindicate this report, too, if necessary, from beginning to end." Henry Foote, the patron saint of the omnibus approach, was pleased and supportive: "What I heard of it was gratifying to me." Lewis Cass, a member of the committee, also stood by it, deploring all the hip-shooting as it came out of the chute as "not only premature, but injurious." Other moderates on the committee tried to counter the vitriol. New York's Daniel Dickinson believed that "in the adoption of this bill lies the only chance of securing any government for the territories, at least during this session of Congress." Indiana's Jesse Bright said, "Verily it looks as though there are some among us who intend not to be satisfied with any measure or measures that have the appearance of a compromise."[7]

In the train of Clay's presentation of the committee's report, the barrage of amendments and motions to change it or jettison it began in earnest. Stephen Douglas moved to table the joint California-territories bill and get on to admitting California separately. It failed 28–24. Jefferson Davis introduced an amendment to guarantee the right to carry slaves into the territories. William Seward reintroduced the Wilmot Proviso. Clay parried them and neither went anywhere.

Indeed, nothing seemed to be going anywhere. By mid-May, Foote, who saw himself now in the "work of pacification" despite holding "views of a very ultra southern cast," was wringing his hands. "It is with feelings of profound regret," he said, "that I have witnessed the progress of a debate so little, as it seems to me, marked with that spirit of reciprocal moderation and forbearance so important to a pacific and satisfactory settlement of existing differences." He had "hoped that a season had at last arrived when we would be able to consult together calmly, and to interchange our views freely without resorting at all to the language of criminations and censure." Foote then censured Yulee, who had been attempting to throw a wrench into the machinery and had just concluded an anti-Northern outburst that Foote described as a "specimen" of that sort of "heated declamation."[8] Soon after his election in 1845, Yulee had converted from Judaism to Christianity. He was a plantation owner-slaveholder from Florida with an anticompromise mind-set, ready to consider secession.

Foote went on to say that he too believed the South was in a fight against "dishonor and injustice," but he wanted "to assist in reestablishing those ties of fraternal affection which once so strongly bound together the whole body of our countrymen, which have been so alarmingly enfeebled of late, and which, it is to be feared, are of this moment in danger of utter extinction." Yet he was not without optimism. He predicted that "the indications now so apparent everywhere in favor of the plan of settlement before us will continue to multiply upon our vision, until the acclamations of twenty millions of people shall be heard to break forth upon the consummation of the scheme of *peace*, of *conciliation*, and of *compromise*, which is to mark the year 1850 as the most happy and most glorious in our national annals."

Alabama's Jeremiah Clemens did not see it. "I tell the Senator," he told Foote, "that not withstanding his seeming confidence, it is wholly impossible for this bill to pass without material amendment. It is lingering through a wretched existence now by the mere sufferance of its enemies. We could have strangled it at its birth—three of us could have killed it yesterday—we can lay it on the table today." Clemens called Foote that "co-laborer" with Clay. He could remember Foote in better days when "I found him so fiery a yokefellow I was nearly broken down in trying to keep up with him." Now, he said, "we are as wide apart as the poles."[9]

As unique in the Senate as Yulee was Pierre Soulé of Louisiana, the first and only exile from the French Pyrénées to sit in that body. Soulé, a celebrated criminal lawyer, was a brash, imperious, revolution-minded man to whom tact was a somewhat alien trait. He was addicted to dueling pistols and saw secession as inevitable. He was the next senator ready with a set speech, on May 21. "Sir," Soulé said, "I wish it was a *compromise*—a *real* compromise—containing *mutual* concessions—and a *fair* compromise containing *equivalent* concessions." If it were, he said, he would support it "with all my heart." But "I do not see in these measures any such compromise, nor indeed any compromise at all. . . . The South *gives*, the North *takes*."[10]

Clay had been carefully monitoring all the Southern dissenters. On May 21, the same day of Soulé's attack on the compromise, he rose to parry their shots. "Sir," Clay said, "this finding fault, and with the aid of a magnifying glass, discovering defects, descrying the little animalculae which move on the surface of matter, and which are indiscernible to the naked natural eye, is an easy task, and may be practiced without any practical benefit or profitable result." Give us instead a better plan, he charged. "I find myself in a peculiar and painful position . . . assailed by extremists everywhere . . . by those in high as well as those in low authority."

That said, he plunged into a seering rebuttal of Soulé, whom he apparently believed of low authority:

> No part of this compromise seems to receive the commendation of the Senator from Louisiana, or to afford him any solace or satisfaction. . . . It is said that nothing has been done for the South in the establishment of these territorial governments; nothing in this measure of compromise. What, sir? Is there nothing done for the South when there is a total absence of all congressional action on the delicate subject of slavery; when Congress remains passive, neither adopting the Wilmot proviso, on the one hand, nor authorizing the introduction of slavery on the other? . . . What were the South complaining of all along? . . . Their great effort, their sole aim has been for several years to escape from that odious proviso. The proviso is not in the bill. The bill is silent; it is nonactive on the subject of slavery. The bill admits that if slavery is there, there it remains. The bill admits that if slavery is not there, there it is not. The bill is neither southern nor northern. It is equal; it is fair; it is a compromise.

The bill "has left the field open to both"—to be decided by the people of the territory when applying for statehood, which was what Southerners argued for all along.

But it was high authority Clay was really after now, not the Soulés of the Senate. Through with Soulé, he turned his guns on Zachary Taylor. The president was sitting in the White House and sticking by his own plan with a heart hardened toward what Clay was trying to do. Considering it "a very painful duty," Clay hit the president with a simile: "Here"—counting them off on the five fingers of his left hand—"are five wounds—one, two, three, four, five—bleeding and threatening the well being, if not the existence of the body politic. What is the plan of the President? Is it to heal all these wounds? No such thing. It is only to heal one of the five, and to leave the other four to bleed more profusely than ever, by the sole admission of California, even if it should produce death itself." Clay had seen "with profound surprise and regret, the persistence . . . of the Chief Magistrate of the country in his own peculiar plan. I think that in the spirit of compromise, the President ought to unite with us."

Clay found it reprehensible that Taylor stuck bullheaded to his own single-barreled scheme, leaving Utah with no government at all and New Mexico with a military government under a mere lieutenant colonel. The Texas-New Mexico boundary dispute was left unaddressed, and there was no suggested adjustment of the fugitive slave question or any arrangement for dealing with slavery and the slave trade in the District of Columbia.[11]

James Pike was impressed with Clay's "tempestuous demonstration." Clay, he wrote in the *New York Tribune*, "was on his high horse again yesterday. He made a rattling, thundering, smashing speech. He came down upon Mr. Soulé and upon the Administration like a wolf on the fold. . . . His oratory teaches us to see how it is that an Irishman can enjoy a shillalah fight with his best friend." Pike thought that Clay "displayed the spirit and the fire of youth. Deep, pervading passion spoke in his impetuous gestures and his purple countenance. . . . His voice was never more flexible or more trumpet-toned. He thundered and lightened and stormed amain. He shook his hoary locks, gray with three and seventy winters. His features gleamed with demoniac energy. Withering blasts came from his mouth. He rained down censures and imprecations. He seemed to wing his way through and over the Senate chamber like a hawk over the frightened flock of a barn-yard."[12]

Senator Thomas Hart Benton was less impressed. "If there had been more fingers there might have been more wounds," he growled. "When the fingers gave out [the wounds] gave out."[13]

Neither was Webster impressed: "I think Mr. Clay is in danger of eclipsing his glory. Why attack the President?" Webster believed that Clay "with all his talents, is not a good leader, for want of temper. He is irritable, impatient, & occasionally over-bearing; & drives people off."[14]

Solomon Downs, a member of Clay's Committee of Thirteen, who supported the compromise generally, said he could not agree with Soulé, his colleague from Louisiana, any more than Clay could. Downs would have rather seen the odious Wilmot proviso come up, on which all Southerners could agree. Instead he regretted that this one had Southern senators disagreeing with one another. According to Downs, "We have at no time had so favorable a compromise offered us as this. If we reject it, it will be utterly impossible that we should ever get so far again towards a fair and reasonable compromise on this subject." It was the best chance perhaps ever to settle the question "fairly and honorably, and without blood." Take up its provisions, amend them, reject them if you will, Downs urged his fellow Southerners, "but do not kill them by crying out 'mad dog.' "[15]

Stung by Downs's words, surprised by Clay's attack, and not a little upset, Soulé returned to the floor on May 24 to deny that he desired no compromise. He believed that Clay had dealt with him "ungraciously and arrogantly" and that he had been "strangely misconceived" by Downs. He lashed out at Down's argument that this was the best deal the South was likely to get. "Has it come to this, Mr. President," Soulé asked, "that when we are pleading for our just and constitutional rights, we are to kneel down in supplication before the North, and be content and rejoice that we meet not at her hands a still worse treatment?" Then for Clay's benefit he said, "Let the bill before us be amended and improved in those parts which, in my opinion, are not only obnoxious, but threaten the utter annihilation of southern rights and equality, and I am willing to yield it a most cordial support." Clay, though dubious, said he was happy to hear it.[16]

Southern voices continued to sing out in the Senate chamber. Virginia's James Mason, speaking for himself this time, not Calhoun, came down hard against abolishing either slavery or the slave trade in the District of Columbia. The Virginia legislature, he reported, had called that bill "a direct attack upon the institutions of the southern States" that must be "resisted at every hazard." If passed, the legislators wanted the governor to convene them to consider redress. Mason warned that "no law which excludes the institution of slavery in any territory below the line adopted in 1820 will ever be tolerated, or . . . be endured." His position aligned him against both the California and Texas boundary provisions of the bill, since parts of California and the land claimed by Texas fell below that line and would be lost to slavery forever. The line itself was hard enough to endure, Mason said. He hated it and deplored its ever being agreed to at all, but there it was, looming still as a line of compromise, for the sake of peace between the North and South. Georgia's venerable John Berrien noted that Mason's idea would hack 4.5 degrees latitude from the southern half of the proposed state of California and make slavery optional where it was now prohibited.[17]

Augustus Dodge of Iowa was no Southerner, but he was by now "sick, sore, and tired" of all this: "Though this measure is one that does not please me in all its parts, I shall swallow it in order to get the subject out of the halls of Congress."[18] Dodge, like Yulee and Soulé, was a first of sorts in the Senate. He was the son of a sitting senator—Henry Dodge of Wisconsin, Benton's close friend. Jessie Benton Frémont, Senator Benton's daughter, had said to Augustus when he was sworn in only days after his father in December 1848, "I am sure you will be the best-behaved man in the Senate, on the ground that a dutiful son will be exceedingly decorous in the immediate presence of his father."[19] Generally, he was. Father and son did not always vote the same way but generally both favored compromise.

Clay was also sick, sore, and tired of the process. The summer heat had been intense, and he drove out to Riversdale when he could to "breathe country air." "I have spoken a great deal (much more than I wished) in the Senate," he wrote. "I am a good deal debilitated but still struggling for the Compromise." But his optimism was waning. "The Administration, the Abolitionists, the Ultra Southern men, and the timid Whigs of the North are all combined against it. Against such a combination, it will be wonderful if it should succeed."[20]

On May 30, Andrew Butler, who only two months before had announced Calhoun's passing in the Senate, rose to be a messenger of death once more. Another colleague, Franklin Harper Elmore, sent by the South Carolina governor to replace Calhoun, had also died, after less than a month in the Senate. "My heart sinks under the melancholy duty, . . ." he sadly began.[21] Butler, a wealthy South

Carolina planter with 1,000 acres and sixty-four slaves, was a man given to impassioned speeches powerfully illustrated and seething with scathing wit and humor. He had been a judge of the South Carolina Court of Common Pleas and often, since coming to the Senate, had wished himself back there. He was a faithful representative of the slaveholding interests. But he was also a moderate in his heart, yearning for an unsevered Union.

Death announcements appeared to be Butler's lot in life. While in the House of Representatives, he had informed the members of the death of two colleagues. And now there went Elmore, who had died in his lodgings the night before, his place in the Senate having been but "a transit to a common tomb" with the man he succeeded.[22] Elmore, who had read law in Butler's office, was fifty-one years old when he died. He had been a congressman and in the ten years before his appointment to the Senate the widely respected president of the Bank of the State of South Carolina. His voice had been heard only once in the Senate, the day he had first answered when his name was called by the secretary. Funeral services were held on the next day, Friday, with the president attending.

More than one senator wanted to get away from the gloom and rancor for a while. William Dayton of New Jersey moved that the Senate adjourn for the first three days of the next week to take up the carpets. It was customary to fit the chamber with alternate carpets for the summer session. Clay objected. He considered the Senate's business critical. Besides, he liked the carpets that were there, preferring them to any others that might be put down. So the Senate did not adjourn.[23]

Still smarting from Clay's knock of his lack of a proposal of his own, Soulé came in with an amendment to the California bill. California's southern border would be the 36° 30' line. That part below the line would be made into a separate Territory of South California and organized similarly to Utah, to apply for statehood with or without slavery, as its people desired. Clay was delighted to see Soulé present a project rather than just himself.[24]

The first amendment that was roundly debated, however, was the one Davis introduced, which would require territorial legislatures to protect every form of property, including slaves. This proposal clashed directly with Cass's and Douglas's popular sovereignty position. An amendment by Salmon P. Chase of Ohio to negate Davis's was rejected 30–25, on a mainly North-South split. Then Davis's amendment was also rejected, by the same margin, with a slightly different voting alignment. Seward immediately injected the Wilmot Proviso again, which was just as immediately voted down 33–23.

Amendments were now flying in from every quarter. Some, engineered for only minor adjustments to the omnibus, were being accepted. Others were being batted away or ruled out of order, with much arguing over what was out of order. Some of the amendments simply struck out a word or a short phrase, in what was developing into a war of words. Clay was at his seat carefully monitoring everything that was coming in, objecting to some, not objecting to others.

On June 6 Jefferson Davis complained that "All this Congress has done has been to scatter seeds of excitement over the country. It would be fortunate indeed if we sat fewer days and fewer hours." He said this as he was opposing a resolution to move the hour of meeting daily up from noon to eleven o'clock, adding even more hours. Clay favored it, "to meet the present crisis and exigency." Clemens, in an amending mood, moved to make an even earlier start: ten o'clock. That time was rejected, but eleven o'clock was agreed to.[25]

The Senate was now considering the one issue of all those in the omnibus that could pitch the country into a civil war overnight— the Texas-New Mexico boundary impasse. Clemens had come in the next morning, June 7, with a far more day-ruining resolution than a time change. He wanted to trash the idea of Texas ceding the disputed territory to New Mexico and getting its bills paid. Clemens would give all the territory outright to Texas. Clay vigorously objected to this one, saying it would put New Mexico under the permanent domination of Texas. This was perhaps what Clay meant when he had said on May 13, "the crisis of the crisis has arrived."[26]

On this issue, Henry Clay and Zachary Taylor were in rare agreement. Before coming to Washington to assume the presidency, Taylor had told Ethan Allen Hitchcock, one of his officers in the U.S.-Mexican war, that he had made up his mind that he was "opposed to the pretension of Texas to the Rio Grande" and that "Congress ought to define her limits."[27] However, Texans were unmoved by Taylor's view of the matter. Governor Peter Hansborough Bell believed that "those who would deny our claim [to the New Mexico territory] would continue to do so, were it placed before them in characters written with a sunbeam."[28] Southerners generally called denial of the Texas claim the "usurpation of New Mexico."[29]

Taylor's resolve had calcified even more since coming to Washington. When word reached him that Texans might soon march on New Mexico and seize its claim by force, the president vowed that he would resist with federal troops. He had marched into Texas before and he would do it again. He knew the way. In April he told Alfred Pleasonton, an army officer about to join his command in New Mexico, "These Southern men in Congress are trying to bring on civil war. They are now organizing a military force in Texas for the purpose of taking possession of New Mexico and annexing it to Texas, and I have ordered the troops in New Mexico to be reinforced, and directed that no armed force from Texas be permitted to go into that territory." If there were not enough soldiers there to do that, Taylor told Pleasonton, "I will be with you myself . . . before those people shall go into that country or have a foot of that territory. The whole business is infamous, and must be put down."[30]

Taylor was pushing Congress. He was about to send a message to the Hill to the effect that the territory in dispute belonged to the federal government and "ought so to remain until the question of boundary shall have been determined by some competent authority."[31]

In the Senate on June 7 the Clemens amendment was beaten down 37–17. Foote then brought forward the first of "certain other amendments" he had been promising, also on the Texas-New Mexico boundary bill. His nemesis, Senator Benton, vowed that on Monday next he would make a motion to postpone indefinitely the entire compromise bill.[32]

On the next day, Saturday, June 8, the Senate turned to Foote's three-headed amendment. It would rivet the Lone Star State's northern boundary at 34 degrees north latitude, carving two degrees of New Mexico above El Paso out for Texas. It would not include Santa Fe, which was at 36.5 degrees, the northern limit of the Texas claim. With Foote's amendments Texas would keep title to all territory it had held in 1836, when it won its independence from Mexico. The amendments also reaffirmed the validity of the Texas resolutions of annexation as a slave state.

Amendments to Foote's resolutions began coming in. Clay and others confronted both the amendments and the amendments to the amendments, standing fast for the committee's version. Vice President Fillmore interrupted periodically to rein in the invective. "It is not in order," he ruled, "to make personal allusions," to which the offending senator replied to the effect, "I have made none," or

"I was speaking of the remarks of the Senator, and not of him individually," or "I am not charging any improper motives."[33]

On Monday, June 10, as promised, Benton moved to postpone consideration of the compromise bill to March 4, 1851, and then proceeded to speak at length on his motion, which, he said, "supersedes all other motions, and which, itself, can only be superseded by a motion still more stringent—the motion to lay on the table." The postponement would be an indefinite one since March 5, 1851, would be "a day certain . . . beyond the life of the present Congress." Benton's aim in this matter was what it had been from the start—to get rid of this "parcel of old bills." This, Old Bullion argued, should have been done long ago. Instead, the bills that ought to have been considered singly had been "carried out by the committee, and brought back again, bundled into one, and altered just enough to make each one worse; and then called a compromise—where there is nothing to compromise—and supported by a report which cannot support itself." He argued that the compromise was "an old dish of distress" served up by Clay, who was "returning among us" after an absence of several years and beginning again "where he left off," pacifying a noncrisis ponied up by politicians. Benton called the whole affair "this comedy of errors."[34]

However, on Wednesday, June 12, Benton withdrew his motion to let voting proceed on other amendments, and the debate swung back to the testy Texas-New Mexico boundary issue. Seward, as hardline as ever, argued that Texas was not entitled to any of New Mexico. Therefore there was no reason to buy it from Texas. It had no title, Seward insisted, its claim was groundless. His position was that the president should do as he vowed to do: decide the matter in New Mexico's favor by force of arms if necessary.

Foote was soon on his feet calling Seward "a counselor to bloodshed and violence," which brought Fillmore's gavel down with a warning to Foote that "it is not in order to speak in such a manner of any Senator." But Foote would not let up. "Sir," he insisted, "it is worse than that 'higher law'. . . it is worse than any of those execrable sentiments that we are from time to time compelled to hear." But neither would Seward back off. He promised to "vote to strike out every feature of the bill, as fast as they are proposed. If we cannot break the bill down by a common opposition, I am willing to take it to pieces joint by joint, limb by limb."[35]

While Seward and Foote were going at one another, Benton's distaste for Clay and Clay's for him, bubbling just under the surface, erupted. Benton accused Clay of being the author of a damning letter against him, even though it was signed by another man. "He will not get off by standing behind anybody else," Benton shouted. "No man will get off from me in that way." Over calls for order by other senators and the vice president, Clay shouted back, "I repel with scorn and indignation the imputation that I am the author of that letter. I hurl it back to him, that he may put it in his casket of calumnies where he has so many other things of the same sort."[36] This exchange was entirely too hot. The Senate voted immediately to adjourn.

Back in session on Friday, June 14, there was a motion again to adjourn for three days for the sake of changing the carpets and cleaning the chamber. This one was from David Yulee. Clay objected again, noting that all such motions invariably came from those opposed to the compromise bill. "Washington surrendered his sword in an uncarpeted room," Clay hissed, "and yet we must adjourn three days, when the whole country is in a crisis, to take up a carpet. . . . I hope we shall not adjourn till we get through this bill." The motion was voted down.[37]

The Texas boundary question was still front and center, and there was now a motion from Tennessee's Hopkins L. Turney to strike that entire section from the bill, leaving the question unresolved. It was a motion, Alabama Senator William King believed, that "will pretty much settle the fate of the bill, and of the other amendments that may be anticipated and hoped for." Southerners assailed the ultra-Northern position that Texas had no right to the disputed land, and the vote to strike the issue from the bill failed, 27–24, not on a North-South split as usual but on a vote for or against the Omnibus Bill.[38]

On Saturday, June 15, there was finally a compromise on the carpets. The Senate agreed that when it adjourned Thursday next, it would stay out to the Monday following, to let the chamber be cleaned and the carpets changed. Clay this time agreed.

On Monday the debate continued to roll—across the new carpets. The amendments continued to come, with Southern senators proposing measures to keep access to the territories open until states were formed with or without slavery and with Free-Soilers trying to freeze them out. Clay stood on the alert to ward off seriously crippling amendments. On June 19 the Senate rejected another Davis amendment that would repeal any preexisting Mexican law in the new territories that restricted the right of all U.S. citizens to carry their property to the territories—this after first rejecting a Hale amendment to Davis's amendment to except slave property. Clay was disgusted:

> "Mr. President, I must own that a hundred times almost, during the progress of this bill, have I been quite ready to yield, and say, for one, I withdraw from all further efforts for the passage of this bill. I never have seen a measure so much opposed—so much attempted to be thwarted. We exhibit the spectacle of a *see-saw*, putting the least weight on one side, while there is an obstruction of the balance on the opposite side. Whilst all parties are, or ought to be, desirous of harmonizing the country, and of restoring once more tranquility, difficulties almost insuperable, upon points of abstraction, upon points of no earthly practical consequence, start up from time to time, to discourage the stoutest heart in any effort to accommodate all these difficulties.[39]

The midsummer heat was oppressive, and the approach of the cholera season, which generally set in during August, was a nagging concern. Clay kept on prodding, moving that the Senate meet earlier each day "to ascertain what is to be the fate of this bill . . . here we have been nearly two whole months upon a single bill, and if any man can see when the question is to terminate, I own, for one, that I am in utter darkness." The time of convening had slipped back to noon. Clay wanted to roll it up to eleven o'clock again. When Hale said he would vote against any meeting an hour early, Clay said, "I supposed so . . . the Senator from New Hampshire is in his usual vocation. There has not been a proposition for dilatory proceedings in relation to this bill, since its origin to this moment, to which he has not lent his aid, his countenance, and his support. He is in his accustomed vocation." The earlier time was agreed to, 30–17.[40]

The subject was now back on California. Soulé had come on with a long speech and an amendment opposing its immediate admission. His idea was to bounce back California's petition for admission for further conditions and modifications, postponing admission indefinitely. This proposal catapulted Douglas to his feet for a two-hour reply. California's sin, Douglas said, "her only crime—was that she chose, in the plenitude of her wisdom and power to exclude the institution of slavery from her borders." Daniel Webster followed Douglas, lining up with him to urge California's admission at once.[41]

On Monday, June 24, Robert W. Barnwell was sworn in as Franklin Elmore's and John Calhoun's successor, with hopes for a longer life. Barnwell had been a college friend of noted Massachusetts orator Edward Everett and celebrated essayist Ralph Waldo Emerson at Harvard, two ardent antislavery men. But back home he had been a signer of South Carolina's ordinance of nullification in 1832. He was an out-and-out firebrand who despaired that Southern civilization was "doomed," but that it "must go out in blood." If the Union could be saved, he believed, it would only be by an extension of the Missouri Compromise line that would divide California into two states. He was on his feet on June 27, three days after his swearing in, arguing for an extension of the line to the Pacific—dividing the property—with all restrictions of slavery lifted south of that line. If that could not be done, he said, then the slavery question could not be resolved within the Union.[42]

Barnwell was not alone. Jefferson Davis was convinced the bill could "never be so amended by the Senate as to receive my vote." Instead of an amendment, he now had an ultimatum—the Missouri Compromise line or nothing. The convention of Southern states that had come out of Calhoun's "Southern Address" the year before had met in Nashville earlier in June and endorsed it as its own ultimatum—the only thing it could fully agree upon. The convention had turned out to be a far meeker meeting than had been envisioned. It had quietly adjourned after calling for an extension of the line as a compromise solution, if there was to be one, and agreeing to meet again after the current session of Congress ended to reassess the situation. The outcome of the Nashville convention was seen by many as the signal of a likely acceptance of the compromise in the South, if one could ever be hammered out. Davis saw the Nashville ultimatum as the ultimatum of his constituents in Mississippi, and the least he would settle for short of all the territories being thrown open to Southerners and their slaves. "If the territory cannot be enjoyed in common, it should be divided," he said. He was ready, therefore, to vote to lay the omnibus into its deserved "tomb."[43]

Saturday, June 29, was a very hot day, and a day when Northern senators were rising to put renewed heat on the Southerners. James Cooper, a Pennsylvania Whig and a member of the Committee of Thirteen, took the floor to say the subject had been "exhausted of all its novelty." He granted that the package was not the most he could have wished—he had voted for the Wilmot Proviso—but "the best which was practicable under the circumstances." He believed it better than Taylor's plan. John Davis, Webster's colleague from Massachusetts, echoed the Northern ultraist point of view, saying that all the concession in the compromise plan was by the North. William Upham, a Whig from Vermont, deplored "the storm that is beating so pitilessly upon us" and condemned the South as its originator.[44]

It was July now. On the second day of this hot new month, David Yulee pressed a resolution to adjourn the Congress sine die on August 1. The ever-vigilant Henry Clay rose to his feet once more, deploring any such thought without settling these pressing questions. A month did not appear to him to be nearly enough time. "I would as soon quit the field of battle at the moment when our arms were directed against a foreign enemy," Clay said, "aye, sooner flee from such a field of battle, than I would quit my post here, and leave the country in the position in which it would be left if we do not settle these matters." Webster rallied to Clay's side. Hale rallied to Yulee's—an unholy alliance of slaveholder and slave hater, polar opposites politically and philosophically nonetheless both against the bill for entirely different reasons. Yulee's motion was postponed for two weeks, to be reassessed then.[45]

The drumbeat from the North continued. Seward told the Senate that the omnibus's conditions for Texas, New Mexico, Utah, and the District of Columbia were "equally *unreasonable, injurious,* and *oppressive.*" He demanded that the bill be subdivided. What Seward really sought—as always—was the Wilmot Proviso, "the proviso of freedom." If he could not have that, he would not then surrender to "the riddling covenant contained in this bill," with its "misshapen chaos of fair-seeming forms, and mischiefs manifold . . . this unwieldy, rickety ark."[46]

By July 3 more moderate voices were rising above the clamor but were hardly less abusive of the compromise and the compromiser. For John Bell, "this subject is, from day to day, becoming more complicated, and new difficulties interposed to any harmonious adjustment." He called the compromise package a "piece of political joinery" that fell short. "Sir," he said, "when giants set their hands to a work, we expect something more than the product of ordinary mortals; something more than the mere expedient of a day, a measure to answer a temporary emergency." Instead, what he saw in the handiwork of this particular giant, Henry Clay, was "the cloud in the distance, surcharged with the elements of the hurricane."

Foote, who continued to be as pesky an everyday presence on the floor as Clay was a vigilant one, now interrupted Bell. "I have no doubt," Foote said, "that it [the Omnibus Bill] will save the country from the most serious present evils, and impending perils more serious than any we have ever heretofore encountered; and I believe it will be sustained by this and all future generations." Bell disagreed: "No, sir; the question at the North will be renewed and agitated with increased bitterness, mingling in all elections, as heretofore. The chance, slender as it may be . . . that slavery may be extended into New Mexico, will be sufficient to keep all the elements of agitation in full blast at the North; while at the South the excitement originally produced by this state of sentiment at the North, will find no abatement in its tendency to sectional alienation and animosity."

No, sir, Foote countered, "if this measure passes, abolition is dead forever; free-soilism is prostrated, and the demagogues of the hour will cease to keep up their warfare over the country." To that Bell replied, "there is some danger that [the agitation] will become more serious, and that this compromise . . . may not only fail to heal . . . the bleeding wounds . . . but that it will not even stanch it."

A supporter of the president's plan, which he praised for the "true genius, sagacity, and statesmanship displayed in it," Bell also wanted to say something positive about Taylor, who was holding fast against Clay's compromise. Southern Whigs had approached the president late in June and in early July to seek his backing for the compromise, but he would not budge. Taylor, Bell said, is "hawked at, pursued, denounced, reviled through the five hundred presses of the Opposition, and in the speeches of the most distinguished and powerful leaders in the Senate, at a time of the most imminent peril to the peace of the country, as if all the elements of human passion and malice had united to overwhelm and destroy him." Indeed, Bell added, the president is "struggling between Scylla and Charybdis, with Hell Gate just in front, or rear, as you may choose to place it. All the metaphors, similes, and other figures of speech drawn from the perils of ocean navigators, would be inadequate to portray the obstructions thrown in the way of the President, in his arduous navigation of the ship of State at the present moment."[47]

Willie Mangum, having sat through the two-day duration of Bell's presentation, called it "the most prosing speech in concentric circles I have seen or heard."[48] The various buttings-in on Bell's speech prompted William King, the senior member, to say, "I have never known, till this session, such constant interruptions of individuals when addressing the Senate." The vice president had noticed these interruptions as well "with a degree of pain," but Fillmore said they were allowed by the rules if the interrupted senator yielded for them.[49]

On July 8 anxious eyes were glancing from the chamber to the White House, where Taylor was reported ill. In closing his speech on the compromise, Truman Smith of Connecticut echoed Bell with ringing praise for the president. "He has my unreserved confidence." Smith said. "I believe in him—in his moderation, his sense of justice, his firmness and unflinching resolution, his sagacity, his wisdom, and especially in his entire devotion to the true welfare of our common country. He has not only my confidence, but my heart; and I consecrate all that I am, and all I hope to be, to his service."[50]

NOTES

1. Clay, *Papers*, 10:710.
2. Ibid., 709; Wentworth, *Congressional Reminiscences*, 26–27, 27 n.
3. Joseph H. Parks, "John Bell and the Compromise of 1850," *Journal of Southern History* 9 (August 1943): 330.
4. Joseph H. Parks, *John Bell of Tennessee* (Baton Rouge, LA, 1950), 7, 173, 240, 244.
5. This brief summary of the committee's recommendations is from *Congressional Globe*, 31st Cong., 1st sess., 944–46.
6. National Archives, "Westward Expansion and the Compromise of 1850," 21.
7. This immediate reaction to the committee's report, with the exception of Pike's comment in the *New York Tribune*, is all from *Congressional Globe*, 31st Cong., 1st sess., 948–56. Pike's comment is quoted in National Archives, "Westward Expansion and the Compromise of 1850," 43.
8. *Congressional Globe*, 31st Cong., 1st sess., Appendix, 579–80.
9. Foote's further views and his exchange with Clemens are in ibid., 580, 585–86.
10. Ibid., 635.
11. Clay's attacks on Soulé and Taylor are in ibid., 612–16.
12. Pike, *First Blows of the Civil War*, 71–72.
13. *Congressional Globe*, 31st Cong., 1st sess., Appendix, 677.
14. Webster, *Papers*, 105, 121.
15. *Congressional Globe*, 31st Cong., 1st sess., Appendix, 639, 636–37.
16. Soulé's retort is in ibid., 784–85, 788–89.
17. Ibid., 649–50, 653–54.
18. *Congressional Globe*, 31st Cong., 1st sess., 1086.
19. Lewis Pelzer, *Augustus Caesar Dodge* (Iowa City, IA, 1908), 138.
20. Clay, *Papers*, 10:733, 736, 759, 763.
21. *Congressional Globe*, 31st Cong., 1st sess., 1105.

22. Ibid.

23. Ibid., 1107–8.

24. Ibid., 1113.

25. The two quotes are from ibid., 1139, 1140.

26. *Congressional Globe*, 31st Cong., 1st sess., Appendix, 567.

27. Hitchcock, *Fifty Years in Camp and Field*, 349.

28. Kenneth L. Neighbours, "The Taylor-Neighbors Struggle over the Upper Rio Grande Region of Texas" *Southwestern Historical Quarterly* 61 (April 1958): 458.

29. Hunter, "Correspondence," 114.

30. Alfred Pleasonton in a letter to Thurlow Weed, September 22, 1876, in Barnes, *Memoir of Thurlow Weed*, 180.

31. Richardson, *Compilation of the Messages and Papers of the Presidents*, 5:48.

32. *Congressional Globe*, 31st Cong., 1st sess., 1165.

33. Ibid., Appendix, 798.

34. Ibid., 676–77, 684.

35. The Seward-Foote exchange is from ibid., 860–63.

36. Ibid., 867.

37. *Congressional Globe*, 31 Cong. 1st sess., 1210.

38. Ibid., Appendix, 867.

39. Ibid., 929.

40. *Congressional Globe*, 31 Cong., 1st sess., 1298–99.

41. Ibid., Appendix, 852, 984.

42. John Barnwell, ed., "Hamlet to Hotspur: Letters of Robert Woodward Barnwell to Robert Barnwell Rhett," *South Carolina Historical Magazine* 77 (October 1976): 255–56; *Congressional Globe*, 31st Cong., 1st sess., Appendix, 992.

43. *Congressional Globe*, 31st Cong., 1st sess., Appendix, 993–94, 997.

44. Ibid., 1004–5, 1009, 1014, 1017.

45. *Congressional Globe*, 31st Cong., 1st sess., 1329–30.

46. Ibid., Appendix, 1022–24.

47. Bell's comments and Foote's counterthrusts are from ibid., 1088–89, 1096–97, 1099.

48. Mangum, *The Papers of Willie P. Mangum*, 5:180.

49. *Congressional Globe*, 31st Cong., 1st sess., Appendix, 1100.

50. Ibid., 1186.

CHAPTER ELEVEN

CHANGING THE GUARD

SOUTH CAROLINA'S Andrew Butler held the floor on July 9—with a speech on the compromise bill this time not an obituary. Butler, who saw "the channel of separation being "worn deeper and deeper every day," was up, calling Free-Soilers and abolitionists the "codfish aristocracy."[1] And he did not mean it as a compliment.

An hour into his speech, he abruptly stopped. A foreign visitor in the gallery described the scene. Daniel Webster, standing before Butler, was staring sadly at him out of those two cavernous eyes and "indicating with a deprecatory gesture that he must interrupt him on account of some important business." Butler bowed and fell silent. "A stillness as of death reigned in the house, and all eyes were fixed upon Webster, who himself stood silent for a few seconds, as if to prepare the assembly for tidings of serious import. He then spoke slowly and with that deep and impressive voice which is peculiar to him."[2]

"A very great misfortune is now immediately impending over the country," Webster said. "The President of the United States cannot live many hours."[3] "A thrill, as if from a noiseless electric shock," the foreign visitor in the gallery later wrote, "had passed through the assembly." She felt herself grow pale.[4] Webster moved that the Senate adjourn, and it was immediately agreed to. At 10:30 that night, Zachary Taylor died.

It had all started on Thursday, July 4. The president had gone out with his family and several heads of departments to celebrate Independence Day at the laying of the cornerstone of the Washington Monument. It was one of the most stifflingly hot days yet in the very hot summer. Before leaving his carriage at the monument Taylor had complained of dizziness and headache. He sat on a small ill-shaded stand in the open under the glaring sun for three hours, for two of those subjected to a speech by Henry Foote. The president, who "did not know how to retreat," toughed it out.[5]

Back at the White House, weary, hungry, and thirsty, he overindulged on iced milk and cherries. In the evening he was to attend a party hosted by Robert C. Winthrop for his friends, North and South. Fillmore, Cobb, Webster, Horace Mann—even Benton and Foote, "in juxtaposition"—were to be there.[6] Taylor sent his regrets; he was not feeling well. Soon after, he was seized by a violent attack of cholera morbus—acute gastroenteritis—with its attendant cramps, indigestion, diarrhea, and vomiting. However, he did not consider himself seriously ill. He had a history of intestinal disorders. But by midnight he was much worse. The illness persisted through Saturday and two more physicians were called in. On Sunday, Taylor said to his physician, "In two days I shall be a dead man."[7]

By Monday the doctors had checked the visible stages of the cholera morbus, but typhoid fever had set in, accompanied by acute mental distress. The physicians and the president's family became alarmed. By evening hope was abandoned. Rumors of the president's distress had gotten out. That night and the next morning bulletins were issued to crowds who had gathered in front of the White House seeking news. The *Republic*'s bulletin said, "The President is laboring under a bilious remittent fever, following an attack of serious cholera morbus; and is considered by his physicians seriously ill."[8] At 3:30 Tuesday morning—it was now July 9— the crisis miraculously seemed to pass and the crowds were told he was out of immediate danger. Bells were rung and bonfires lit in celebration. Officials flocked to the White House with congratulations. Shortly before noon Webster called on the president. But as he was returning to the Senate chamber, word followed him that Taylor had abruptly plunged into a relapse and was unlikely to live through the day. The doctors had taken him off the medicine and said he was in God's hands. Webster had interrupted Butler's speech to give the Senate that sad report. A bulletin went out to the crowds that the president was dying and that he had been told he had not many hours to live. "You have fought a good fight," the president told one of the physicians, "but you cannot make a stand."[9]

As he was dying, Taylor said, "I have always done my duty; I am ready to die; my only regret is for the friends I leave behind me."[10] At his bedside Varina Davis struggled to tear the distraught Margaret Taylor away from her husband's body. The dead president's wife "would listen to his heart, and feel his pulse, and insist he did not die without speaking to her."[11] At the Department of State a midnight bell rang out the news and in a few moments mourning bells in every church steeple in the city were tolling.[12]

Fillmore, informed of Taylor's death by the cabinet, was stunned. "I have no language to express the emotion of my heart," he said. "The shock is so sudden and unexpected that I am overwhelmed with grief."[13] The next day he formally announced "this most afflicting bereavement" to the Congress, assuring them that "it has penetrated no heart with deeper grief than mine." He sent a note to the senators that because of the "lamented death," he would "no longer occupy the chair of the Senate." In another message to both houses, he said, "A great man has fallen among us"; we are "a nation in tears."[14]

Fillmore appeared in the hall of the House of Representatives to take the oath of office before the entire Congress. He was attended by a committee from the two houses and accompanied by the members of Taylor's cabinet. The chief justice of the Circuit Court of the District of Columbia, William Cranch, appointed one-half century earlier by President John Adams, administered the oath. Benton noted that it was an inaugural "marked with solemnity without joy." Fillmore delivered no address. He bowed following the brief ceremony and left the hall to begin serving his nation in tears.[15]

The two houses of Congress spoke eulogies of praise and regret. Congressman Thomas H. Bayly of Virginia said, "Sir, in the very midst of the tempest, when the storm is howling about us, and when all is uncertainty and alarm, the captain has been unexpectedly swept from the deck."[16] Robert Winthrop, who had a knack for saying the right thing in times of bereavement, said, "In any strife which may await us his name [was] worth to us an army with banners."[17] Solomon Downs, the senator from Taylor's home state of Louisiana, offered resolutions "suitable to the occasion" and said, "Let us, then, bury in the tomb of our departed President all sectional feelings and divisions, and unite, once more, in that spirit of cordial good will and brotherly love which united our forefathers in the earlier days of the Republic." William King of Alabama said, "The country has reason to deplore the death of a great man, and, I must be permitted to add, a good man." He said, "If errors were committed, I shall draw the curtain over them."[18] On July 11, King became president pro tem of the Senate, replacing Fillmore in the chair.

Taylor's body lay in state in the East Room of the White House on July 12 in a lead coffin enclosed in another of mahogany, with silver fittings. Thousands filed past to view the great soldier's body. The next day, Saturday, July 13, came in cool, with a clear sky and a fanning breeze. Funeral salutes with beating drums began at sunrise and continued throughout the morning. At noon, the Reverend Smith Pyne, rector of St. John's Episcopal Church, conducted services at the executive mansion. The president's remains were then carried and laid to rest in the Congressional Burying Ground with a "funeral pageant" befitting a fallen warrior—"painfully magnificent," Seward thought.[19] A cortege of more than a hundred carriages stretched for more than two miles down the length of Pennsylvania Avenue. There were twenty honorary pallbearers, young Francis O. French wrote in his diary, "composed of all the great men of this land, but the real pall bearers were some of the soldiers who served under Genl. Taylor during the wars of Florida [the Seminole wars] and Mexico."[20]

Indeed, French had never seen so many soldiers in one place in his young life. Leading the huge force of 1,500 regulars and volunteers from thirty military units was Winfield Scott himself, general in chief of the army, mounted on a prancing charger and wearing a richly embroidered uniform topped with a high, yellow-plumed hat. He presented a figure, a reporter from the *National Intelligencer* wrote, "well calculated to fill the eye and to swell the heart with patriotic pride." It was, he wrote, "at once an elevating and a moving sight to behold such a Hero as Taylor followed to the grave by such a Hero as Scott."[21] Congressman David Outlaw believed Scott in his full military regalia was the best part of the whole funeral.[22]

The funeral car rode on wheels carved from solid blocks of wood. It was overhung by a high canopy of black silk overlaid with a large gilt eagle and shrouded in curtains of black and white silk in alternating festoons with rosettes, fringes, and tassels. The car was drawn by eight pale white horses, each led by a turbaned black groom in white oriental costume. Behind it was led Old Whitey with holsters and inverted spurs on his saddle. The war horse, the reporter from the *National Intelligencer* wrote, "stepped proudly," it seemed, "with a military air."[23] The procession was wailed along to the burying ground by tolling bells, bellowing cannon, and "plaintive strains of music." Mrs. Taylor lay in her bed in the White House "trembling violently when bands 'blared the funeral music' " and "cannon boomed to announce the final parting." Triple volleys were fired over the fallen soldier-president's vault, where the coffin would remain until autumn, when his remains would be removed to the family cemetery on the Beargrass Creek plantation in Kentucky.[24]

Taylor had been president only sixteen months, but William Seward said, "I never saw grief, public grief, so universal and so profound."[25]

〜 Now all eyes turned to Fillmore, whom George Templeton Strong in New York called Taylor's " 'accidental' successor, of whom nobody knows much, and in whom no party puts any very special trust or faith."[26] A story made the rounds that the new president wanted a new carriage. A veteran White house attendant, "Old Edward" Moran, took him to see a bargain being offered by its owner leaving town. "This is all very well, Edward," Fillmore said, "but how would it do for the President of the United States to ride around in a second-hand carriage?" "But sure," Old Edward said, "your Ixellency is only a sicond-hand Prisident!"[27] It was the second time that the reins of the national government had been passed on to a president not elected to the office by the people.

Fillmore had climbed to the top of American politics on a very different path from Zachary Taylor. The new president was fifty years old, a handsome man of average height, of "striking appearance," portly, with "broad, heavy, florid features." His hair was gray, his eyes blue. He was dignified, courteous, engaging, polished, intelligent, and always meticulously dressed. It was said that he would be picked out in any crowd "as a man far above the average."[28]

He was self-made. Unlike Taylor, Fillmore's background was rooted in poverty. The son of a New York tenant farmer, he was semi-illiterate growing up, raised on backbreaking work in the fields. In his teens he was apprenticed to a textile mill. There, acutely aware of his ignorance and wanting to make something of himself, he carried a dictionary in his pocket and read every book in a neighbor's library. On his way up he taught school, became a law clerk, and then a lawyer. He settled in Buffalo to become a prominent citizen with a highly successful law practice. There he became a leader of the Whig Party, and in 1828 he was elected to the state legislature. In 1832 he was sent to Congress and in his final term, in 1842, was chairman of the powerful Ways and Means Committee and hailed by Whigs for steering the Tariff of 1842 through the House. In 1844 he was defeated, by a small margin, in a reach for the governorship of New York. In 1848, to his astonishment, he found himself Zachary Taylor's vice presidential running mate.[29]

Fillmore was an ineloquent speaker, a stranger to metaphor and simile, but what he said was to the point and packed power. He took pride in regularity. "I have taken but one dose of medicine in

Millard Fillmore
U.S. Senate Historical Office

thirty years," he was to say, summing up his life years later, "and that was forced upon me unnecessarily. I attribute my good health to the fact of an originally strong constitution, to an education on a farm and to life-long habits of regularity and temperance. I never smoked or chewed tobacco. I never knew intoxication. Through-out all my public life I maintained the same regularity and systematic habit of living to which I had previously been accustomed. I never allowed my usual hours for sleep to be interrupted. The Sabbath I always kept as a day of rest."[30]

He had married Abigail Powers, the daughter of a Baptist minister, a tall, spare, graceful woman with auburn hair, light blue eyes, and a fair complexion. She was impressively well informed; before marrying Fillmore she had been a schoolteacher. She abhorred Washington, refusing to go there until after her husband became president. In delicate health, she was reserved with strangers and not given to mingling in society. But she presided at official White House dinner parties and was well thought of in the capital. She was fond of music, and their son sang to her every evening, accompanied by their daughter on the piano.[31] Mrs. Fillmore felt about Washington rather as Fillmore's father felt about it. The old man, eighty years old and known as "Squire Fillmore," came to visit his son in the White House. When he was about to leave, he was urged to remain a few days longer—he had been something of a hit in Washington. "No, no!" he protested. "I will go. I don't like it here; it isn't a good place to live; it isn't a good place for Millard; I wish he was at home in Buffalo."[32]

Fillmore was firmly antislavery, but he had presided over the tumultuous Senate with a steady, dignified, and impartial hand. He had had a falling out with the Weed-Seward faction of the party in New York over patronage, and his ascendancy now promised no good for Seward. Zachary Taylor's cholera morbus had killed the New York senator's influence at the top. It had put him on the outside looking in. Seward lamented, "Providence has at last led the man of hesitation and double opinions, to the crisis, where decision and singleness are indispensable." Fillmore's ascendancy also promised grief for Free-Soilers and antislavery Whigs, for he favored Henry Clay's compromise. When Taylor fell, their prop was gone. They themselves were in free fall. "So we go," Seward moaned, "in this changing world!"[33]

Alexander C. Bullitt, the former editor of the *Republic*, had said, when he heard of Taylor's death, "I mourn for the kind-hearted old man as I would for a father. He never acted wrong on his own motion. The filibustering knaves who practiced upon his credulity and good nature will now get their deserts, and justice will be done to all parties."[34] Now it was Fillmore who decided who got what. He moved swiftly, rooting out Seward men and replacing them with conservative Whigs wherever possible. He swept out Taylor's cabinet with the idea of naming either Clay or Webster as secretary of state. Clay called on him and urged him to take Webster, which Fillmore did. The new cabinet had four slave-state men, but they were moderates. And it was a cabinet that tilted toward compromise. With Webster now dominating, the administration's influence would swing squarely behind Clay's compromise.

Robert C. Winthrop was sent by Massachusetts to fill Webster's vacated seat in the Senate. He acknowledged that "Webster and I are on perfectly good terms, but some of his peculiar friends regard me with a basilisk eye, and bitterly reproach my not having followed in his footsteps."[35] But Winthrop, a moderate, would also seek compromise.

There were some issues, despite his political housecleaning, on which Fillmore would be Taylor reincarnated. One was the Texas-New Mexico boundary question. Webster had told Congressman Henry Hilliard, "Mr. Hilliard, if General Taylor had lived we should have had civil war."[36] Webster was talking about the border question and Taylor's threat to use force to thwart the Texas claim. Fillmore was with Taylor on this one. He was just as ready to use force to derail the Texas intention. He viewed any Texas move into U.S. territory in New Mexico as an intrusion, under the protection of no lawful authority. He would resist such willful trespass by force if necessary, "however painful the duty," just as Taylor had vowed to do. At the same time he was about to call on Congress for "an immediate decision or arrangement or settlement of the question."[37]

Southerners had continued to argue the Texas-New Mexico issue with Taylor virtually up to the day of his death. On July 3, the day before the president fell ill, Robert Toombs had visited him, after Taylor had ordered the military governor at Santa Fe to use troops to forcibly resist any attempted Texas takeover. Toombs had warned Taylor that this new policy would drive him and every other Southern Whig into open opposition and that the entire South would rush to the side of Texas if New Mexico should forcibly resist. Taylor had again denied the validity of the Texas claim, calling it "the damnedest pretext of a title." He vowed again to take up arms against such a hostile assault, if the territory's only inhabitants were Comanche Indians, until Congress settled the matter. He told Toombs he was a soldier who knew his duty and would do it whatever the consequences. Toombs later told a friend, "The worst of it is, he will do it."[38]

Alexander Stephens, greatly agitated, threatened to initiate impeachment proceedings against Taylor and sent a strong open letter to the president, which the *National Intelligencer* ran on July 4. Little Alec wrote that "the first *Federal gun* that shall be fired against the people of Texas, without the authority of law, will be the signal for the freemen from the Delaware to the Rio Grande to rally to the rescue. . . . Be not deceived, and deceive not others. . . . When the 'Rubicon' is passed, the days of this Republic will be numbered . . . the cause of Texas, in such a conflict, will be the cause of the entire South." This threat had been made by Southerners before, but this one, from this particular pro-Union Southern Whig, had been reprinted across the country.[39]

The Southern Whigs would find they could no more persuade Fillmore, a politician, on this issue than they could persuade Taylor, a soldier. What they could take some comfort in, however, was the fact that the wall against the compromise bill in the Senate was now down.

NOTES

1. *Congressional Globe*, 31st Cong., 1st sess., Appendix, 1252, 1248.
2. Bremer, *The Homes of the New World*, 2:52.
3. *Congressional Globe*, 31st Cong., 1st sess., 1362.
4. Bremer, *The Homes of the New World*, 2:52.
5. Wentworth, *Congressional Reminiscences*, 9.
6. David Outlaw to Emily Outlaw, July 6, 1850, Outlaw Papers.
7. "Reminiscences of Washington," 250.
8. Dyer, *Zachary Taylor*, 405.
9. Poore, *Perley's Reminiscences*, 1:378.
10. *Congressional Globe*, 31st Cong., 1st sess., 1363.
11. Varina Davis to her parents, July 10, 1850, in *Jefferson Davis: Private Letters, 1823–1889*, ed. Hudson Strode (New York, 1966), 63.
12. This account of Taylor dying owes much to Rhodes, *History of the United States*, 1:176–77; Poore, *Perley's Reminiscences*, 1:378; "Reminiscences of Washington," 250, 538; and Dyer, *Zachary Taylor*, 405–6.
13. Richardson, *A Compilation of the Messages and Papers of the Presidents*, 5:51.
14. *Congressional Globe*, 31st Cong., 1st sess., 1363, 1366.
15. Benton, *Thirty Years' View*, 2:767.
16. *Obituary Addresses Delivered on the Occasion of the Death of Zachary Taylor. . . .* (Washington, DC, 1850), 54.
17. Winthrop, *A Memoir of Robert C. Winthrop*, 129.
18. *Congressional Globe*, 31st Cong., 1st sess., 1363, 1365.
19. Seward, *Seward at Washington*, 146.
20. French, *Growing Up on Capitol Hill*, 13.

21. *Obituary Addresses Delivered on the Occasion of the Death of Zachary Taylor*, 101.

22. David Outlaw to Emily Outlaw, July 18, 1850, Outlaw Papers.

23. *Obituary Addresses Delivered on the Occasion of the Death of Zachary Taylor*, 97.

24. I am indebted for this description of the funeral to "Reminiscences of Washington," 538; Julian, *Political Recollections*, 94; Dyer, *Zachary Taylor*, 407; and Davis, *Private Letters*, 62.

25. Seward, *Seward at Washington*, 144.

26. Strong, *Diary*, 17.

27. James Morgan, *Our Presidents* (New York, 1954), 109.

28. This brief physical description of Fillmore is a tapestry woven from Poore, *Perley's Reminiscences*, 1:379; Carroll, *Twelve Americans*, 448; Smith, *The Presidencies of Zachary Taylor and Millard Fillmore*, 43; and Rhodes, *The History of the United States*, 1:178.

29. I got a great deal of help in this account of Fillmore's rise to the top from Smith, *The Presidencies of Zachary Taylor and Millard Fillmore*, 43–46.

30. Fillmore, "Millard Fillmore Papers," xxxv, xxxvi.

31. Thanks go to "Reminiscences of Washington," 539, for this description of Mrs. Fillmore.

32. Poore, *Perley's Reminiscences*, 1:385–86.

33. Seward, *Seward at Washington*, 145, 148.

34. Parmelee, "Recollections of an Old Stager" (vol. 47, September 1873): 590.

35. Winthrop, *A Memoir of Robert C. Winthrop*, 143.

36. Hilliard, *Politics and Pen Pictures*, 231.

37. Richardson, *Compilation of Messages and Papers of the Presidents*, 5:69, 71–72.

38. Mark J. Stegmaier, "Zachary Taylor versus the South," *Civil War History* 33 (September 1987): 227–28.

39. Alexander Stephens, public letter to Zachary Taylor, July 4, 1850, Box 2N243, in Guy Morrison Bryan Papers, Eugene C. Barker Texas History Center, University of Texas, Austin. For an excellent, comprehensive history of the Texas-New Mexico boundary dispute see Mark J. Stegmaier, *Texas, New Mexico, and the Compromise of 1850: Boundary Dispute and Sectional Crisis* (Kent, OH, 1996).

CHAPTER TWELVE

WRECK OF THE OMNIBUS

WITH TAYLOR LAID in his vault in the Congressional Burying Ground and Fillmore raised from his chair in the chamber to a loftier station, the Senate turned again to the Gordian knot that was binding the compromise.

Clay deplored the "oppressive state of the weather."[1] It was stultifyingly hot, and the Senate chamber and his rooms at the National Hotel were ovens. But he had resumed his station on the floor, standing watch over the onslaught of amendments. Foote continued floating measures to adjust the package, allegedly trying to make it work. Seward continued throwing occasional amendments, like grenades, into the hopper to outlaw slavery in the territories. Benton continued to plant his land mines against the compromise, lobbying in harness with Northern foes of the compromise who wanted single-measure consideration for California. Southerners continued their drumbeat of support for the Texas claim to the New Mexico territory.

John P. Hale continued to be disgusted with the process. "I have sat here some five or six months listening to speeches," he complained. Worse, he saw no end to it. "I am tired of this," he said, and moved to lay the compromise on the table and kill it, for he hated it more than he hated the speeches. "Instead of undertaking to probe [Clay's five wounds] to the bottom," Hale said, the compromise applies but "a superficial plaster over the surface, deceiving the eye, but leaving all the elements of death and putrification to strive beneath it."[2]

On July 17, Webster seized the floor, seeking "to harmonize opinions as far as I can . . . to facilitate some measure of conciliation . . . and give the country repose." He argued that if California is first admitted immediately, as it should be, then it will follow that something must and will be done before adjournment to settle the question of the New Mexico territory. "I shall never consent to leave this session of Congress," he pledged, "until some provision be made for New Mexico." The next day Virginia's Senator

Robert M. T. Hunter rose to say, "I have never in my life risen to speak with more reluctance than I do at this time" but then spoke Southern doctrine for upward of an hour and one-half. At one point, Foote jumped in. "Will the gentleman allow me just one word?" he asked, a request that drew snickers, for Foote was constitutionally unable to hold any comment to just one word. He then put things in such a way as to raise protests from other senators, including his Mississippi colleague Jefferson Davis, and was called periodically to order by the chair.[3]

Clay was even more disgusted with things than Senator Hale. "The measure," he said, "has received very little aid, very little countenance, from any side of the House." He longed for the question to be "settled definitively, settled one way or the other," for "really, the state of my health is such as to render it absolutely necessary for me to repair to some sea-bathing place, so as to endeavor to invigorate it a little." On July 22, he spoke for more than four hours, painting "a rapid view of some of the objections" to the bill. "The subject," he mused, "has presented one of the most extraordinary political phenomena that I ever witnessed . . . a united Senate almost in favor of all the measures in detail . . . but opposed to them when they came to be presented unitedly to be acted on." He argued that it "contains all that is necessary to give peace and quiet to the country." Furthermore, he believed "from the bottom of my soul, that the measure is the reunion of this Union. I believe it is the dove of peace, which, taking its aerial flight from the dome of the Capitol, carries the glad tidings of assured peace and restored harmony to all the remotest extremities of this distracted land." He pled with his colleagues, "Let us go to the altar of our country and swear, as the oath was taken of old, that we will stand by her . . . that we will pass this great, comprehensive, and healing system of measures, which will hush all the jarring elements, and bring peace and tranquility to our homes. . . . Will you go home and leave all in disorder and confusion, all unsettled, all open? . . . We shall stand condemned in our own consciences, by our own constituents, and by our own country."[4]

David Outlaw, impressed, wrote to his wife that Clay spoke "with a power and animation and eloquence worthy of his palmiest days."[5] Horace Mann rather agreed, saying, "Nothing but the prowess of Clay could have kept the breath in [the Omnibus Bill] to this time."[6] But Clay was clearly losing patience with the ultraists on both ends of the political spectrum. When Robert Barnwell, South

Carolina's replacement for John C. Calhoun and Franklin Elmore, vowed he would raise his sword against the Union if his state's rights were invaded or its peace and liberty disturbed, Clay tore into him. "If he pronounced the sentiment . . . of raising the standard of disunion and of resistance to the common Government," Clay hissed, "whatever he has been, if he follows up that declaration by corresponding overt acts, he will be a traitor, and I hope he will meet the fate of a traitor." Moreover,

> I do not regard as my duty what the honorable Senator seems to regard as his. If Kentucky to-morrow unfurls the banner of resistance unjustly, I never will fight under that banner. I owe a paramount allegiance to the whole Union—a subordinate one to my own State. When my State is right—when it has cause for resistance—when tyranny, and wrong, and oppression insufferable arise—I will then share her fortunes; but if she summons me to the battle-field or to support her in any cause which is unjust against the Union, never, *never*, will I engage with her in such a cause.[7]

David Outlaw wrote his wife, "No arrangement which can or will be made will satisfy South Carolina, and it is useless to attempt it. Her leading statesmen have satisfied themselves, that they made a bad bargain, by entering into the Union, and they are desirous of getting out of it."[8]

A weeklong hailstorm of amendments and amendments to amendments—attempts to force a vote, table the measure, postpone it, or simply to adjourn—followed Clay's speech, and all were rejected. Then, finally, in a bewildering, fast-moving scenario, the end came. Suddenly, on the last day of July, with the weather as hot as ever, the vehicle flew out of Clay's control and wrecked. A new set of senators who had been lying back, participating very little in a substantial way—James Pearce of Maryland, William Dawson of Georgia, James Bradbury of Maine, David Yulee of Florida, David Atchison of Missouri, Joseph R. Underwood of Kentucky—launched a flurry of amending measures. New Mexico, the heart of the Omnibus Bill, was stripped from it. A Yulee motion struck the Texas-New Mexico boundary section, an Atchison motion eliminated California statehood. Everything in the bill was suddenly yanked away—everything but a law to establish a territorial government of Utah, without a ban on slavery. The Omnibus Bill was left an empty shell, "a most lame and impotent conclusion of four or five months' labour," wrote a disgusted Outlaw.[9]

Its enemies, North and South, were ecstatic. "Their vehicle is gone," Benton crowed, "all but one plank. . . . The omnibus is over-turned, and all the passengers spilled out but one. We have but Utah left—all gone but Utah!"[10] Horace Greeley, reporting from the scene, wrote, "And so the Omnibus is smashed—wheels, axles and body—nothing left but a single plank termed Utah. I even saw the gallant driver abandoning the wreck between six and seven this evening, after having done all that man could do to retrieve, or rather to avert the disaster. . . . There was nothing left but to grin and bear it."[11] Greeley continued, "These wearisome, never-end-ing discussions—eight months of them close . . . with the same dreary record of nothing really done. The heavens are brass, the earth is crisp and sweltering, the very breeze is sulphurous, Sa-hara-like, and still as the Hon. Members continue to spout, and spout, day after day, as unflaggingly as though oratory were an art newly invented!" The *Charleston Mercury*, at the opposite end of the journalistic spectrum from Greeley, editorialized, "Now what was the secret fate of Mr. Clay's bill? It was a cheat, a charlatan's device for hiding the diseases of the body politic momentarily, and claiming the reward of curing them . . . this small statesmanship of expedients. . . . We do not say that this controversy can be settled in the Union at all. We doubt if it can be."[12]

Clay, the "gallant driver," said, "We have presented to the coun-try a measure of peace, a measure of tranquility; one which would have harmonized, in my opinion, all the discordant feelings which prevail. That measure has met with a fate not altogether unexpected, I admit . . . but one which . . . I deplore extremely."[13] He walked out of the chamber disheartened and disgusted—"as melancholy," the correspondent of the *New York Express* thought, "as Gaius Marius over the ruins of Carthage."[14]

Believing the compromise failed "namely owing to one of the most extraordinary co-operations of Ultras, from the North and South, which was ever witnessed in a deliberative body," Clay, "a good deal jaded with the long session, and arduous labors," left Washington for Newport, Rhode Island, and the healing waters of the Atlantic.[15] Through the long months he had never been absent when the compromise was being debated. Often ill and feeble, wracked by his cough, he had spoken on the floor seventy times in defense of the bill.[16] But he was not completely without hope. Ear-lier he had said that if the Omnibus Bill "is not to carry, if defeat awaits it, I will not yet despair of the country. I will still hope that others under better auspices . . . will bring forward some great, comprehensive, healing measure to reunite the union of our country."[17]

Stephen Douglas, the chairman of the Senate's Committee on the Territories, had started in politics in the presidential campaign of 1828, ripping down handbills opposing Andrew Jackson as fast as they were pasted on walls and fences in his native Vermont. He was fifteen then, and already a Jacksonian and a Democrat for life.[18] He had been elected to the Senate from Illinois in 1846 after a brief layover in the House. He was short, brash and aggressive, and full of explosive energy. Blessed with great oratorical powers, he excelled in furor and conflict. He was a perfect chairman of the committee, for he was an avid expansionist who had vowed to make America *"an ocean-bound republic"* from the Atlantic to the Pacific.[19]

Ben Perley Poore, the Washington journalist, describing him, wrote, "His dark eyes, peering from beneath piercing brows, gleamed with energy, mixed with an expression of slyness and sagacity."[20] It was said of Douglas that his head was not quite as large as Webster's but it was modeled on it.[21] It was, in another contemporary's view, "an immense head—in height, and breadth and depth—in indications of solidity and force, you cannot find its equal in Washington. There is power under that massive brow, and resolution in that grim mouth; no doubt at all of that."[22]

He was, one who knew him said, "a good mixer. There was no company in which he could not be a congenial companion." In dress he was "the glass of fashion." And in temperament he was a doer. The same friend said, "In an emergency he immediately took in the situation and acted with promptness. While other men were considering, he would meet the crisis."[23] He was about to meet this crisis.

Only thirty-six years old, one of the three youngest senators, Douglas had never had much faith in the Omnibus Bill. He favored Clay's compromise—indeed, had been the author of most of the legislation it was based upon. He had gone along with the omnibus approach, knowing it would fail, and marking time. In mid-March he had said in praise of Clay, "He set the ball in motion which is to restore peace and harmony to the Union. He was the pioneer in the glorious cause, and set a noble example, which many others are nobly imitating." Douglas's objective from the beginning had been "to get a vote upon something practical."[24] To

Stephen A. Douglas
Library of Congress

that end he had been vigorously pushing for a vote on California statehood.

After the omnibus crashed, Douglas moved in and grabbed the compromise helm. He wrote two Illinois friends, in a private letter,

I regrett [sic] it very much, altho I must say that I never had very strong hopes of its passage. By combining the measures into one Bill the Committee united the opponents of each measure instead of securing the friends of each. I thought from the beginning that they made a mistake in this respect. I declined being a member of the committee of 13 for this reason & for the same reason opposed the appointment of the committee. . . . I gave the Bill of Mr Clay my active & unwavering support down to its final defeat. . . . [It] was defeated by a union between the Free Soils and disun[ion]ists & the administration of Gen'l Taylor. All the power & patronage of the Govt was brought to bear against us, & at last the allied forces were able to beat us. . . . But let it always be said of old Hal that he fought a glorious & a patriotic battle. No man was ever governed by higher & purer motives.[25]

Now, with the slate wiped clean, Douglas had a better idea. It was clear to him that although there was no workable majority for the Omnibus Bill, there were sectional blocs in favor of each measure separately.

Douglas would now pick up the pieces of Clay's compromise, as Clay had hoped somebody would, and ram them through one by one, working one bloc, then the other, to build majorities for each. He began immediately to introduce separate bills, as he had wanted to do from the start. Indeed, he had been working toward that end behind the scenes in his committee. He had also been working the House, in private meetings with allies there to prepare the groundwork in case the bill failed and he could put the compromise through and send it over to them piece by piece. In fact, Douglas had arranged earlier with John McClernand of Illinois, his chief ally in the House, to introduce similar bills in their respective houses. "Thus," he wrote his two Illinois friends, "will all the Bills pass the Senate & I believe the House also. When they are all passed you see they will be collectively Mr Clay's compromise, & separately the Bills Reported by the committee on Territories four months ago. . . . We have great confidence that we will yet be able to settle the whole difficulty before we adjourn."[26]

On August 1, the day after the omnibus crashed, the bill for a territorial government in Utah was read a third time and passed. That same day Douglas began steering through the California bill as well as the testy Texas-New Mexico boundary proposal calling for Texas to drop its claim and accept $10 million instead. Debate on those two measures went on side by side, and the Texas bill passed first, 30–20. Twelve votes were against it from slave-state senators, eight from the free states. Then California statehood passed 34–18, the yeas all from fifteen Northern Democrats, eleven Northern Whigs, four Southern Whigs, and Senators Chase, Hale, Benton, and Houston. The nays were all from the South—and all Democrats but three. On August 15 the bill for a territorial government for New Mexico without the Wilmot Proviso passed 27–10, the nays all from the North. On August 26 a tightened Fugitive Slave Law was passed, 27–12, the nays mainly from Northern Whigs; fifteen Northern senators did not vote. Abolition of the slave trade in the District of Columbia passed on September 16 by a 33–19 vote, with thirteen Southern Democrats and six Southern Whigs voting no.[27]

By the time Clay returned from the seashore in late August, Douglas had virtually jammed the Great Pacificator's entire compromise package through the Senate, one bill at a time, as he predicted he would do—based solidly on popular sovereignty and greatly abetted in rallying votes by Millard Fillmore's newly supportive White House. Only four senators voted for all five of the compromise bills—Augustus Dodge, the good son, was one of them, but not his father, who voted for only two. The father, Henry, was a tough-minded former sheriff, soldier, U.S. marshal, and governor of the Wisconsin territory, who went armed with pistols and a bowie knife, even on civic occasions. Young Dodge, also tough minded if not as well armed, supported the compromise bag and baggage despite his antiblack, proslavery sentiments. The other three senators who voted for all five bills were Sam Houston of Texas, Daniel Sturgeon of Pennsylvania, and John Wales of Delaware. Douglas would have, but he was unavoidably absent when the Fugitive Slave law came to a vote. Clay also would have, but he was away at the seashore.

As they were passed in the Senate, the bills were sent to the House, where a membership equally schism-rent and divided had been waiting, consuming, David Outlaw thought, "nine months in idle, and worse than idle debate."[28] The House had not been into generating comprehensive compromise legislation of its own, but it had been heavy into speechmaking about it. In the month between May 8 and June 11, fifty-eight congressmen had delivered hour-long or longer speeches. Only thirteen spoke in favor of the omnibus compromise that was agonizing the Senate.[29] Robert Toombs on June 15 delivered a fire-eating speech that Alexander

Stephens admired in particular. It "produced the greatest sensation in the House that I ever witnessed by any speech in that body," Stephens said. "It created a perfect commotion."[30]

With bills fabricated in the Senate now coming to the House, the *New York Herald* commented, " 'Look to the Senate,' was at one time the watchword. 'Look to the House,' is now the cry."[31] The end of August and the beginning of September were something of a down time in Washington. According to Congressman Outlaw, "The city is as dull as can be imagined. The strangers who come here, stay but a short time. The streets look dull. Every body looks dull—every body feels dull."[32]

That changed in the House when the first bills arrived from the Senate in early September. The Texas boundary-debt and New Mexico territory measures, the first to come, were bound together into what was called the "little omnibus," and almost half of the senators went over to the hall of the House to see what would happen with it.

Douglas had carefully spaded the ground in the House to engineer a rapprochement between House Democrats and Whigs—McClernand and William Richardson of Illinois, on one hand; Toombs, Stephens, Linn Boyd, and Thomas Clingman on the other, with the Speaker, Howell Cobb, playing a strong parliamentary and mediating hand. McClernand and Richardson had organized others of the Illinois Democratic contingent in the House—William H. Bissell,Thomas J. Harris, Timothy R. Young—into a solid phalanx supporting the compromise.

McClernand was from Shawneetown, in heavily Democratic southern Illinois. He was wiry, wired, energetic, and dark eyed, with a long thin face anchored to a prominent nose. His scholarly research and theatrical speaking style had made him well known in that end of the state and won him the sobriquet, the "Grecian Orator." He had been in politics since he was twenty-four years old. The Whig *Sangamo Journal*, not a friend, described him as having "a singular propensity for office." McClernand had been elected to the House with Douglas in 1843, and his early speeches in Congress had been so intense he once had to be gavelled to silence. He was a hard-line expansionist but a bitter enemy of the Wilmot Proviso and a solid backer of Douglas's popular sovereignty. He had been working in harness with Douglas on the compromise for some time, since April 3, when they introduced companion measures in their respective houses to admit California as a free state, to organize

Utah and New Mexico as territories without a slavery restriction, and to keep slavery in the District of Columbia. Since things were testy on the House floor, McClernand carried two pistols and a bowie knife. But he had played the role of compromiser through-out the debate, primarily behind the scenes.[33]

McClernand's Democratic stablemate, William Richardson, working hand-in-hand with him on the compromise, sat in Douglas's former House seat. Richardson was seen by one observer as a "strong coarse man," big, powerful, muscular, and lovable, with an enormous nose and mouth and "fine eyes." His voice could be heard "like a fire-bell over the clatter of engines in the street."[34]

Linn Boyd, a Kentucky Whig and chairman of the House Com-mittee on the Territories, was working closely with Douglas and his two Democratic allies in the compromise fight. Boyd was a strik-ingly handsome man—a journalist thought him "one of the finest looking men in Congress"—of tireless energy. He was a farmer with little formal education, who had begun his public life as a sheriff. Now he was one of the most respected men in the House, a master parliamentarian. Too long a widower, in April he had married a Pennsylvanian, Ann Rhey Dixon, a relative of Millard Fillmore.[35]

Boyd had framed the "little omnibus," saying, "I think we have talked enough—in God's name let us act."[36] His measure reached the floor on September 4 and for the next three days the House was in chaos. Agitated members left their seats, spilled into the aisles, and clustered about the Speaker's desk. Calls to order had little soothing effect on the uproar. But on September 6 the House ap-proved the engrossment of the bill for a third reading—a step tan-tamount to passage. Shouts, whistles, and stamping feet rocked the hall. The Senate reporter noted "a sort of unpremeditated *allegro* whistle," which he had never heard before on the floor of the House. "The other tokens of glorification," he wrote, "were of a less musi-cal order." Cobb overworked his gavel but was met with shouts, "Let them stamp! It is all right!" Passage followed a few minutes later, 108–97.[37]

This broke the logjam. Everything had been riding on it. Quickly now, the other parts of the compromise marched across the House floor. On September 7 the California and Utah bills passed. George Templeton Strong, the Wall Street lawyer, noted in his diary, "Con-gress has acted at last on the great Southern problem; passed the Texas and California bills, checked the Southern chivalry in the generation of gas, and blighted the hopes of Billy Seward and his gang of incendiaries, who wanted to set the country on fire with civil war that they might fill themselves with place and profit in the confusion."[38]

Horace Mann, who was holding out for Free Soil and the "absolute security" of the Wilmot Proviso, was disgusted. "Here are twenty, perhaps thirty, men from the North in this House," he said, "who, before Gen. Taylor's death, would have sworn, like St. Paul, not to eat nor drink until they had voted the proviso, who now, in the face of the world, turn about, defy the instructions of their States, take back their own declarations, a thousand times uttered, and vote against it. It is amazing; it is heart-sickening." And he grieved, "The slaveholders have overthrown principles, and put them to rout as Napoleon did armies." There were times when Mann admitted to feeling like "going into sackcloth and ashes for human nature."[39] This was probably one of those times.

On September 12 the Fugitive Slave Bill was passed in the House. This was a tough one for a lot of Northerners, who feared the wrath of their abolitionist constituents. Thirty-one Northern members voted for it. Thirty-three Northerners, however, were either absent or paired or dodged the vote, causing the irascible Pennsylvania Whig, Thaddeus Stevens, to say, "I suggest that the Speaker should send a page to notify the members on our side of the House that the Fugitive Slave bill has been disposed of, and that they may now come back into the hall."[40] Congressman Outlaw, an ardent but procompromise Southerner, said, "This stealing of slaves produces more irritation, more heart-burning, among slaveholders, than all other causes combined. It furnishes more material for agitation than any thing else, because it is a practical evil which we suffer, and a palpable wrong which the North commits, which comes home to the business and bosoms of men."[41]

The bill as finally passed put the Fugitive Slave Law under exclusive federal jurisdiction. It set up a procedure authorizing U.S. commissioners, following summary hearings on cases of runaway slaves, to issue warrants for their arrest and certificates for returning them to their masters. An affidavit by the slave's master would be accepted as sufficient proof of ownership. Commissioners would be paid $10 for each certificate granted but only $5 for each refused, a differential certain to be bitterly denounced as prejudicial by abolitionists. Commissioners could call bystanders with summonses if necessary to enforce the law. Fugitives claiming to be free men were denied the right of trial by jury and their testimony was not to be admitted as evidence in any proceedings under the law. Heavy penalties would greet any evasion or obstruction. Marshals and deputies refusing to execute the warrants would be liable to a $1,000 fine. In cases where the fugitives escaped by dint of official negligence, the marshal might be sued for the value of the slave. Citizens preventing the arrest of a fugitive or helping to hide him were subject to a like fine, imprisonment for up to six months, and civil damages for each slave so lost. This bill was going to bring no end of trouble from up North, the haven already to an estimated 30,000 runaways worth nearly $15 million.[42]

On September 17 the bill abolishing the slave trade in the District of Columbia was passed. The president signed it, the last of the bills, on September 20. The various pieces of the compromise were law. Outlaw was speaking for more than one congressman when he wrote home, "I trust they will carry healing on their wings throughout the Republic."[43]

The key to the final tortuous passage of the compromise had been the steady backing of the Northern Democrats and Southern Whigs, who made up the political middle in each section. The California bill was clearly a compromise for the North, the New Mexico bill and the Fugitive Slave Law were concessions to the South. The Texas-New Mexico boundary bill and the bill to end the slave trade, but not slavery, in the District of Columbia were standoffs.

On the last day of September the exhausted Congress adjourned precisely at noon. It had been grappling with the crisis for ten months, 302 days—days blackened by acrimony and driven by strong sectional differences—the longest session in its history. Henry Clay wrote Lucretia in the final days saying he had been "much benefited by the Sea bath & air" of Newport, but "never have I been so tired of a Session of Congress or so anxious to get home."[44] He had finally said something every senator could agree with.

NOTES

1. *Congressional Globe*, 31st Cong., 1st sess., Appendix, 1270.
2. *Congressional Globe*, 31st Cong., 1st sess., 1391; ibid., Appendix, 1271.
3. This lineup of senators from Webster to Foote is in ibid., Appendix, 1266–67, 1382, 1393.
4. Clay's feelings and words are from ibid., 1398, 1404–5, 1407, 1413.
5. David Outlaw to Emily Outlaw, July 22, 1850, Outlaw Papers.

6. Mann, *Life of Horace Mann*, 304.

7. *Congressional Globe*, 31st Cong., 1st sess., Appendix, 1414.

8. David Outlaw to Emily Outlaw, July 25, 1850, Outlaw Papers.

9. Ibid., August 1, 1850.

10. *Congressional Globe*, 31st Cong., 1st sess., Appendix, 1484.

11. Quoted in Hamilton, *Prologue to Conflict*, 111.

12. Both quotes are from National Archives, "Westward Expansion and the Compromise of 1850," 42.

13. *Congressional Globe*, 31st Cong., 1st sess., Appendix, 1486.

14. *New York Express*, August 2, 1850, quoted in Parks, "John Bell and the Compromise of 1850," 354.

15. Clay, *Papers*, 10:793–94.

16. Parton, *Famous Americans of Recent Times*, 48–49.

17. *Congressional Globe*, 31st Cong., 1st sess., Appendix, 1400.

18. Robert W. Johannson, *Stephen A. Douglas* (New York, 1973), 9.

19. *Congressional Globe*, 28th Cong., 2d sess., Appendix, 68.

20. Poore, *Perley's Reminiscences*, 1:317.

21. Dyer, *Great Senators*, 129.

22. Halstead, *Three against Lincoln*, 119.

23. Clark E. Carr, *Stephen A. Douglas: His Life, Public Services, Speeches, and Patriotism* (Chicago, 1909), 42, 46.

24. *Congressional Globe*, 31st Cong., 1st sess., 662; ibid., Appendix, 375.

25. Stephen Douglas to Charles H. Lanphier and George Walker, August 3, 1850, in *The Letters of Stephen A. Douglas*, ed. Robert W. Johannsen (Urbana, IL, 1961), 191–93.

26. Ibid., 192–93.

27. I had much help in compiling this rundown of the voting from Rhodes, *History of the United States*, 1:181–82.

28. David Outlaw to Emily Outlaw, August 31, 1850, Outlaw Papers.

29. Smith, *The Presidencies of Zachary Taylor and Millard Fillmore*, 148.

30. Stephens, *A Constitutional View of the Late War*, 2:217.

31. *New York Herald*, September 6, 1850, quoted in Holman Hamilton, "Kentucky's Linn Boyd and the Dramatic Days of 1850," *Register of the Kentucky Historical Society* 55 (July 1957): 189.

32. David Outlaw to Emily Outlaw, August 30, 1850, Outlaw Papers.

33. Richard L. Kiper, *Major General John Alexander McClernand: Politician in Uniform* (Kent, OH, 1999), 2, 5–11; with incidental descriptive material from Hamilton, "Kentucky's Linn Boyd and the Dramatic Days of 1850," 186.

34. Halstead, *Three against Lincoln*, 13, 22; Hamilton, "Kentucky's Linn Boyd and the Dramatic Days of 1850," 186.

35. I am indebted for this brief picture of Linn Boyd to Hamilton, "Kentucky's Linn Boyd and the Dramatic Days of 1850," 185–88.

36. *Congressional Globe*, 31st Cong., 1st sess., 1697.

37. Ibid., 1764.

38. Strong, *Diary*, 19.

39. Mann, *Life of Horace Mann*, 283, 289, 322, 332; Rhodes, *History of the United States*, 1:184.

40. Rhodes, *History of the United States*, 1:183.

41. David Outlaw to Emily Outlaw, July 29, 1850, Outlaw Papers.

42. This estimated number and value of runaway slaves in the North is from Clingman, *Selections from Speeches and Writings*, 240.

43. David Outlaw to Emily Outlaw, September 10, 1850, Outlaw Papers.

44. Clay, *Papers*, 10:800.

EPILOGUE
End of an Era

SENATOR DANIEL DICKINSON of New York, who had done his duty by the compromise, exulted that "the mad current of disunion which threatened to overwhelm us" had been short-circuited, and "the dark and angry waves" rolled "back from the holy citadel."[1]

On the Saturday night after the House passed the "little omnibus" and the California and Utah bills, and the deadly current had died and the angry waves had receded, "wild jubilation" rocked Washington. There were bonfires and belching cannon salutes for the next twenty-four hours. All-night processions of celebrants roamed the streets looking to serenade the lawmakers responsible for the miracle. The main buildings in Washington were lit and illuminated, and exultant crowds shouted, "The Union is saved!" Also lit were Douglas, Foote, and others after it was suggested that this was "a night on which it was the duty of every patriot to get drunk." Douglas and Foote did their duty. As Linn Boyd wrote his new bride, "it found us all litterally [sic] boiling over with gladness."[2]

A Washington friend wrote James Buchanan in Pennsylvania, "One thing is certain, that every face I meet is happy. All look upon the question as settled and no fears are felt in relation to the movements in either the South or North. I can scarcely realize that I am now surrounded and conversing with the same men I heard in warm and angry discussion but a few days ago. The successful are rejoicing, the neutrals have all joined the winning side, and the defeated are silent."[3]

Since his Seventh of March speech, Webster confessed, "there has not been an hour, in which I have not felt a 'crushing' weight of anxiety, & responsibility. I have gone to sleep at night, & waked in the morning, with the same feeling of 'eating care.'" But he told a friend in early October, "I can now sleep anights. We have gone thro' the most important crisis, which has occurred since the foundation of the Government; & what ever party may prevail, hereafter, the Union stands firm. Faction, Disunion, & the love of mischief

187

are put under, at least, for the present, & I hope for a long time."
He believed that the country had "had a providential escape from
very considerable dangers."[4]

Much was still riding on hope as city after city in the country
celebrated. Alabama's William King, the president pro tem of the
Senate, spoke for the hopeful but dubious when he adjourned the
Senate sine die: "Whether the action of Congress will allay [the]
excitement, restore harmony, and bring about a better state of feeling in the country, remains to be seen."[5] Ohio's Salmon Chase and
Tennessee's John Bell were among the dubious. For Chase, "The
question of slavery in the Territories has been avoided. It has not
been settled."[6] As for Bell, "The crisis is not past; nor can perfect
harmony be restored to the country until the North shall cease to
vex the South upon the subject of slavery."[7]

At the root of the doubt was the misgiving that the compromise had failed to crack the nubbin of the tough nut of slavery in
the territories—that it had skirted the problem rather than solved
it. The compromise carried no formula to guide the future. The same
North-South division over slavery in the territories lingered. It was
suggested that Congress perhaps had passed a lawsuit rather than
a law; that it was an "armistice" rather than "a true compromise."[8]

Some sour notes were sounding throughout the country, too.
Northern radicals regretted the lost opportunity to emphatically
exclude slavery from the territories. They condemned the Fugitive
Slave Law and promised to obstruct its enforcement. Radical Southerners mourned the admission of California as a free state and felt
an abiding foreboding of doom over the loss of sectional balance.

But happier notes were rising above the sour ones. Millard
Fillmore wrote Governor Hamilton Fish of New York on September 9, "The long agony is over. I have just approved and signed
bills settling the disputed boundary between Texas & New Mexico
& Utah. Though these several acts are not in all respects what I
would have desired, yet, I am rejoiced at their passage, and trust
they will restore harmony and peace to our distracted country."
He considered it "in its character final and irrevocable." He would
tell the Congress in his first annual message on December 2 that
the compromise measures "are regarded by me as a settlement in
principle and substance—a final settlement of the dangerous and
exciting subjects which they embraced. . . . By that adjustment we
have been rescued from the wide and boundless agitation that surrounded us, and have a firm, distinct, and legal ground to rest

upon." He exhorted his countrymen to "rally upon and maintain that ground as the best, if not the only, means of restoring peace and quiet in the country and maintaining inviolate the integrity of the Union."[9]

Henry Clay said, "The fact is no longer doubtful that the fires are extinguished and extinguishing daily in the furnaces of the country."[10] Resolutions of grateful amen flocked to the hopper. Whatever else might be happening, the storm and fury had gone out of Congress. It was "no longer an arena of wrath and wrangling."[11]

Some congressmen and senators, however, would be going home to trouble and disrupted futures—and not only in a North unhappy with the Fugitive Slave Law. Many people in volatile Georgia, a key Southern state, were unhappy, which did not bode well for Howell Cobb, Robert Toombs, and Alexander Stephens, the state's powerful triumvirate in the House. Excitement was at a high pitch in the so-called Empire State of the South. The radical Democratic press there assailed the compromise and threatened disunion. The *Columbus Sentinel* on September 2 wrote, "We have all along contended that the admission of California would fill to overflowing the poisoned cup of degradation which the North has for years been preparing for the South. . . . We now abandon the Union as an engine of infamous oppression. We are for secession, open unqualified secession. Henceforth we are for war upon the government; it has existed but for our ruin and to the extent of our ability to destroy it, it shall exist no longer." The *Columbus Times*, the *Savannah Georgian*, and the *Augusta Constitutionalist* echoed this firebrand sentiment.[12]

A struggle for control of Georgia's constitutional convention convening in December found Cobb, Toombs, and Stephens frantically trying to load it with sentiment favorable to the compromise. They succeeded. The convention adopted a preamble and set of resolutions called the "Georgia Platform" that pledged the state's support for the compromise and the Union as long as the South's constitutional rights were secure and the North remained faithful to the compromise. "We ought [not] to grumble now," Toombs wrote; "no cause for secession exists." Seeking to rally political muscle behind this positive position, the Constitutional Union Party was organized. Cobb, the driving force, was picked in June 1851 to run for governor on its ticket against a Southern Rights Party candidate, Charles J. McDonald, a popular two-time governor of the state. Cobb was elected by a lopsided majority. Georgia in the end had spoken unmistakingly for the compromise, against disunion and secession.[13] So did most other Southern states.

It turned out that the doubters were right about the questionable long-term durability of the compromise, however. Despite all his efforts to pacify crises of the Union over the better part of one-half century, Henry Clay's compromises tended to paper over the problem rather than solve it. It was said of him that he crafted policy that postponed evil consequences rather than permanently prevented them. His compromises were temporary in effect, damping the problem for a time, only to have the trouble erupt more virulently later. The Missouri Compromise, although it lasted thirty years, was only a truce that would break out into fiercer conflict in 1850. The Compromise of 1850 was also only a truce that would end ten years later in a death-dealing civil war.

This last great compromise would begin unraveling in only four years. In 1854 its final architect and principal author, Stephen Douglas, would set its undoing in motion with the Kansas-Nebraska bill, which repealed the Missouri Compromise line and with it the only restriction on slavery in the territories. It had not been Douglas's intention to undo the Compromise of 1850, but, bent on development of the American West and under pressure from the South, he had to make concessions. And the concessions he made shattered the wall of the compromise. With the passage of the Kansas-Nebraska bill, slavery might now be admitted anywhere in the territories wherever popular sovereignty might put it. The glue that had held the country together and prevented civil war was no longer holding. It deteriorated even further nearly three years later with the Dred Scott decision, in which the Supreme Court ruled that Southerners could take their slaves—deemed property by the court—into any territory, which wholly undercut Douglas's popular sovereignty policy. All of this was not only to wreck the Compromise of 1850 but also to wreak political havoc. By the middle of the 1850s, the Whig Party, schizophrenic with its Northern and Southern halves, was unable to survive the buffeting of the slavery issue and died, to be replaced by the new, surging Republican Party.

Following this fast-moving train of events, nothing, it appeared, could now be compromised. Pacification, even as a temporary measure, became unattainable. The only solution was civil war, and it would break, a terrible swift storm, in 1861. The Compromise of 1850 was a compromise only in the sense that it would be the last one before no compromise was possible. It had simply bought the Union a decade of time.

〜 Besides, the pacificators were gone. Clay and Webster died before the end of 1852. They, with Calhoun, had been giants, the three of them a trio unrivaled in the nation's history. The *Charleston Daily Courier* had called them "the *three Great Men of America* . . . towering in colossal proportion and pyramidal eminence above all rivalry," riding high "in the admiration and the hearts of their countrymen."[14] "When *they* spoke," one writer said, "America listened, and when they were thinking, America was still." When they were sitting in the Senate, "you felt as you looked down from the gallery, that the Senate was full, whoever else was present or whoever was away."[15]

Their modern-day joint biographer, Merrill Peterson, has written, "Their arrival on the political stage announced a new era of American statesmanship, and their departure forty years later brought it emphatically to a close." They had come together in the House of Representatives for the first time in 1813 from three main points of the political compass: East, West, and South. They had come together in the Senate for the first time in 1832 and immediately became its "master spirits." Peterson calls them "the legitimate successors of Washington, Adams, and Jefferson." They "became part of the furniture of American memory."[16]

Calhoun had been first to die, as we know, in the midst of the wrangling over the Compromise of 1850. Clay was next. His health had steadily declined after the tumult of 1849–50. Throughout the winter and spring of 1851–52, he had been confined almost wholly to his rooms in the National Hotel, clearly dying. About half-past eleven in the morning, June 29, 1852, he died, "before the foliage of summer was sere."[17]

President Fillmore said, "The tolling bells announced the death of the Hon. Henry Clay. Though this event has been long anticipated, yet the painful bereavement could never be fully realized."[18]

By six o'clock that evening Pennsylvania Avenue was draped in black. Even the hall of the rival Democratic Party was deeply shrouded. The outpouring of grief for Clay in death became as palpable as the outpouring of acclaim for him in life. "A great national sorrow hung over us," a Washingtonian wrote.[19] Virginia's Democratic Senator Robert M. T. Hunter, never Clay's ally, said, "His memory is as imperishable as American history itself, for he was one of those who made it."[20] Horace Greeley lamented, "I profoundly loved Henry Clay. . . . I loved him for his generous nature, his gallant bearing, his thrilling eloquence, and his life-long devotion to what I deemed our country's unity, prosperity, and just renown."[21]

A newspaper that was his political foe wrote, "Alas! who can realize that Henry Clay is dead! Who can realize that never again that majestic form shall rise in the council-chambers of his country to beat back the storms of anarchy which may threaten, or pour the oil of peace upon the troubled billows as they rage and menace around? Who can realize that the workings of that mighty mind have ceased—that the throbbings of that gallant heart are stilled— that the mighty sweep of that graceful arm will be felt no more, and the magic of that eloquent tongue, which spake as spake no other tongue besides, is hushed—hushed forever!"[22]

As Clay was dying, Webster, that other great tongue, now the sole survivor of the trio, said, "Mr. Clay is a great man; beyond all question a true patriot. He has done much for his country. . . . I think, however, he was never a man of books, a hard student; but he has displayed remarkable genius. I never could imagine him sitting comfortably in his library, and reading quietly out of the great books of the past. He has been too fond of this world to enjoy anything like that. He has been too fond of excitement—he has lived upon it."[23]

Now, for Clay, the excitement and the life were over. In Washington on July 1, the day of his funeral, nearly every house, public building, schoolhouse, and church was draped in black. The coffin was carried through a huge jam in the Capitol rotunda to the Senate chamber for the service, conducted by Clement M. Butler, the chaplain of the Senate. Afterward it was moved to the rotunda, making Clay the first statesman ever to lie there in state. Thousands trooped past the bier. The next morning the coffin was put on cars and sent, with an escort of senators and congressmen, home to Lexington, Kentucky, passing en route through mourning crowds in Baltimore, Philadelphia, New York, Albany, Buffalo, Cleveland, Cincinnati, and Louisville. In Philadelphia, its first stop, the body lay in state in Independence Hall. In New York, as the funeral car passed slowly by, drawn by eight white horses, "every public place on the line of route was decorated with insignia emblematic of grief, and inscriptions and mottoes, some of which were very expressive, fell upon the eye, and awakened many thoughtful and sad emotion."[24]

⁓ Scarcely three months after Clay was laid to rest in Lexington, Webster, still Fillmore's secretary of state, followed, dead of cirrhosis of the liver, the legacy of a life of heavy drinking. He died at Marshfield on a clear October Sabbath, when "the winds of autumn" had swept "the stern New England shores,"[25] and "when all nature seemed hushed in repose"[26]—just a few days before the 1852 presidential election. The timing brought to mind the irony that Webster "went down to his grave with the firm conviction that he had been defrauded of the Presidency by the jealousy and intrigues of his rivals. He entertained no doubt that the great mass of his countrymen were anxious to make him President, but were overruled and thwarted by the party leaders."[27]

Between seven and eight o'clock the parish church bell in Marshfield rang out the melancholy news, tolling nine times to announce the death of a male, then seventy times to count the years of the deceased. Everybody knew who it was. The cries rose, "It must be that Daniel Webster is dead"; "The pride of our nation has fallen"; "Our great neighbor and townsman is no more."[28]

At the end, passing in and out of consciousness, Webster had opened his eyes and stared at those gathered around his bed. He asked, "Have I wife, son, doctors, friends—are you all here?—have I on this occasion said anything unworthy of Daniel Webster?" Reassured, he closed his eyes, opened them again, and said, "I still live." Then he died.[29]

"Daniel Webster is dead!!!!!" young Francis French wrote in his journal in Washington. "His giant intellect is at rest forever. No more shall his voice be lifted up in behalf of the dearly beloved Constitution of his country: no more shall we hear its majestic tones echo through the national legislative halls. He is dead!"[30] Henry Hilliard said, "We heard of his death as we should have received the intelligence of a national calamity."[31] Ralph Waldo Emerson, the great essayist and New England intellectual, wrote, "The sea, the rocks, the woods, gave no sign that America and the world has lost the completest man. . . . Nature had not in our days, or not since Napoleon, cut out such a masterpiece."[32]

President Fillmore proposed a state funeral. But Webster had left instructions for something private and simple at Marshfield.

So instead, on a golden Indian summer day, he lay in an iron coffin under the shade of a large tree in front of the house at Marshfield. His body was dressed in his blue coat with gilt buttons, his hands were folded on his breast, and his face wore that sad, serious smile so familiar to his friends in his later years. The village pastor conducted the services; then the upper half of the coffin was closed and the body was carried to the burial ground on the estate on a platform car drawn by two black horses. On either side of the coffin walked the pallbearers, six husky weather-browned farmers and fishermen, neighbors selected by Webster himself—a simple Marshfield man being borne to his grave by simple Marshfield pallbearers. He wanted to be buried in this fashion with "a mere New England funeral . . . in a manner respectful of his neighbors." Such New England luminaries as Franklin Pierce, Edward Everett, and Rufus Choate walked the mile to the burial ground behind the car "through a line of saddened forms and faces on each side." Webster's friend, George Ticknor, did not doubt that more than 10,000 mourners had come to see the great statesman to his final rest in a scene "inexpressibly solemn and sad."[33]

It was perhaps just as well that Clay and Webster were gone. They would have abhorred living in an America at war with itself, where all hope for compromise had also died.

NOTES

1. Webster, *Private Correspondence*, 393.
2. For this picture of celebrating Washington I drew on Nevins, *Ordeal of the Union*, 343; Hamilton, " 'The Cave of the Winds,' " 350–51; and Hamilton, "Kentucky's Linn Boyd and the Dramatic Days of 1850," 192.
3. J. M. Foltz to James Buchanan, September 8, 1850, quoted in Nevins, *Ordeal of the Union*, 343.
4. Webster, *Papers*, 143, 144, 155.
5. *Congressional Globe*, 31st Cong., 1st sess., 2072.
6. Ibid., 1859.
7. Parks, *John Bell*, 262.
8. Potter, *The Impending Crisis*, 113.
9. Smith, *The Presidencies of Zachary Taylor and Millard Fillmore*, 195; Richardson, *Messages of the Presidents*, 5:93.
10. *Congressional Globe*, 31st Cong., 2d sess., 114.
11. Hamlin, *The Life and Times of Hannibal Hamlin*, 216.
12. Brooks, "Howell Cobb and the Crisis of 1850," 289, 289 n.
13. The grist for this summary of the situation in Georgia and the newspaper quote are drawn from ibid., 290–94. The Toombs quote is from Brooks, "Howell Cobb Papers" (September 1921), 47.
14. Quoted in Peterson, *The Great Triumvirate*, 5.

15. Parker, *The Golden Age of American Oratory*, 120.

16. Peterson, *The Great Triumvirate*, 5–6.

17. *Obituary Addresses on the Occasion of the Death of the Hon. Daniel Webster*, 50.

18. Fillmore, "Millard Fillmore Papers," 367.

19. Remini, *Henry Clay*, 782.

20. U.S. Congress, *Obituary Addresses, Henry Clay*, 23.

21. Greeley, *Autobiography*, 166.

22. Quoted by Abraham Lincoln in his eulogy on Clay in Abraham Lincoln, *Collected Works*, ed. Roy P. Basler, vol. 2 (New Brunswick, NJ, 1955), 122.

23. Parton, *Famous Americans of Recent Times*, 29–30 n.

24. Joan Sayers Brown, "The Funeral of Henry Clay," *Antiques Magazine* 112 (July 1977): 110.

25. *Obituary Notices on the Occasion of the Death of the Hon. Daniel Webster*, 50.

26. Sargent, *Public Men and Events*, 2:393.

27. Parmelee, "Recollections of an Old Stager" (vol. 45, October 1872): 750–51.

28. Harvey, *Reminiscences and Anecdotes of Daniel Webster*, 447.

29. Jones, *Lords of Speech*, 46–47.

30. French, *Growing Up on Capitol Hill*, 70–71.

31. Hilliard, *Politics and Pen Pictures*, 265.

32. Alexander, *The Famous Five*, 51.

33. This picture of Webster's funeral is from "Reminiscences of Washington," 665–66; and Ticknor, *Life, Letters, and Journals*, 2:283.

BIBLIOGRAPHY

Alexander, Holmes. *The Famous Five*. New York: Bookmaker, 1958.

Allen, William C. *History of the United States Capitol: A Chronicle of Design, Construction, and Politics*. Washington, DC: Government Printing Office, 2001.

American National Biography. Edited by John A. Garraty and Mark C. Carnes. 24 vols. Published under the auspices of the American Council of Learned Societies. New York: Oxford University Press, 1999.

Ames, Herman V. "John C. Calhoun and the Secession Movement of 1850." American Antiquarian Society *Proceedings*. New series. 28 (April 1918): 19–50.

Annals of Congress.

Arnston, Paul, and Craig R. Smith. "The Seventh of March Address: A Mediating Influence." *Southern Speech Communication Journal* 40 (Spring 1975): 288–301.

Baker, Richard Allan. *The Senate of the United States: A Bicentennial History*. Malabar, FL: Robert E. Krieger, 1988.

Baltimore Sun.

Barnes, Thurlow Weed. *Memoir of Thurlow Weed*. 1884. Reprint, New York: Da Capo Press, 1970.

Barnwell, John, ed. "Hamlet to Hotspur: Letters of Robert Woodward Barnwell to Robert Barnwell Rhett." *South Carolina Historical Magazine* 77 (October 1976): 236–56.

Bartlett, Irving H. *Daniel Webster*. New York: W. W. Norton, 1978.

Benton, Thomas Hart. *Thirty Years' View: or a History of the Working of the American Government for Thirty Years, from 1820 to 1850*. 2 vols. 1856. Reprint, New York: Greenwood Press, 1968.

Birkner, Michael. "Daniel Webster and the Crisis of the Union, 1850." *Historical New Hampshire* 37 (Summer/Fall 1982): 151–73.

Boller, Paul F., Jr. *Presidential Anecdotes*. New York: Oxford University Press, 1981.

Boston Whig.

Bremer, Fredrika. *The Homes of the New World: Impressions of America*. 3 vols. London: Arthur Hall, Virtue & Company, 1853.

Brent, Robert A. "Between Calhoun and Webster: Clay in 1850." *Southern Quarterly* 8 (April 1970): 293–308.

Brooks, Robert P. "Howell Cobb and the Crisis of 1850." *Mississippi Valley Historical Review* 4 (December 1917): 279–98.

_____. "Howell Cobb Papers." *Georgia Historical Quarterly* 5, no. 2 (June 1921): 39–52; no. 3 (September 1921): 35–47.

Brown, Everett Somerville, ed. *The Missouri Compromises and Presidential Politics, 1820–1825: From the Letters of William Plumer, Jr.* St. Louis: Missouri Historical Society, 1926.

Brown, Joan Sayers. "The Funeral of Henry Clay." *Antiques Magazine* 112 (July 1977): 110–11.

Bryan, Guy Morrison. Papers. History Center, University of Texas, Austin.

Burns, James MacGregor. *The Vineyard of Liberty.* New York: Alfred A. Knopf, 1981.

Calhoun, John C. *The Papers of John C. Calhoun.* Edited by Robert L. Meriwether and Clyde N. Wilson. Vol. 26. Columbia: University of South Carolina Press, 2001.

_____. "Correspondence of John C. Calhoun." Edited by J. Franklin Jameson. *Annual Report of the American Historical Association for the Year 1899.* Vol. 2. Washington, DC: Government Printing Office, 1900.

Carr, Clark E. *Stephen A. Douglas: His Life, Public Services, Speeches and Patriotism.* Chicago: A. C. McClurg, 1909.

Carroll, Howard. *Twelve Americans: Their Lives and Times.* 1883. Reprint. Freeport, NY: Books for Libraries Press, 1971.

Chambers, William Nisbet. *Old Bullion Benton: Senator from the New West.* Boston: Little, Brown, 1956.

Charleston Daily Courier.

Clay, Henry. *The Papers of Henry Clay.* Edited by Melba Porter Hay et al. 10 vols. Lexington: University Press of Kentucky, 1991.

Clay, Thomas Hart. *Henry Clay.* Philadelphia: G. W. Jacobs, 1910.

Cleveland, Henry. *Alexander H. Stephens in Public and Private.* Philadelphia: National Publishing Company, 1866.

Clingman, Thomas L. *Selections from Speeches and Writings of Hon. Thomas L. Clingman.* Raleigh, NC: John Nichols, 1877.

Cole, Arthur C. *The Whig Party in the South.* Washington, DC: American Historical Association, 1913.

Coleman, James P. "Two Irascible Antebellum Senators: George Poindexter and Henry S. Foote." *Journal of Mississippi History* 46 (February 1984): 17–27.

Colton, Calvin. *The Last Seven Years of the Life of Henry Clay.* New York: A. S. Barnes, 1856.

Columbus (Georgia) Sentinel.

Congressional Globe.

Craven, Avery O. *The Coming of the Civil War.* New York: Charles Scribner's Sons, 1942.

_____. *The Growth of Southern Nationalism, 1848–1861.* Volume 6 of *A History of the South.* Edited by Wendell Holmes Stephens and E. Morton Coulter. Baton Rouge and Austin: Louisiana State University Press and the Little Fund for Southern History of the University of Texas, 1953.

Crist, Lynda Lasswell. "A 'Duty Man': Jefferson Davis as Senator." *Journal of Mississippi History* 51 (November 1989): 281–95.

Curtis, George Ticknor. *The Last Years of Daniel Webster: A Monograph*. New York: D. Appleton, 1878.

_____. *Life of Daniel Webster*. 2 vols. New York: D. Appleton, 1870.

Cuyler, Theodore Ledyard. *Recollections of a Long Life: An Autobiography*. New York: Baker & Taylor, 1902.

Daniel, John W., ed. *Life and Reminiscences of Jefferson Davis by Distinguished Men of His Times*. N. p.: Eastern Publishing Company, 1890.

Davis, Jefferson. *The Papers of Jefferson Davis*. Edited by Lynda Lasswell Crist, Mary Seaton Dix, and Richard E. Beringer. Vol. 4. Baton Rouge: Louisiana State University Press, 1983.

_____. *Private Letters, 1823–1889*. Edited by Hudson Strode. New York: Harcourt, Brace & World, 1966.

Davis, Varina Howell. *Jefferson Davis, Ex-President of the Confederate States of America: A Memoir by His Wife*. 2 vols. 1890. Reprint, Freeport, NY: Books for Libraries Press, 1971.

Davis, William C. *The Union That Shaped the Confederacy: Robert Toombs and Alexander H. Stephens*. Lawrence: University Press of Kansas, 2001.

Degler, Carl N. "There Was Another South." *American Heritage* 11 (August 1960): 52–55.

Dictionary of American Biography. Edited by Allen Johnson et al. 22 vols. New York: Scribner, 1946–1958.

Dodd, William E. *Statesmen of the Old South; or from Radicalism to Conservative Revolt*. New York: Macmillan, 1911.

Douglas, Stephen A. *The Letters of Stephen A. Douglas*. Edited by Robert W. Johannsen. Urbana: University of Illinois Press, 1961.

Dyer, Brainerd. *Zachary Taylor*. Baton Rouge: Louisiana State University Press, 1946.

Dyer, Oliver. *Great Senators of the United States Forty Years Ago*. New York: Robert Bonner's Sons, 1889.

Eaton, Clement. *Henry Clay and the Art of American Politics*. Boston: Little, Brown, 1957.

_____. *A History of the Old South*. New York: Macmillan, 1949.

_____, "Everybody Liked Henry Clay." *American Heritage* 7 (October 1956): 26.

Eisenstadt, Arthur A. "Daniel Webster and the Seventh of March." *Southern Speech Journal* 20 (Winter 1954): 136–47.

Emerson, Ralph Waldo. *The Complete Essays and Other Writings of Ralph Waldo Emerson*. Edited by Brooks Atkinson. New York: Modern Library, 1940.

Farrell, John J., ed. *Zachary Taylor, 1784–1850, Millard Fillmore, 1800–1874: Chronology, Documents, Bibliographical Aids*. Dobbs Ferry, NY: Oceana Publications, 1971.

Fehrenbacher, Don E. *Chicago Giant: A Biography of "Long John" Wentworth*. Madison, WI: American Research Center, 1957.

_____. *The South and Three Sectional Crises*. Baton Rouge: Louisiana State University Press, 1980.

Fillmore, Millard. "The Millard Fillmore Papers." Edited by Frank H. Severance. Vol. 10. *Publications of the Buffalo Historical Society.* 1907.

Follett, Mary Parker. "Henry Clay as Speaker of the United States House of Representatives." In *Annual Report of the American Historical Association for the Year 1891*. Vol. 1. Washington, DC: Government Printing Office, 1892.

Foner, Eric. "The Wilmot Proviso Revisited." *Journal of American History* 56 (September 1969): 262–79.

Foote, Henry S. *Casket of Reminiscences*. 1874. Reprint, New York: Negro Universities Press, 1968.

Foster, Herbert Darling. "Webster's Seventh of March Speech and the Secession Movement, 1850." *American Historical Review* 27 (January 1922): 245–70.

Freehling, William W. *Road to Disunion*. Vol. 1. *Secessionists at Bay, 1776–1854*. New York: Oxford University Press, 1990.

French, Benjamin Brown. *Witness to the Young Republic: A Yankee's Journal, 1828–1870*. Edited by Donald B. Cole and John J. McDonough. Hanover, NH: University Press of New England, 1989.

French, Francis O. *Growing Up on Capitol Hill: A Young Washingtonian's Journal, 1850–1852*. Washington, DC: Library of Congress, 1997.

Gardiner, Oliver Cromwell. *The Great Issue: or The Three Presidential Candidates*. New York: William C. Bryant, 1848.

Giddings, Joshua R. *Speeches in Congress*. Boston: John P. Jewett, 1853.

Gobright, Lawrence A. *Recollection of Men and Things in Washington during the Third of a Century*. Philadelphia: Claxton, Renwen & Haftelfinger, 1869.

Going, Charles B. *David Wilmot, Free Soiler*. New York: D. Appleton, 1924.

Greeley, Horace. *The American Conflict: A History of the Great Rebellion*. 2 vols. Hartford, CT: O. D. Chase, 1864–1866.

_____. *The Autobiography of Horace Greeley: or Recollections of a Busy Life*. New York: E. B. Treat, 1872.

Green, Constance M. *Washington: Village and Capital, 1800–1878*. Princeton, NJ: Princeton University Press, 1962.

Halstead, Murat. *Three against Lincoln: Murat Halstead Reports the Caucuses of 1860*. Edited by William B. Hesseltine. Baton Rouge: Louisiana State University Press, 1960.

Hamilton, Holman. *Prologue to Conflict: The Crisis and Compromise of 1850*. Lexington: University of Kentucky Press, 1964.

_____. *Zachary Taylor: Soldier in the White House*. Indianapolis: Bobbs-Merrill, 1951.

_____. " 'The Cave of the Winds' and the Compromise of 1850." *Journal of Southern History* 23 (August 1957): 331–53.

_____. "Democratic Senate Leadership and the Compromise of 1850." *Mississippi Valley Historical Review* 41 (December 1954): 403–18.

_____. "Kentucky's Linn Boyd and the Dramatic Days of 1850." *Register of the Kentucky Historical Society* 55 (July 1957): 185–95.

Hamlin, Charles Eugene. *The Life and Times of Hannibal Hamlin*. Cambridge, MA: Riverside Press, 1899.

Harmon, George D. "Douglas and the Compromise of 1850." *Journal of the Illinois State Historical Society* 21 (January 1929): 453–99.

Harvey, Peter. *Reminiscences and Anecdotes of Daniel Webster*. Boston: Little, Brown, 1877.

Heidler, David S. *Pulling the Temple Down: The Fire-Eaters and the Destruction of the Union*. Mechanicsburg, PA: Stackpole Books, 1994.

Hilliard, Henry W. *Politics and Pen Pictures at Home and Abroad*. New York: G. P. Putnam's Sons, 1892.

Hitchcock, Ethan Allen. *Fifty Years in Camp and Field*. Edited by W. A. Croffut. 1909. Reprint, New York: Books for Libraries Press, 1971.

Hodder, Frank H. "The Authorship of the Compromise of 1850." *Mississippi Valley Historical Review* 22 (March 1936): 525–36.

Hofstadter, Richard. *The American Political Tradition and the Men Who Made It*. New York: Vintage Books, 1974.

Holt, Michael F. *The Rise and Fall of the American Whig Party: Jacksonian Politics and the Onset of the Civil War*. New York: Oxford University Press, 1999.

Hubbell, John T. "Three Georgia Unionists and the Compromise of 1850." *Georgia Historical Quarterly* 51 (September 1967): 307–23.

Hunter, Robert M. T. "Correspondence of Robert M. T. Hunter, 1826–1876." Edited by Charles H. Ambler. In *Annual Report of the American Historical Association for the Year 1916*. Vol. 2. Washington, DC: Government Printing Office, 1918.

Jackson Mississippian.

Jefferson, Thomas. *The Works of Thomas Jefferson*. Edited by Paul Leicester Ford. Vol 12. New York: G. P. Putnam's Sons, 1905.

Johannsen, Robert W. *Stephen A. Douglas*. New York: Oxford University Press, 1973.

Johnson, Gerald W. *America's Silver Age: The Statecraft of Clay-Webster-Calhoun*. New York: Harper & Brothers, 1939.

_____. "Great Man Eloquent." *American Heritage* 9 (December 1957): 74–77.

Johnston, Richard Malcolm, and William Hand Browne. *Life of Alexander H. Stephens.* Philadelphia: J. B. Lippincott, 1878.

Jones, Edgar Dewitt. *Lords of Speech: Portraits of Fifteen American Orators.* Chicago: Willett, Clark, 1937.

Julian, George W. *Political Recollections, 1840 to 1872.* 1883. Reprint, Miami, FL: Mnemosyne, 1969.

Ketchum, Richard M. "Faces from the Past: Zachary Taylor." *American Heritage* 14 (October 1963): 52–53.

Kiper, Richard L. *Major General John Alexander McClernand: Politician in Uniform.* Kent, OH: Kent University Press, 1999.

Kirwan, Albert D. *John J. Crittenden: The Struggle for the Union.* Lexington: University of Kentucky Press, 1962.

Lanman, Charles. *The Private Life of Daniel Webster.* New York: Harper & Brothers, 1852.

Lewis, Walker, ed. *Speak for Yourself, Daniel: A Life of Webster in His Own Words.* Boston: Houghton Mifflin, 1969.

Lightfoot, Alfred. "Henry Clay and the Missouri Question, 1819–1821." *Missouri Historical Review* 61 (January 1967): 143–65.

Lincoln, Abraham. *Collected Works of Abraham Lincoln.* Edited by Roy P. Basler. Vol. 2. New Brunswick, NJ: Rutgers University Press, 1955.

Linden, Glenn M. *Voices from the Gathering Storm: The Coming of the American Civil War.* Wilmington, DE: Scholarly Resources, 2001.

Ludlum, Robert P. "Joshua R. Giddings, Radical." *Mississippi Valley Historical Review* 23 (June 1936): 49–60.

Lyman, Samuel P. *The Public and Private Life of Daniel Webster.* 2 vols in 1. Philadelphia: John E. Potter, 1852.

Lynch, William O. "Zachary Taylor as President." *Journal of Southern History* 4 (August 1938): 279–94.

Mackay, Alex. *The Western World; or Travels in the United States in 1846–47.* 1849. Reprint, New York: Negro University Press, 1968.

Macmillan Information Now Encyclopedia: The Confederacy. New York: Simon & Schuster, 1998.

MacNeil, Neil. "The House Shall Chuse Their Speaker . . ." *American Heritage* 28 (February 1977): 26–31.

Malen, James C. "The Motives of Stephen A. Douglas in the Organization of Nebraska Territory: A Letter Dated December 17, 1853." *Kansas Historical Quarterly* 19 (November 1951): 321–53.

Mangum, Willie P. *The Papers of Willie Person Mangum.* Edited by Henry Thomas Shanks. 5 vols. Raleigh, NC: State Department of Archives and History, 1956.

Mann, Mary Tyler. *Life of Horace Mann.* Boston: Willard Small, 1888.

Martin, John M. "William R. King and the Compromise of 1850." *North Carolina Historical Review* 39 (October 1962): 500–518.

Martineau, Harriet. *Retrospect of Western Travel*. 3 vols. 1838. Reprint, New York: Greenwood Press, 1969.

Maury, Sarah Mytton. *The Statesmen of America in 1846*. Philadelphia: Carey & Hart, 1847.

McClure, Alexander K. *Colonel Alexander K. McClure's Recollections of a Half a Century*. Salem, MA: Salem Press Company, 1902.

Montgomery, H. *The Life of Major General Zachary Taylor*. Auburn, NY: Derby, Miller and Company, 1849.

Moore, Glover. *The Missouri Controversy, 1819–1821*. 1953. Reprint, Gloucester, MA: Peter Smith, 1967.

Morgan, James. *Our Presidents*. New York: Macmillan, 1954.

Morris, Richard B., ed. *Encyclopedia of American History*. New York: Harper & Brothers, 1953.

Morrison, Chaplain W. *Democratic Politics and Sectionalism: The Wilmot Proviso Controversy*. Chapel Hill: University of North Carolina Press, 1967.

National Cyclopaedia of American Biography. 63 vols. New York: James T. White, 1898–1984.

Neighbours, Kenneth F. "The Taylor-Neighbors Struggle over the Upper Rio Grande Region of Texas in 1850." *Southwestern Historical Quarterly* 61 (April 1958): 431–63.

Nevins, Allan. *Ordeal of the Union*. Vol. 1. *Fruits of Manifest Destiny, 1847–1852*. New York: Charles Scribner's Sons, 1947.

New York Express.

New York Herald.

New York Journal of Commerce.

New York Tribune.

Outlaw, David. Papers. Southern Historical Collection, University of North Carolina, Chapel Hill.

Parker, Edward G. *The Golden Age of American Oratory*. Boston: Whittemore, Niles & Hall, 1857.

Parks, Joseph Howard. *John Bell of Tennessee*. Baton Rouge: Louisiana State University Press, 1950.

———. "John Bell and the Compromise of 1850." *Journal of Southern History* 9 (August 1943): 328–56.

Parmelee, T. N. "Recollections of an Old Stager." *Harper's New Monthly Magazine* 45 (August 1872): 445–48, (September 1872): 600–605, (October 1872): 750–53; 46 (December 1872): 92–97, (January 1873): 270–75; 47 (September 1873): 586–91, (October 1873): 753–60; 49 (June 1874): 110–18.

Parton, James. *Famous Americans of Recent Times*. Boston: Ticknor & Fields, 1867.

Pelzer, Louis. *Augustus Caesar Dodge*. Iowa City, IA: State Historical Society of Iowa, 1908.

Persinger, Clark E. " 'The Bargain of 1844' as the Origin of the Wilmot Proviso." In *Annual Report of the American Historical Association for the Year 1911.* Vol. 1. Washington, DC: Government Printing Office, 1913.

Peterson, Merrill D. *The Great Triumvirate: Webster, Clay, and Calhoun.* New York: Oxford University Press, 1987.

_____. *Olive Branch and Sword: The Compromise of 1833.* Baton Rouge: Louisiana State University Press, 1982.

Phillips, Ulrich B. *The Life of Robert Toombs.* New York: Macmillan, 1913.

_____, ed. "The Correspondence of Robert Toombs, Alexander H. Stephens, and Howell Cobb." In *Annual Report of the American Historical Association for the Year 1911.* Vol. 2. Washington, DC: Government Printing Office, 1913.

Pike, James S. *First Blows of the Civil War: The Ten Years of Preliminary Conflict in the United States from 1850 to 1860.* New York: American News Company, 1879.

Poage, George R. *Henry Clay and the Whig Party.* Chapel Hill: University of North Carolina Press, 1936.

Polk, James K. *The Diary of James K. Polk during His Presidency, 1845 to 1849.* 4 vols. Edited by Milo Milton Quaife. Chicago: A. C. McClurg, 1910.

Poore, Benjamin Perley. *Perley's Reminiscences of Sixty Years in the National Metropolis.* 2 vols. Philadelphia: Hubbard Brothers, 1886.

Potter, David M. *The Impending Crisis, 1848–1861.* Completed and edited by Don E. Fehrenbacher. New York: Harper & Row, 1976.

Remini, Robert V. *Henry Clay: Statesman for the Union.* New York: W. W. Norton, 1991.

"Reminiscences of Washington." *Atlantic Monthly* 46 (December 1880): 799–810; 47 (February 1881): 234–50, (April 1881): 538–47, (May 1881): 658–66.

Rhodes, James Ford. *History of the United States from the Compromise of 1850 to the McKinley-Bryan Campaign of 1896.* 8 vols. 1892–1919. Reprint, Port Washington, NY: Kennikat Press, 1967.

Richardson, James D., ed. *A Compilation of the Messages and Papers of the Presidents, 1789–1897.* Vol. 5. Washington, DC: Government Printing Office, 1897.

Richmond Enquirer.

Rozwenc, Edwin C., ed. *The Compromise of 1850.* Problems in American Civilization. Boston: D. C. Heath, 1957.

Russel, Robert R. "What Was the Compromise of 1850?" *Journal of Southern History* 22 (August 1956): 292–309.

Sangamo (Illinois) Journal.

Sargent, Epes. *The Life and Public Services of Henry Clay.* Edited by Horace Greeley. Auburn, NY: Derby & Miller, 1852.

Sargent, Nathan. *Public Men and Events from the Commencement of Mr. Monroe's Administration, in 1817, to the Close of Mr. Fillmore's Administration, in 1853.* 2 vols. Philadelphia: J. B. Lippincott, 1874.

Scarborough, Katherine. *Homes of the Cavaliers*. New York: Macmillan, 1930.

Schott, Thomas E. *Alexander H. Stephens of Georgia: A Biography*. Baton Rouge: Louisiana State University Press, 1988.

Schuckers, J. W. *The Life and Public Services of Salmon Portland Chase*. New York: D. Appleton, 1874.

Schurz, Carl. *Life of Henry Clay*. 2 vols. Boston: Houghton Mifflin, 1887.

Scott, Winfield. *Memoirs of Lieut.-General Scott, Written by Himself*. 2 vols. New York: Sheldon, 1864.

Seager, Robert, II. "Henry Clay and the Politics of Compromise and Non-Compromise." *Register of the Kentucky Historical Society* 85 (Winter 1987): 1–28.

Seward, Frederick W. *Seward at Washington as Senator and Secretary of State: A Memoir of His Life, with Selections from His Letters, 1846–1861*. New York: Derby & Miller, 1891.

Shoemaker, Floyd Calvin. *Missouri's Struggle for Statehood, 1804–1821*. 1916. Reprint, New York: Russell & Russell, 1969.

Simms, Henry H. *A Decade of Sectional Controversy, 1951–1861*. 1942. Reprint, Westport, CT: Greenwood Press, 1978.

Simpson, John Eddins. *Howell Cobb: The Politics of Ambition*. Chicago: Adams Press, 1973.

Smith, Elbert B. *Magnificent Missourian: The Life of Thomas Hart Benton*. Philadelphia: J. B. Lippincott, 1958.

_____. *The Presidencies of Zachary Taylor and Millard Fillmore*. Lawrence: University Press of Kansas. 1988.

Smith, O. H. *Early Indiana Trials and Sketches*. Cincinnati: Moore, Wilstach, Keys, 1858.

Smith, William Ernest. *The Francis Preston Blair Family in Politics*. 2 vols. New York: Macmillan, 1933.

Smith, W. L. G. *Fifty Years of Public Life: The Life and Times of Lewis Cass*. New York: Derby & Jackson, 1856.

Stegmaier, Mark J. *Texas, New Mexico, and the Compromise of 1850: Boundary Dispute and Sectional Crisis*. Kent, OH: Kent State University Press, 1996.

_____. "Zachary Taylor versus the South." *Civil War History* 33 (September 1987): 219–41.

Stenberg, Richard R. "The Motivation of the Wilmot Proviso." *Mississippi Valley Historical Review* 18 (March 1932): 535–41.

Stephens, Alexander H. *A Constitutional View of the Late War between the States*. 2 vols. Philadelphia: National Publishing Company, 1868–1870.

Stephens, Robert Grier. "The Background and Boyhood of Alexander H. Stephens." *Georgia Review* 9 (Winter 1955): 386–97.

Stevens, Frank E. "Life of Stephen Arnold Douglas." *Journal of the Illinois Historical Society* 16 (October 1923–January 1924): 247–673.

Strong, George Templeton. *The Diary of George Templeton Strong: The Turbulent Fifties, 1850–1859*. Edited by Allan Nevins and Milton H. Thomas. New York: Macmillan Company, 1952.

Sunderland, Byron. "Washington as I First Knew It." *Records of the Columbia Historical Society* 5 (1902): 195–211.

Talmadge, Arthur White. *The Talmadge, Tallmadge, and Talmage Genealogy*. New York: Grafton Press, 1909.

Thompson, William Y. *Robert Toombs of Georgia*. Baton Rouge: Lousiana State University Press, 1966.

Ticknor, George. *Life, Letters, and Journals of George Ticknor*. 2 vols. 6th ed. Boston: James R. Osgood, 1876.

Trent, William P. *Southern Statesmen of the Old Regime*. New York: Thomas Y. Crowell, 1897.

U.S. Congress. *Biographical Directory of the United States Congress, 1774–1989*. Bicentennial ed. Washington, DC: Government Printing Office, 1989.

_____. *Obituary Addresses Delivered on the Occasion of the Death of Zachary Taylor, President of the United States. . . .* Washington, DC: William M. Belt, 1850.

_____. *Obituary Addresses on the Occasion of the Death of the Hon. Daniel Webster, of Massachusetts, Secretary of State for the United States*. Washington, DC: Robert Armstrong, 1853.

_____. *Obituary Addresses on the Occasion of the Death of the Hon. Henry Clay*. Washington, DC: Robert Armstrong, 1852.

U.S. National Archives and Records Administration, Center for Legislative Archives. "Westward Expansion and the Compromise of 1850." In *Congress and the Shaping of American History*, Vol. 1, *1789–1869*. Washington DC: unpublished.

Van Deusen, Glyndon G. *The Life of Henry Clay*. Boston: Little, Brown, 1937.

Varon, Elizabeth R. " 'The Ladies Are Whigs': Lucy Barbour, Henry Clay, and Nineteenth-Century Virginia Politics." *Virginia Cavalcade* 42 (Autumn 1992): 72–83.

Virginia Free Press.

Webster, Daniel. *The Letters of Daniel Webster*. Edited by C. H. Van Tyne. 1902. Reprint, New York: Greenwood Press, 1968.

_____. *The Papers of Daniel Webster*. Edited by Charles M. Wiltse and Michael J. Birkner. Vol. 7. Hanover, NH: University Press of New England, 1986.

_____. *The Private Correspondence of Daniel Webster*. Edited by Fletcher Webster. 2 vols. Boston: Little, Brown, 1857.

Weed, Thurlow. *Autobiography of Thurlow Weed*. Edited by Harriet A. Weed. 1883. Reprint. New York: Da Capo Press, 1970.

Weisenburger, Francis P. *The Passing of the Frontier, 1825–1850*. Columbus, OH: Ohio State Archaeological and Historical Society, 1941.

Wentworth, John. *Congressional Reminiscences: Adams, Benton, Clay, Calhoun, and Webster*. Chicago: Fergus, 1882.

Whipple, Edwin P., ed. *The Great Speeches and Orations of Daniel Webster with an Essay on Daniel Webster as a Master of English Style*. Boston: Little, Brown, 1919.

Whittier, John Greenleaf. *The Complete Poetical Works of John Greenleaf Whittier*. Boston: Houghton Mifflin, 1910.

Wiltsie, Charles M. *John C. Calhoun, Sectionalist, 1840–1850*. Indianapolis: Bobbs-Merrill, 1951.

Winthrop, Robert C., Jr. *A Memoir of Robert C. Winthrop*. Boston: Little, Brown, 1897.

Woodburn, James A. "The Historical Significance of the Missouri Compromise." In *Annual Report of the American Historical Association for the Year 1873*. Washington, DC: Government Printing Office, 1894.

Young, John Russell. *Men and Memories: Personal Reminiscences*. Edited by Mary D. Russell Young. 2d ed. New York: F. Tennyson Neely, 1901.

Young, William T. *Sketch of the Life and Public Services of General Lewis Cass*. Detroit: Markham & Elwood, 1952.

INDEX